PRAISE FOR *AIN...*

"A fierce, full-bodied examination of our ...
pop culture and feminism. Read it!"

—**JANET MOCK**, author of *Surpassing Certainty:*
What My Twenties Taught Me

"Proving himself a worthy member of the BeyHive, Kevin Allred takes us on a journey through Beyoncé's greatest hits and expansive career—peeling back their multiple layers to explore gender, race, sexuality, and power in today's modern world. A fun, engaging, and important read for long-time Beyoncé fans and newcomers alike."

—**FRANCHESCA RAMSEY**, author of *Well, That Escalated Quickly:*
Memoirs and Mistakes of an Accidental Activist

"*Ain't I a Diva?* explores the phenomenon of Beyoncé while explicitly championing not only her immense talent and grace but what we can learn from it. In this celebration of Beyoncé, and through her, other Black women, Allred is giving us room to be exactly who we are so that maybe we, too, can stop the world then carry on!"

—**KEAH BROWN**, author of *The Pretty One:*
On Life, Pop Culture, Disability,
and Other Reasons to Fall in Love with Me

"Kevin Allred is a writer who approaches the topic of Beyoncé's role and impact on the culture with nuance and skill. Keenly aware of his position and privilege as a white cis male, Allred centers and amplifies Black feminist voices in his writing as he explores themes of race, gender, and class in Beyoncé's career. Applying a feminist reading to her music, Allred illuminates and introduces ideas that are timelier now than ever before. This is a must-read for any fan of Beyoncé and of fascinating feminist discourse."

—**ZEBA BLAY**, senior culture writer, *HuffPost*

AIN'T I A
DIVA?

Beyoncé and the Power of Pop Culture Pedagogy

KEVIN ALLRED
Foreword by Cheryl Clarke

FEMINIST
PRESS
AT THE CITY UNIVERSITY
OF NEW YORK
NEW YORK CITY

Published in 2019 by the Feminist Press
at the City University of New York
The Graduate Center
365 Fifth Avenue, Suite 5406
New York, NY 10016

feministpress.org

First Feminist Press edition 2019

 This book was made possible thanks to a grant from
New York State Council on the Arts with the support
of Governor Andrew M. Cuomo and the New York
State Legislature.

 This book is supported in part by a grant from the Shelley &
Donald Rubin Foundation.

First printing June 2019

Cover illustration by Emerald Pellot
Cover and text design by Drew Stevens

Library of Congress Cataloging-in-Publication Data
Names: Allred, Kevin, 1981- author.
Title: Ain't I a diva? : Beyoncé and the power of pop culture pedagogy /
    Kevin Allred ; foreword by Cheryl Clarke.
Description: First Feminist Press edition. | New York, NY : Feminist Press,
    2019. | Includes bibliographical references.
Identifiers: LCCN 2018048370 (print) | LCCN 2018060604 (ebook) | ISBN
    9781936932610 (ebook) | ISBN 9781936932603 (pbk.)
Subjects: LCSH: Beyoncé, 1981---Criticism and interpretation. | Popular
    music--History and criticism. | Sex in music. | Feminism and music.
Classification: LCC ML420.K675 (ebook) | LCC ML420.K675 A73 2019 (print) |
    DDC 782.42164092--dc23
LC record available at https://lccn.loc.gov/2018048370

To all the PB students over the years. For being open, fearless, creative, and endlessly curious.

To all the Black women writers, artists, and activists mentioned within, and more. For opening my eyes.

And, of course, to Beyoncé Giselle Knowles-Carter. For everything.

CONTENTS

FUTURE

FOREWORD
"AREN'T I AN ARCHIVE?"

WRITING THIS FOREWORD TO KEVIN ALLRED'S *AIN'T I a Diva?: Beyoncé and the Power of Pop Culture Pedagogy* brings me almost full circle. Feminist and lesbian-feminist presses—from *Conditions* magazine (1976–1990) and Kitchen Table: Women of Color Press (1980–1992), to Firebrand Books (1984–2000) and Sinister Wisdom Press (1976–present)—have supported my work since 1977. The Feminist Press (1970–present) has been part of that history and still is.

> By placing her own *body* on display, even while also expressing *agency* and *pleasure* . . . Beyoncé highlights the additional constraints placed on Black women . . . trying to access a *sex-positive feminism* . . . and *a different . . . politics* . . . that re-creates *empowered sexuality* . . . with *Black women at the center*. (164–65, emphasis mine)

I cherish these watchwords of Black feminism: "body," "agency," "pleasure," "sex-positive," "different," "empowered sexuality," and putting "Black women at the center." And does Beyoncé give us all this? Kevin Allred fervently believes so. And I want to believe with him. Anyone who, like Allred, is such a staunch believer in Black women and Black feminism is all right with me.

Entering graduate school and developing a "deepening queer identity and feminist political consciousness" collided with Allred's desire to "link Beyoncé's work to larger phenomena and politics" (xxi). And Allred challenges us throughout *Ain't I a Diva?* to do likewise. Beyoncé's work becomes a portfolio of Black feminist thought for Allred and for students in his class. He uses the prodigious Black pop icon to reference most of the equally prodigious Black feminist thinkers/ speakers since Sojourner Truth and her fabled "Ain't I a Woman?" declamation. He draws partially upon it for the title of his book. (Although historian Deborah Gray White claims that Sojourner Truth said, "*Aren't* I a woman," not "*Ain't* I a woman." Thus, the title of her first groundbreaking book on Black women in slavery: *Ar'n't I a Woman* (1985). In *Sojourner Truth: A Life, A Symbol* (1996), historian Nell Irvin Painter claims Truth might never have said these words at all—"ain't" or "aren't." I'll venture Beyoncé—in all her middle-class Blackness—would say "aren't.") Allred also takes the "diva" designation of *Ain't I a Diva?* from Beyoncé's gangsta-girl video of the same name.

"Diva is a female version of a hustla," so Beyoncé says in the video, while she and her backups reprise the lyrics: "I'm-a a diva." And she is. Diva Beyoncé swaggers in very high heels down the middle of a street, chewing gum—her favorite tough-chick gesture—and setting a car on fire.

Studying Bey videos became a nightly regimen for Allred, as he compiled and collected information and materials for future use. That future use became the course "Politicizing Beyoncé," which may have contributed to a burgeoning academic field known as Beyoncé Studies. And there is plenty to study, of which Allred presents a trove of evidence. He claims a "diva is intersectional" (5) because, as he demonstrates, Beyoncé integrates "education, pop culture, and honest conversation across difference, history, and politics, in solidarity with a longer Black feminist trajectory and deep appreciation of the sources" (xi). In the appendix is his syllabus, which is a generous act and will enable anyone who has the courage and savvy to instruct and self-instruct.

Centering Beyoncé, Allred makes a catalog—writ large—of the work of forty years of Black feminist political and social theorists, literary critics and theorists, novelists, poets, essayists, performance artists, journalists, filmmakers, and visual artists. Allred calls them all in: from the pioneers Toni Cade Bambara,

Barbara Christian, Audre Lorde, and Flo(rynce) Kennedy; to the more contemporary likes of Angela Davis, Kimberlé Crenshaw, and bell hooks; to younger innovators like Staceyann Chin, Kara Keeling, Kara Walker, and Janet Mock. He even includes reference to my own "Lesbianism: An Act of Resistance" from the foundational *This Bridge Called My Back: Writings by Radical Women of Color* (1981), edited by Cherríe Moraga and Gloria Anzaldúa. Queen Bey is ensconced in this archive. I welcome her and will enjoy being there with her.

In a 2016 piece for *The New Yorker*, Hilton Als claims that Beyoncé gives the world "formulas" in *Lemonade*, "instead of diving deeper into her art." Formulaic or not, I consider Beyoncé's *Lemonade* (2016) a "magnum opus." And so does Allred. And like Beyoncé, it is a tour de force. Allred reads *Lemonade* as a reference to Toni Morrison's own magnum opus, *Beloved* (1987), as well as to Julie Dash's pinnacle film, *Daughters of the Dust* (1991). I like his play, in chapter 4, "Ghosts of Slavery ~~Past~~," on Morrison's concept in *Beloved* of rememory as "thought pictures" of slavery, or, as he calls it *out*, "[slavery's] racist afterlife," which is everywhere "a repellent palimpsest, always lurking" (84). The traumatic past, and not just ours but others' as well, may present itself at any moment. If slavery's thought pictures are everywhere—and they are—then Beyoncé's *Lemonade* is just such a thought picture—with all its haunting visuality and musicality. Thus, the strike-through of "Past." Slavery is never *past*. The ghosts of slavery are always behind, ahead, and around us, as Audre Lorde tells us in her brilliant volume of poetry *Our Dead Behind Us* (1986)—they are there pushing us forward.

Allred stays away from interpreting *Lemonade* as a parable of hubby Jay-Z's infidelity, and instead engages it as Beyoncé's critique of America's infidelity, its bankrupt promises to African Americans of equal treatment, which grow more bankrupt by the day. This graver infidelity is borne out as we view scenes in *Lemonade* of poor and displaced Black people in New Orleans after the disaster of Hurricane Katrina, with no help in sight from the George W. Bush administration. This was rehearsal for the treatment of the people of Puerto Rico by the Trump administration in the wake of Hurricane Maria in 2017. (At least Bush and Bill Clinton raised money for the long-term relief of Katrina survivors.) In this way, Beyoncé's *Lemonade* becomes another forceful visual archive of US betrayal of its citizens. Again, Allred joins Beyoncé's visual reference in *Lemonade* to the injustices done to Katrina survivors with Morrison's literary indictment of the evils of slavery in *Beloved*. And in his book, he puts the two in conversation:

Beyoncé has long been sitting in the same cemetery as Morrison, attempting to listen to highly vocal ghosts. The ghost of Beloved herself, actually, might be hiding in the repellent landscape of 'Déjà vu,' and déjà vu as a phenomenon is just another form of rememory. (84)

Definitely. But Beyoncé has not been "sitting in that cemetery" as long as Morrison has been "sitting in that cemetery." Come on. However, Beyoncé may be able to *sit with* Ms. Morrison in that cemetery, but always in deference to the Black feminist thinkers who came before.

Full disclosure: Kevin Allred joined my graduate class, "Feminism: Theory and Practice," in the fall of 2008. (Beyoncé was nowhere on the syllabus, though she would have been a boon.) The course was always an experiment in melding activism and theory: i.e., how do we nurture our practice, and how do we practice an integrated struggle? Allred—as were many of the students—was well-versed in Black feminist studies, and his whiteness didn't get in the way of his knowledge or participation in the class. *Ain't I a Diva?* is evidence of his scholarly commitment to placing Black women at the center of our struggle for an empowered sexuality. Signs of this commitment were apparent in our class, even without Beyoncé.

Allred takes up similar experiments in his book, engaging a host of Black feminist conceptual frameworks and theoretical inspirations in order to parse out the titular diva's work. Melissa Harris-Perry's "crooked room" theoretical metaphor captivates Allred. The crooked room is an apt and adept conceit of the constraints Black women must struggle against. The crooked room opens the way to a whole system of repressions. In referencing Zora Neale Hurston's apocryphal memoir, *Dust Tracks on a Road* (1942), Allred recounts Hurston's realization that the "entire organization of the world was counter to things that made her glad. . . . Hurston also realized that to seize happiness, she'd have to stand straight in a crooked room, tilt the room to *her* footfalls" (124–25). And because of Black women's resistance to yielding to the crooked room, we have, as Monique W. Morris reveals in *Pushout: The Criminalization of Black Girls in Schools* (2016), the early criminalization of Black girls for the slightest infractions against the rules of our social institutions. "And still we rise," as Maya Angelou says in one of her more well-known poems.

Ain't I a Diva? identifies Beyoncé as a practitioner of Black feminism. *Ain't I a Diva?* has made me realize how indispensable discography and videography are to literary study, and how both enrich the humanities. This book gives me a model of how pop culture can teach and what an exceptional teacher Allred must be. Those of us who teach so rarely talk about how we do it. Let's put Black women at the center of everything progressive, as Allred advocates. (But, damn, aren't we overworked as it is?) After a year like 2018, when we lost both Aretha Franklin (b. 1942) and Nancy Wilson (b. 1937), two popular Black culture chanteuses, I am happy we have the talent, acumen, glamour, and ambition of Beyoncé Giselle Knowles. We must continue to study her work, especially *Lemonade*, for now. Thanks to Kevin Allred's important intervention, we will—in the classroom and in the street.

—*Cheryl Clarke*
January 2019

INTRODUCTION
SCHOOLIN' LIFE

I WAS SETTLING INTO BED AT MIDNIGHT ON FRIDAY, December 13, 2013—the exact moment Beyoncé bent the entire music industry to her will. I grabbed my phone from the nightstand to check social media one last time, and as I clicked on the Instagram icon, the first thing to pop up was a post from Beyoncé that read simply, "Surprise!" My eyes went wide. "Drunk In Love" (though no one knew the song at the time) played over a video montage while that now-iconic pink font announced: "*BEYONCÉ*. Visual album. 14 songs. 17 videos. Available now." It was not a drill. Zero marketing or promotion, no teaser single. A paradigm shift in the way music was released. I threw my phone across the room, tossed my blankets to one side, hopped up, and darted to my computer. I pulled up iTunes and started the download as fast as my fingers could click after inevitably fumbling my password and cursing once or twice at the top of my lungs. Forgetting sleep completely, I stayed up well into that first night soaking up sounds and lyrics from the surprise record like a sponge. I watched from start to finish, the way Beyoncé intended the project to be consumed, and then immediately returned to songs and videos that stuck out as instant favorites. I couldn't get enough.

Beyoncé's digital drop may not seem like a major political event, but the landscape of the music industry immediately shifted. Countless artists have since tried to re-create the same surprise impact, to varying degrees of success. The phrase "pulled a Beyoncé" gets bandied about now as part of the pop culture lexicon, with its own entry on Urban Dictionary. The industry quickly changed its overall release structure to coalesce worldwide, with new music coming out on Fridays, mirroring the truly legendary release of *BEYONCÉ*. Earlier that summer, Beyoncé had retreated from public life. She'd stopped giving interviews and began communicating with the public almost entirely through sporadic Instagram posts and her website, defying the demands and expectations society places on its most popular celebrities. Her silence not only amplified the impact of the surprise release in December but also marked a monumental shift in Beyoncé's public relations toward a new survival strategy. She set strict boundaries in order to carve out a meaningful life for herself as both a private person and a public artist. As a Black woman in an industry run almost exclusively by rich white men, where Black women were never meant to attain the level of power she has, her 2013 feat is even more earth-shattering.

Oprah Winfrey calls transformative, split-second sea changes "Aha! moments": instances when things shift and reform, on either a small or large scale. And as a featured guest on Nicki Minaj's song "Feeling Myself," Beyoncé boasts about that December 2013 night in just those terms. She explains to any lingering doubters that she effectively changed the game: "I stopped the world." It might sound hyperbolic, but it's not bragging when it's true; Beyoncé stopped the world. More than once now. Each of her subsequent releases have come as additional surprises or initiated further radical shifts in previously tested music promotion and marketing strategy. She emphasizes that "world stop" in the music with a break of silence, ended a few seconds later with the command, "Carry on." And we did. We have. And we'll continue to anticipate each and every time Beyoncé will stop the world. Not just because she consistently delivers innovative, interesting music and visuals, but because she creates cultural Aha! moments across the globe.

To quote some wise words from writer and cultural critic Janet Mock that served as a backbone to her MSNBC series *So POPular!*, pop culture is so much more than a guilty pleasure, it's an "access point"— for education, entertainment, critical inquiry, politics. One that is available and accessible to most everyone in one form or another, unlike often exclusionary academic theory or biased formal education. Pop culture teaches us, and sometimes pop culture can stop our world. Those electrifying and sometimes suspenseful moments are when pop culture gets powerfully translated into politics, when what entertains us also educates. And if we're paying critical attention, they're when we, as an audience, change too. Beyoncé's music is built on countless Aha! moments. Not just regarding the music industry, but encompassing the entire organization of society and our various roles in it. Beyoncé may not hold any formal teaching credentials, but she can definitely teach us something, just as she ensured in the chorus to her 2011 track "Schoolin' Life."

*

Full disclosure: I was late to the BeyHive. I wasn't living in a cave, so of course I knew of Destiny's Child and Beyoncé. I bought *The Writing's on the Wall* on CD and bopped to "Bills, Bills, Bills," "Survivor," and later "Crazy in Love," but my musical tastes shifted all over the place; Beyoncé was constantly there, but in the background. It wasn't until I heard *B'Day*, her second solo album in 2006, that I become a full-fledged Beyoncé devotee. Something visceral and immediate about the sounds of *B'Day* grabbed me by the collar, shook me, and never let go. While *Dangerously* in Love and B'Day both start off with infectious, horn-fueled singles featuring Jay-Z, the recordings couldn't be more different. Listen to the first thirty seconds of each track back-to-back. "Crazy in Love" finds Jay calling the shots, with Beyoncé's classic "Uh-oh, uh-oh, uh-oh, oh-no-no" providing background punctuation, whereas "Déjà Vu" begins with Beyoncé's sultry but commanding voice calling in the bass before the music even starts. In a complete reversal, Jay then complements her with intermittent "Uhs" and "Uh-huhs." She continues to call in the rest of the instruments before *allowing* Jay himself to enter the song with his verse. He quickly tries to claim that he "runs the bass, hi-hat, and the snare," but any close listener knows it's a bald-faced lie. Beyoncé just called each in one by one. She's in control.

The opening of "Déjà Vu" stands as an astute inverse to "Crazy in Love" in order to mark a major artistic transformation in the direction of Beyoncé's career. She'd always featured empowerment in her music, solo and with Destiny's Child, but this new Beyoncé was also unapologetically and aggressively beginning to seize the means of production from record labels and the music industry. Though she would finally attain creative autonomy in 2010 through her own Parkwood Entertainment, Beyoncé planted the seeds of her eventual sovereignty in B'Day. Listening today, I'm always transported back to those initial moments of excitement, feeling shaken up by Beyoncé's new sound and presence. A sound and presence rooted in defiance of a record label that hadn't been supportive of *Dangerously in Love* until it started producing multiple number-one singles, and in a restorative exhale after playing the weak-willed Deena Jones in *Dreamgirls*. *B'Day*, in my mind, is forever most associated with the rattling opening bass note of "Déjà Vu" that refuses to be contained.

The audio levels of *Dangerously in Love* and *B'Day* are like night and day too. "Crazy in Love" is energetic but confined, bass and treble in equal parts, a neatly packaged, restrained studio recording. But that first bass note in "Déjà Vu" rudely breaks through the speaker to slap listeners in the face. The levels get pushed beyond their own limits to ensure a different affective auditory experience. No matter what volume the track is played at, the speakers shake slightly. The phenomenon is known as sonic redlining or clipping, where the sounds get recorded at levels too high to be properly processed as audio; it's literally too much for playback. In extreme cases it can sound like a record or CD is skipping; on *B'Day* it creates a mild, low buzz. The aggressive recording mirrored what Beyoncé spoke to as a business strategy in her later documentary, *Life Is But a Dream*: "Me being polite was not me being fair to myself." Letting others determine how her work and sound would be produced was no longer being fair to herself. *B'Day* was an impolite concept album that emotionally *and physically* moved me via the redlined vibrations. And I liked it. Each record she's released since has built on that same foundation.

My growing Beyoncé obsession coincided with entering graduate school for American studies and women's and gender studies, and my own deepening queer identity and feminist political consciousness. Academically, I was particularly interested in the intersections of race, gender, sexuality, and pop culture, so I wanted to marry my love of this music with critical thinking—to link Beyoncé's work to larger phenomena and politics. Today, countless articles, books, and investigations boast a burgeoning field of Beyoncé studies, but in 2006, serious analyses were few and far between. I eventually came across writing by Daphne Brooks that made my world stop, just like the *B'Day* album itself. The article, "Suga Mama, Politicized," originally published in the *Nation*, functions as passionate cultural analysis and album review simultaneously. Brooks followed the *Nation* article with an extended scholarly piece in the interdisciplinary feminist journal *Meridians* on Black women's soul singing as political activism in times of national catastrophe that also takes Beyoncé as case study. While celebrating the beauty and power of *B'Day*, Brooks argues for readers and listeners to see it alongside more traditionally recognized protest music by Black women, rather than dismiss it as *just* pop music, drawing connections to political work by the likes of Nina Simone, Odetta, Tracy Chapman, Ms. Lauryn Hill, and Martha and the Vandellas, even comparing it to more current artists like Mary J. Blige and Keyshia Cole, of whom she also offers brief, subversive readings.

While critically lauding the album, Brooks presents compelling, unapologetic Black feminist analysis that locates *B'Day* both in the immediate aftermath of 2005's Hurricane Katrina and within a longer history of Black women's subversive cultural production. She convincingly argues that *B'Day* was a complicated response to the ways Black women had been forced to negatively represent and bear the weight of the nation's pain in mass media following Katrina, especially apt given Beyoncé's Creole ancestry and familial ties to the Gulf Coast region. Brooks imagines that Beyoncé was reclaiming a meticulously nuanced political image of Black women with her work—participating in a longer Black feminist historical trajectory, with which I was also familiar and in which I was deeply interested. Reading Brooks, I realized the vibration and feeling I had initially received from listening to the album could be grounded in politics, cultural commentary, and critique. The excess that couldn't be contained by the speakers had a critical counterpart.

Brooks's articles provided a perfect, serendipitous crash course. I began playing around with my own analyses informed by her observations, thinking about Beyoncé's work in other contexts and alongside other writers, using Brooks's example as a map. As far back as *Dangerously in Love*, Beyoncé noted that "harmonies are colors" in the spoken "Beyoncé Interlude," marking a meaningful synesthetic marriage of music and visuals and inviting a deeper analytic dive, particularly into the visual aspect of her work. What else was Beyoncé hiding beneath the surface? Just like *BEYONCÉ* and *Lemonade* to come, *B'Day* was essentially a visual album with a video for each song, so there was ample material to pore over. The videos were just released later on a separate DVD, more like bonus features or anthology than integral elements, so many paid them less mind. Late nights watching and rewatching Beyoncé videos, searching for deeper meanings and associations, taking furious notes, and compiling them all for future use became a regular pastime.

At my first opportunity, I assigned Daphne Brooks's initial article to my own full class of students in an introductory gender studies course. It provided an exciting template to discuss race, gender, and sexuality within the context of something with which students were often already familiar. The days I assigned the article always found students engaged in intense and animated conversation, much more so than during other sessions. Students who had never spoken in class before finally had everything to say, and weren't scared to speak up. Some students balked and said Beyoncé couldn't possibly be trying to be political or make statements in her music, that this was all coincidence and conjecture. Others were amazed and quickly convinced that she was being subversive and making major political statements about Katrina in unconventional ways.

Students in these intro courses came from a wide variety of backgrounds, majors, and identities. Each group is unique in specific composition, but diversity in perspectives in the classroom was a constant. I taught students from many different racial, ethnic, and class backgrounds, as well as multiple sexualities and gender identities, though groups did tend to include a higher number of women than men by virtue of being located in a women's and gender studies department. College students often consider these intro courses easy ways to satisfy university diversity requirements. Instructors are lucky when students enroll already passionate about the topic. One of the main goals of these courses is to pitch women's and gender studies as a major or minor any student might consider more in-depth, to show how race, gender, and sexuality impact the ways society is set up and the ways everyone moves through the world. In rooms of forty-five or fifty usually rowdy and disinterested college students, the sustained conversation around

Beyoncé's music and newly elicited fervor about the topics this focus inspired, even if just for a day or two, felt like the holy grail. What's more, Beyoncé engaged the room in ways that both highlighted differences (whether in identity among students in the classroom or in society at large) and passionately encouraged connection across those differences. Students shared an excitement for the material from their own unique perspectives. As she'd later proclaim on 2016's "Formation," Beyoncé was already "caus[ing] all this conversation" in the classroom nearly a decade prior.

Meanwhile, Beyoncé released *I Am . . . Sasha Fierce*, another concept album rife with politics of gender, sexuality, and identity. The historical context was obviously different—the album was not situated in a particular geography like *B'Day*—but contained other subtle, subversive politics about race, marriage, and gender roles, perfect for unpacking gendered expectations in society. I started asking students to meditate on the lyrics of "If I Were a Boy" as a way to deconstruct stereotypical, gendered double standards—a skill they were then asked to apply to other pop songs of their choosing. Again, they couldn't get enough. The exercise connected the sometimes-theoretical course material directly to their everyday lives and the music they regularly consumed. At the same time, I was enjoying *myself* more than ever before, as a teacher and critical fan, facilitating and participating in the conversations myself. It proved how essential excitement, pleasure, and fun are as elements or core values in building a productive learning environment, just as bell hooks stipulates in *Teaching to Transgress: Education as the Practice of Freedom.* Given the success and enthusiasm that just a couple of examples provided, I kept experimenting with ways to add other songs, concepts, and social issues to the syllabus, kept exploring ways to see the world that revolved around analysis of Beyoncé's music. So why not invite Beyoncé into class for the entire semester?

*

Enter "Politicizing Beyoncé." The course title itself is a bit of a misnomer, though. Beyoncé never needed anyone to politicize her, especially me as a white man. The work she does as a Black woman in an industry (and society) where white men hold most of the power is already inherently political. And since the first time I taught the full course in 2010, she's become progressively more determined to delineate explicitly political layers in her work, while still rarely delivering formal pronouncements on electoral politics. The title wasn't about politicizing Beyoncé as a person— rather, politicizing the gaze through which audiences and the public *see* Beyoncé as an artist and the work she creates. Peeling back the layers of her music to reveal additional influences, references, connections, and even critiques of the ways race, gender, and sexuality have been understood and operate in the world. It meant, to me, learning to locate and talk about the intersections of race, gender, sexuality, class, etc.— their impact and force—through Beyoncé's music, regardless of how removed an individual's identity may be from those intersections. Pragmatically, "Politicizing Beyoncé" was also a quick and catchy phrase meant to grab a student's attention while they flipped through a jam-packed course catalog. And on a purely cosmetic level, "politicizing" served as reference and homage to Brooks's "Suga Mama, Politicized"— the original article that inspired me to create the course.

In the fall of 2010, I got the opportunity to teach a special topics course under the broad heading "Feminist Perspectives." For those unfamiliar, special topics courses in any department typically provide general education credits toward an overall degree, sometimes meet specific university diversity requirements, and count toward that department's major or minor. They give instructors a chance to focus on special interests and research in progress for an entire semester in a collaborative environment with students. I jumped at the opportunity to bring "Politicizing Beyoncé" to life. That fateful semester, students didn't even know they were signing up for a full Beyoncé seminar. Given the snail's pace of university bureaucracy, and the fact that I had been assigned to the special topics course late in the summer, the "Politicizing Beyoncé" subtitle wasn't featured in the catalog. On that first September afternoon, students were . . . shocked, to put it mildly. After some stilted introductory conversation where I asked students what they were expecting, I dropped the ultimate bomb. "This semester we're going to be looking at feminist perspectives of one particular topic," I said, and paused for dramatic effect, almost a beat too long. Then I finished, "And that topic is Beyoncé."

First, there was a wave of disbelief. A couple of students who had been glancing at phones or laptops looked up, confused. One student pulled out their earbuds to see if they'd heard correctly. "Did you say Beyoncé?" Another previously disinterested student yelled, "SHUT UP!" at full volume and unintentionally threw a pen (I ducked!). I couldn't hide my own excitement and amusement either, and doubled over laughing. It was exactly the reaction I'd hoped for. After a couple more minutes of eager questions and chatter, I handed out the full syllabus, and we went through the logistics of the course—journal assignments, research papers, attendance policy, etc. But the energy and interest in the room remained palpable. That energy never diminished over the entire semester, and engagement levels haven't dwindled over subsequent years, though students have been far less surprised about what they were signing up for at the outset.

"Politicizing Beyoncé" was a way to practice carefully analyzing media, using lyrics and music videos as texts themselves, but also a way to create conversations around important social issues while keeping Black feminist voices at the center. I decided early on in organizing the course that I would exclusively assign work by Black women writers, thinkers, artists, and activists alongside Beyoncé's catalog; following Brooks's example, I wanted to put a longer history of Black feminist thought and action in conversation with Beyoncé's music across time. None of the assigned reading would be *about* Beyoncé, but would be selected and positioned to inform her work or draw out particular themes through careful pairing, always organized around the syllabus's central questions: How does Beyoncé challenge our very understanding of the categories of race, gender, class, and sexuality? How does Beyoncé push the boundaries of these categories to make space for and embrace other, supposedly more deviant, bodies, desires, and/or politics? "Politicizing Beyoncé" attempted to undeniably position Beyoncé as a progressive, feminist, and queer icon in an attempt to answer the question: Can her music be seen as a blueprint for social change?

As a white man with certain privileges and access to a classroom, I have also long felt a political responsibility to attempt to subversively marginalize traditional, overrepresented white male voices in any way possible, even though those voices come from the same social position as my own. Black women's voices are still too often only tokenized on syllabi, when included at all. Black feminism is first and foremost about the experience of Black women, and because I can't speak to that experience or identity, I wanted the assigned texts to speak for themselves, to and with one another. I'd been reading Black women's work privately for years after being deeply inspired by individual writers and the field of Black feminist thought overall as a young person, and centered Black women's work in my graduate study as well. It may have been an unlikely area of interest for a white queer kid from Utah, but I do believe listening to Black women holds the answers to building a better world, and wanted to make that truth central to my teaching. The work of the class would be putting the sources into conversation with Beyoncé's music, using them as lenses to uncover hidden lyrical and visual layers in Beyoncé's work. Letting the texts together guide students to ways of seeing always grounded in the intersections of race, gender, sexuality, class, etc.—a hallmark of Black feminist thought even before it became codified as theory or academic discipline.

Of course, some students are more familiar with seeing the world through this lens already, given their own experiences and identities; for others, it is wholly new. In conceptualizing the class, I wanted to cast a wide net and emphasize conversations across differences to reflect the diversity found in the BeyHive and among casual Beyoncé listeners. Her music speaks to many groups, for different reasons. Of course, Black women and LGBTQ+ students, especially queer folks of color, enroll in high numbers, as they comprise major portions of Beyoncé's fan base, but the overall makeup of the class is quite similar to the introductory teaching I was already used to. In fact, I hoped "Politicizing Beyoncé" would function as another kind of introductory course to feminism and issues of social justice solely through Black women's work and voices. I never intended the class to speak *to* or *for* Black women, or any one specific group, as I never could or would do that. Being a white man facilitating the course requires a lot of consideration and self-reflection, as well as deferral to the students in many cases. I obviously have theories about Beyoncé's videos, but try to create space for students as they come to understand the analysis organically and offer their own additional insights. I never lecture—I just prompt discussion with strategic questions and initial ideas. To me, teaching is largely about listening, and improvising. I try to provide a scaffolding to build on, but never impose any particular interpretation of the material as the *only* correct one. A mentor once taught me to think of teaching as choreography, so my plotting of the syllabus was a kind of rough sketch of steps students could infuse with their own energy, experience, and unique movement.

By foregrounding and always speaking from my own identity and privilege in my teaching and analysis, I'm trying to highlight complicities and responsibilities many share in creating and sustaining a society that has hurt so many, while de facto insulating others. I hope that angle encourages students to consider themselves within Patricia Hill Collins's "matrix of domination"—a theory that complicates the simple oppressed/oppressor binary—to expose and interrogate their own levels of power and privilege, whatever they may be. Coming to terms and engaging with one's own privilege in order to recognize its roots and challenge them from that particular vantage point, while simultaneously never speaking over or for others, can help dismantle this unequal society. It's the necessary first step toward solidarity. The classroom is a space where students and instructors alike can discuss these issues in ways that wouldn't likely be as useful or prudent in organizing or activist spaces, though education shares elements with both, and so I wanted to harness what the classroom makes possible, while instilling a critical awareness of and respect for boundaries around identity for those who do wield some privilege.

There are some conversations around Beyoncé's work that are most effectively led and conducted by Black women. Conversations that come out of shared identity with Beyoncé as a Black woman. For instance, I have no place in a conversation around *Lemonade* and the intricacies of Black women's romantic relationships, heterosexual or queer. Those collective dialogues speak to certain pieces of experience I can never access or likely understand. However, I can respectfully listen to learn more, if and when granted the permission to observe, as can others. But I believe Beyoncé's work as a whole is also marketed to and meant to be discussed and analyzed by diverse audiences, even while her references become increasingly and more explicitly Black. By relying on close textual analysis and interpretation, along with healthy doses of admiration, reverence, and humility, it's possible to create those conversations in the classroom with wider audiences. It's about perspective and direction. A large part of Beyoncé's brilliance as an artist lies in how she makes these multiple conversations possible simultaneously—calling out complicities in society, while empowering those that aren't traditionally included in the American project. And always, always centering Black women.

After that first semester in the fall of 2010, the media got wind of my course, and demand grew exponentially. I had no idea that anyone outside those thirty original students would ever hear about it. Since then, I've been lucky enough to teach the full course over a dozen times and be invited to speak about the curriculum around the world, which has been a dream, especially for an adjunct lecturer not typically guaranteed any job security. Beyoncé also continues to release new music, evolve, and expand her empire. The class changes and becomes new again with the passage of time. But the conversations around gender, race, class, and sexuality that take place are as necessary as ever. America's deeply fractured and divided society was put in even starker relief after the 2016 election. Talking about the divides that plague the US and discussing the differences that exist between people—not ignoring them—is increasingly essential to healing this world. Listening to Black women's solutions, especially, is of the utmost importance. In "Age, Race, Class, and Sex: Women Redefining Difference," Audre Lorde says, "Certainly there are very real differences between us. . . . But it is not those differences between us that are separating us. It is rather our refusal to recognize those differences, and to examine the distortions which result from our misnaming them." More recognition, more examination, less misnaming. Beyoncé continues to spark conversations that include all three.

Popular buzzwords like "intersectionality" and "identity politics" are direct Black feminist contributions, though in today's lexicon, they've often been divorced from their histories, resulting in decontextualization from all sides. In that regard, "Politicizing Beyoncé" also seeks to recenter the origins and histories of those terms for those unaware of or intentionally ignoring their sources. The Left often reduces intersectionality to mere representation, identity, or coalition; the Right derisively uses identity politics to claim backlash against straight white men. In either case, the terms get emptied of critical weight and revolutionary potential. Legal scholar Kimberlé Crenshaw coined intersectionality to illuminate the ways Black women's experiences—using discrimination, harassment, and violence as case studies—are wholly erased, relegated to issues of either race or gender and never the complex interplay of power working through multiple, intersecting registers, thus leaving oppressive power masked and running amok. Scholar and founding member of the Crunk Feminist Collective, Brittney C. Cooper, put it this way:

> Intersectionality was never put forth as an account of identity but rather an account of power. That we have taken up intersectionality as a way primarily to speak about ourselves . . . is unfortunate. . . . [I]t often means that we can't think productively about how racism, sexism, classism, heterosexism, ableism, and yes, neoliberalism . . . disadvantage people multiply placed along these axes.

Intersectionality's origins and Cooper's rearticulation highlight it as a lens everyone must necessarily see through.

Similarly, identity politics was coined by the Combahee River Collective (CRC) in 1977 to describe the ways Black women and lesbians are likely predisposed to understand power's nefarious machinations because they experience the force of those interlocking oppressions simultaneously, on personal and intimate levels. The CRC posited the concerns of Black women and Black lesbians, as well as working women and those referred to as Third World Women at the time, as central to a politics able to critique power and address societal problems most effectively. A nonexclusionary politics, but one with Black women at its particular center, that resisted the top-down, rights-based discourse of the United States, in which marginalized groups are only ever partially included in the American project, beginning with those already most privileged in any group. In *How We Get Free: Black Feminism and the Combahee River Collective*, Keeanga-Yamahtta Taylor revisits the CRC's definitive 1977 Black Feminist Statement, mining its continued relevance and its often overlooked anticapitalist demand for a "reorganization of society based on the collective needs of the most oppressed. That is to say if you could free the most oppressed people in society, then you would have to free everyone." Similarly,

Black feminism takes as its guiding principle the idea that when Black women get free, everyone gets free. Identity and experience are obviously central, but the political lens is available and necessary for anyone interested in advocating for progressive social change. Use of the lens doesn't necessarily rely on or require a particular identity.

After years of teaching Beyoncé—or rather, centering Beyoncé while I teach—I wanted to turn what I've learned into a book for a host of reasons. To share what I hope is exciting, thought-provoking analysis of Beyoncé's music. To extend classroom conversations beyond formal university walls. To trace a story of possibly subversive politics layered into Beyoncé's music, or at least highlight the potential to create conversations about subversive politics using Beyoncé's music. To insist that pop culture, and Beyoncé in particular, can be useful, even essential political tools to revitalize education, needed now more than ever. To cultivate critical fandom, inspire fans to always search for deeper meaning in what they love. To prove there is merit in the things that many gatekeepers of the ivory tower pretend to be too smart to enjoy. To demand that more people with privilege become politically engaged, push beyond their own privileged experience (my own included), and recognize those privileges and work from their unique social position in productive solidarity with others. To highlight Black feminism and intersectionality as essential analytic lenses for all people working toward a healthier, more equitable society. To insist that education can also be fun.

I also wanted to record the unique story of "Politicizing Beyoncé" as the first in-depth, semester-long, college-level examination of Beyoncé's larger career, catalog, and artistic, political layers dating back to that first fall 2010 semester. Additional courses have come together in recent years post-*BEYONCÉ*—from a Harvard business study on her marketing innovations and a course focused on image and social media, to a performance studies investigation of gender and race in her work, a deep dive into Black folklore and horror influences in *Lemonade*, and an exploration of feminism and womanism through Beyoncé and Rihanna, among a handful of others. Beyoncé herself has even become more academically involved since 2010 via her BeyGOOD philanthropic endeavors, creating a "Formation Scholars" program for the one-year anniversary of *Lemonade*, and joining with Jay-Z to give away over one million dollars in scholarships during the On the Run II tour. With all these exciting developments and interest in Beyoncé inside and outside the academy, I hope this book also shows that "Politicizing Beyoncé" still offers something unique, exciting, and necessary.

Ain't I a Diva? leads the reader through the most current iteration of the "Politicizing Beyoncé" syllabus and analysis that has emerged from my own work and class conversations. It follows a loose three-part structure—past, present, and future—but one that is thematic, not chronological. Beyoncé's work regularly features the past, historically and metaphorically; a critique of various systems of power in the present; and ways of imagining a better future. Chapters include major pairings students read and study as homework in order to place them in conversation with Beyoncé during class sessions, but I've also attempted to inflect the analysis with additional sources that provide valuable context, some specifically about Beyoncé, that I don't typically ask students to read. Obviously, a book can't fully capture live discussion, but the story and analysis in these pages is pieced together from semesters and years of lively conversation following lines of flight, unpacking layers, and making connections using Beyoncé's music. Plus I've included some notes on my own pedagogical practice. Hopefully, you'll finish the book feeling as if you've taken the class itself, not just read about it, and I hope you'll watch the videos with each chapter as you read, just like students are required to in class, though you're clearly not being graded on your participation. As with the syllabus, I'm purposefully only citing Black women in this book as part of my own political practice and commitment.

Chapter 1 is a condensed version of the first few class sessions: laying the groundwork to approach

Beyoncé as public artist and not private person, plus an introduction to course methodology via a blend of Beyoncé's political conception of a diva and Sojourner Truth's life and speeches. The next three chapters chase ghosts through Beyoncé's catalog, from *Lemonade* backward into American history and her earlier work, reenacting a performative loop. The middle four chapters address stories Beyoncé tells about current intersecting systems of power and control, and how those same systems are normalized and generally haunt society's common sense: beauty standards, sexuality, the Western gender binary, and capitalism. The final three chapters look to building better worlds and healing. Of course, themes spill over and resist containment, just like that first bass note of "Déjà Vu" that grabbed me and still hasn't let go. An epilogue and two appendices finally return to the beginning, and, along with the previous sections, nod to Beyoncé's prescient assertion in *Lemonade*: "The past and the future merge to meet us here." The full book then hopefully turns into its own performative loop that continues to spiral outward. Here we are.

Ultimately, "Politicizing Beyoncé," and now *Ain't I a Diva?*, embrace and attempt to extend the themes of "Schoolin' Life." To blend education, pop culture, and honest conversation across difference, history, and politics, in solidarity with a longer Black feminist trajectory and deep appreciation of the sources. I want to reimagine, from unlikely places, what a political fight might look like, and illuminate various ways individuals can *do* politics and engage politically. I want to create useful conversations that follow the bread crumbs Beyoncé has scattered throughout her music. I hope you'll join me. And I hope, in whatever small way, while reading this book, your world stops. Just a little. Maybe you'll frame an issue differently. In a bold new way. I hope this book leaves you optimistic and inspired, and produces the same enthusiasm Beyoncé's music continues to spark in me and so many others. And then, after worlds stop, as Beyoncé insists in "Feeling Myself," I hope you "carry on." I hope we all carry on as students in Beyoncé's classroom. Connect, critically. Carry on, renewed.

1
AIN'T I A DIVA?

"WHO IS BEYONCÉ?"

It's the first question I ask students to ponder on the first day of class. A question meant to be deceptively complex. A question used to tease out the level of familiarity with Beyoncé students bring to the classroom, any assumptions about her career they might hold, and any various attachments they have to her music. Of course, no prior knowledge or familiarity is necessary—her songs and videos become texts, just like any other readings in any other traditional course. I have, on occasion, had a few students who knew nothing about Beyoncé sign up; they just wanted a break from the monotony of their regular studies. I've even had a Beyoncé antagonist or two enroll to play devil's advocate, but they still have to ground their criticism in textual analysis. All opinions are welcome. It's much more common, however, that students sign up because they're already avid fans—whether or not they claim full-fledged BeyHive membership—or at least casual listeners of pieces or all of Beyoncé's catalog. Some students are new fans; some have been listening for as long as they can remember. As years go by, students even become less likely to know a life before Beyoncé—an eighteen-year-old today was born in 2001 and Destiny's Child's self-titled debut album was released in 1998. Regardless, some students and fans have identity-based attachments; some love the themes and content, even though they don't reflect their own experiences. Most everyone shares a love of the music, though, across backgrounds and identities. In this introductory conversation, I ask students to share it all: what they personally love about Beyoncé, or even (gasp!) things that they aren't as fond of, to draw out some of the above connections. It's a nice way to form camaraderie on the first day, and beats the typical trite icebreaker.

The question also serves as a way to set up one of the foundational aspects of the course that can never be overstated: analysis of Beyoncé will focus on Beyoncé as a performer and artist, not Beyoncé as a private person. So as everyone shares their personal associations and reactions, and even a little gossip, I try to point out the differences between analyzing Beyoncé's performances critically and gossiping or making assumptions about her personal life based on her music—which isn't to say her personal life isn't part of her music, but so much of what the public thinks they know about Beyoncé's personal life is conjecture.

Those watching may suspect certain things, and lyrics and visuals may allude to some interpersonal drama, but they're rarely addressed formally by Beyoncé herself outside of her art. In today's social media culture, fans have near-constant access to their favorite celebrities, but Beyoncé has emphatically drawn a line between her public persona and private life, especially since 2013. She is one of few celebrities, if not the only one of her caliber, with such strictly defined boundaries. That delineation is something that gets highlighted again and again over the course, especially when conversations and analysis veer too close to personal assumptions.

Viewing *Life Is But a Dream*, Beyoncé's 2013 documentary, as a form of visual autobiography together at the beginning of the semester helps drive this point home. The film is a master class in sleight of hand—Beyoncé gives the audience an intimate look at her life and work while still offering few specific facts about her private existence. She literally brings viewers up to the front door of her childhood home in the opening shots, but leaves that door closed, even as she offers vulnerable and intimate behind-the-scenes snippets. All the while, the door serves as a symbolic boundary; it never opens. Those private moments are carefully curated and the audience returns to and moves back from that still-closed door at the end of the film, reminding everyone to respect the barrier between

Beyoncé's private and public selves. To give her space to be an artist and create—the same space and consideration regularly afforded white male artists.

Another introductory exercise I use to highlight Beyoncé as a public artist is to contextualize her place in the longer history of Black women in music. Students are asked collectively to create a timeline of artists who they think map out a trajectory of inspiration, without whom the rise of Beyoncé would have never been possible. To mark the connections between Black women's musical contributions back through time. Many of the artists named during this initial exercise reappear at other moments during the semester too, either named by Beyoncé as specific influences or referenced more generally and artistically through her work or other sources. Bessie Smith, Josephine Baker, Billie Holiday, Sister Rosetta Tharpe, Dinah Washington, Etta James, Nina Simone, Aretha Franklin, Mahalia Jackson, The Supremes, Diana Ross, Tina Turner, Grace Jones, Donna Summer, Natalie Cole, Janet Jackson, Whitney Houston, Ms. Lauryn Hill— just to name a few. Of course, many other artists of other backgrounds and identities play pivotal roles in Beyoncé's development, but the timeline remains focused on Black women in music exclusively.

So, again, who *is* Beyoncé? It's not a question that's meant to be answered, really. It's a question to mull over for the entire course and untold time to come.

Yes, she's a performer, singer, songwriter, actress, visual artist, musical genius, Black woman in the US, business mogul, mother, wife, daughter, sister, icon. She's all those things and countless more. She's also, to quote Jamaican performance poet Staceyann Chin, "Never one thing or the other." Beyoncé is complicated and inhabits multiple identities and positions. I might even add feminist and queer theorist to the list based on analyses of her work. She's all of the above and more; at other times, she's none of those things, and possibly something else entirely. Never one thing or the other. Beyoncé is a piece of history and history in the making. And during a memorable 2008 song, Beyoncé importantly self-identifies as a diva. What is a diva? A diva is also never one thing or another, and a diva is intersectional too. To understand how the idea of the diva functions in Beyoncé's catalog, students must travel back to one of the earliest points in history on the syllabus—not just back through Black women's musical contributions but Black women's activism as well—to Sojourner Truth and her work publicly interrogating race and gender, alongside other systems. All of which get further developed later, but this initial interrogation jump-starts thinking. Obviously, Beyoncé and Sojourner Truth share more differences than commonalities, but it's still useful to name the ways in which Beyoncé might be carrying Truth's truth forward.

Ain't I a Woman?

Sojourner Truth has long been heralded as a Black feminist icon and symbol, representing critique of the often-single-issue focus of both the abolitionist and women's rights movements in the mid- to late 1800s. As Angela Davis states in *Women, Race & Class*, "If most abolitionists viewed slavery as a nasty blemish which needed to be eliminated, most women's righters viewed male supremacy in a similar manner—as an immoral flaw in their otherwise acceptable society." Truth knew society was much more deeply flawed and refused to be silent. Her "Ain't I a Woman?" speech, given at the 1851 Women's Rights Convention in Akron, Ohio, has become a staple in both women's and gender studies and African American studies classrooms. It powerfully critiques a divide that continues to this day in feminist movements. You can find YouTube video performances of the speech by actresses Kerry Washington and Alfre Woodard; it's been memorialized as the title of bell hooks's first book, *Ain't I a Woman: Black Women and Feminism*, and even used by actress and activist Laverne Cox in her university speaking engagements, inflecting the phrase with additional important political commentary on gender.

Trouble is, the version of Truth's speech celebrated today likely never happened. Truth left no first-person writing or records of the "Ain't I a Woman?" speech, as she never learned to read or write, and it was reportedly delivered extemporaneously. She did publish the *Narrative of Sojourner Truth*, as transcribed by a friend, but her speeches don't appear, only her life story. Nell Irvin Painter traces the history of Sojourner Truth in the definitive account of her life, *Sojourner Truth: A Life, a Symbol*. She notes that the version of the speech anthologized today was recorded by Frances Dana Gage in 1863, allegedly from her own twelve-year-old memories of the convention, and is, according to Painter's meticulous research, "by no means the real Sojourner Truth." Despite the inaccuracies and sometimes direct contradictions to the only other record of the speech—by Marius Robinson in 1851, with none of the dramatic flourish of Gage's account, and none of the dialect which might be considered racist when recorded by Gage, especially because Truth was brought up speaking Dutch and likely had none of the speech patterns memorialized—Painter says Gage's account persists because of its power as *performance*.

Though the dramatic phrasing and gestures associated with the speech everyone reads, quotes, and performs today are likely incorrect, the sentiment and content do fall in line with Sojourner Truth's overarching work to dismantle racism and sexism at their intersections. In fact, Truth was often even more radical than she is usually given credit for, fiercely attacking capitalism as the very system from which racial and gender difference are created. Truth was born into slavery around 1797 as Isabella Baumfree (she later adopted the surname Van Wagenen) but escaped with one of her daughters in 1826. She later sued white owners in that same year to have her son returned to her and won, becoming the first Black woman to ever win a lawsuit against a white man, a major feat in and of itself. She eventually took on the name Sojourner Truth, meaning walking truth teller, in 1843 after feeling called by God to spread her message. She toured not unlike a contemporary performer, captivating audiences with both oration and song, preaching religion but also demanding freedom for Black women as an abolitionist and women's rights advocate simultaneously.

Beyoncé and Sojourner Truth are connected through performance and their affective pull on audiences. Truth's commanding presence and charisma were regularly referenced by those who witnessed her speeches. The same are often ascribed to Beyoncé. But the two also connect through content. Truth's tireless attempts to disrupt racism *and* sexism, while capturing the oppression Black women faced in her day, echo through many of Beyoncé's lyrics, visual images, and performances, exceedingly so as her career continues to evolve. Both Beyoncé and Truth contribute to a Black feminist history and trajectory; they just utilize different contexts and strategies. Historical circumstances certainly differ—Truth worked adamantly against the system of her time from an outside position after escaping slavery; Beyoncé works firmly within a capitalist apparatus, but it's possible to find critical commentary on that same system in a close analysis of her music. Both women also crafted public images for themselves divorced from their personal histories and private lives. And they are both examples of uncredited forms of education, of "Schoolin' Life." Education, intellect, and smarts are not just the domain of official institutions or the ivory tower in America; rather, knowledge can come from anywhere—life experience, struggle, political positioning. Truth wasn't able to attend school as a young girl because she was enslaved; Beyoncé left official schooling as a girl to earn capital in the entertainment industry, having been primed for that career since before she could make the decision for herself. Both became powerful symbols for their respective times.

I still assign the "Ain't I a Woman?" speech in class, framing it as performance, not fact, and alongside more accurate snippets of Truth's life as told by Painter and through Truth's own *Narrative*. Just as conversations around celebrity gossip today can teach audiences about what is prized and valued in society, Truth's speech still has the power to pose questions about how and why Truth is remembered as she is, as well as to question what gets forgotten in doing so. The speech and the larger work of Sojourner Truth is a useful historical entry point into the intersection of race and gender—intersectionality long before it was coined by Kimberlé Crenshaw. I also ask students to think about the "Ain't I a Woman?" speech as anti-capitalist critique, to which the syllabus returns in more detail later in the semester. Yes, the erasure of Black womanhood specifically is at the heart of the repeated "Ain't I a woman?" query, but Truth maintained that that erasure was fueled through the economics of slavery via capitalism. The speech focuses on Black women's exclusion, given the work they were often required to do, from the separate spheres white women were afforded. "Look at me! Look at my arm! I have ploughed, and planted, and gathered into barns, and no man could head me. And ain't I a woman?" Truth allegedly exclaimed. She exposed the fact that gender categories and expectations have been used as racist tools throughout history to separate white and Black as well as male and female, all for capitalist gain. Profits over people. Truth positioned work done as an enslaved Black woman—forced planting, ploughing—as a site to uncover the ways intersecting gender, racial, and sexual differences, taken for granted as innate, are actually created and preserved by those reaping the profits.

Beyoncé approaches similar territory by deconstructing what it means to be a diva more than one hundred and fifty years later, performing as her alter ego Sasha Fierce. The lyrics of "Diva" highlight work, albeit in different contexts, to unapologetically demand an answer to Truth's iconic query. Beyoncé simultaneously updates, inflects, and rephrases it with her own unique, contemporary spin, and it's no longer a rhetorical question with performative flourish—it's a merciless, defiant assertion. By thinking about Sojourner Truth alongside Beyoncé, "Ain't I a woman?" slides powerfully into "I'm-a a diva." And Beyoncé's diva takes no prisoners.

Ain't I a Diva?

In today's vernacular, embracing your inner (or outer) diva is not a de facto positive attribute. But that's exactly the reframing Beyoncé attempts in the 2008 song from *I Am . . . Sasha Fierce*. The word "diva" entered English from the Italian for "female deity" in the late nineteenth century and typically referenced the most coveted female role in opera, achieved only after years of dedication to honing talent and craft. However, race, gender, and sexuality all carve out aspects of today's definition of diva, heavily informed by pop culture. A string of popular performance specials on the cable network VH1, beginning in 1998 and airing as recently as 2016, sought to reclaim and celebrate divas, but the term is still often colloquially (mis)understood as a woman who is bossy, difficult, or entitled. Today's pop culture divas may demand attention, but often for notorious, ignoble reasons that have nothing to do with talent. Diva has racial and queer connotations too—an intersectional position all its own. *RuPaul's Drag Race* has celebrated drag divas, campy cattiness overflowing, for mainstream audiences since 2009. Sasha Fierce's diva, comparable to Sojourner Truth's "woman," incorporates these multiple pieces and enacts a complex critique of power from categories often seen as powerless. And like Truth, Beyoncé also hints at the fact that capitalism creates racial, gender, and sexual difference to begin with in "Diva"—while performing her own queer drag parody.

In the opening shot of the music video, Beyoncé shares exactly the definition of diva she wants understood as central to her song and Sasha Fierce performance:

di•va
\ˊdē-və\
plural divas or di•ve
NOUN

1 a successful and glamorous female performer or personality <a fashion diva>;
2 especially : a female singer who has achieved popularity <pop diva>

The definition is altered slightly from Merriam-Webster's, and offering it as an introductory title screen indicates those changes must be significant. She completely leaves out Merriam-Webster's first definition of "prima donna" and then alters the second definition somewhat, splitting it in two to fit her purposes. While the dictionary's definition begins, "a *usually* successful and glamorous female performer or personality" (my emphasis), Beyoncé insists on the success and glamour of her diva, and thus suggests audiences consider the various costs of that success. Under capitalism, success does not always follow talent, but one's success *is* often built on the exploitation or erasure of others, just as the category and separate sphere of womanhood was built off the labor of Black women. Some snide criticism delivered by Sasha Fierce, speaking from an outsider position to expose difficult truths.

Beyoncé then importantly stresses *achievement* in her diva, as opposed to tacit popularity—the achievement and work involved in *becoming* a diva—whereas the dictionary merely deems the diva "a popular female singer." Anyone can be popular and not deserve it. Capitalism especially doesn't care about talent or merit, only profit and hype (popularity). Turn on the radio today and you're bound to see this principle in action. In addition to deconstructing the success and glamour Sasha Fierce invokes in the first part of the definition, Beyoncé is throwing specific shade at those who may receive notoriety or fame without putting in hard work, or have no real talent or skill—those who benefit off the system at the expense of others. In a 2015 Made in America performance of "Diva," Beyoncé sampled words by mixed martial arts fighter Ronda Rousey, naming the one who profits while not studying and cultivating their talent or working hard to achieve their success, in heightened distinction to her redefined diva, a "do-nothing bitch."

When Beyoncé calls out so-called divas for their lax work ethic, there exists a surprising reflection of the way Audre Lorde constantly confronted her various audiences, letting them know that she was vigilantly doing the difficult *work* of challenging all forms of oppression on a daily basis, and demanding to know if they were doing their own version of that work. In "The Transformation of Silence into Language and Action," Lorde states, "Perhaps for some of you here today, I am the face of one of your fears. Because I am woman, because I am Black, because I am lesbian, because I am myself—a Black woman warrior poet doing my work—come to ask you, are you doing yours?" Beyoncé is astutely mirroring Lorde from her own vantage point and confronting her audience with the various ways that the word "work" works. Audre Lorde and Beyoncé both hold themselves to the highest standard, and demand a high standard of their audience. It's easy to simply equate work here with achievements within a capitalist enterprise. And that traditional sense of work is certainly central, evidenced by lyrics that make "getting paid" a priority, but money doesn't always follow the work. Some profit from exploitation of others' work, even getting paid means more than cash in pocket in a Beyoncé performance. To stop there would be to abandon the power of the connection with Lorde and the full critique Beyoncé levels.

In *Life Is But a Dream*, Beyoncé offers an analysis of money as power, not for individual gain but for its revolutionary potential to affect change for better or worse: "It really pisses me off that women don't get the same opportunities as men do. Or money for that matter, because, let's face it, money has given men the power to run the show. It gives men the power to define our values and to define what's sexy and what's feminine. And that's bullshit." Money—as arbiter and driving force in a capitalist system—is the problem. Treating people differently, whether by individual choice or forced by law, can't simply fix the unequal distribution of wealth if the system itself for assigning meaning and power remains intact. Next to Lorde's invocation of work and Beyoncé's redefinition of money, "work" takes on more meaning: the traditional meaning remains, but added is the more implicit notion of doing *political* work to challenge racism, sexism, and homophobia through redefining money and capitalism. Beyoncé sings, "Diva is a female version of a hustla," which is not just a gendered distinction marking who gets credit for what types of work where she keeps gendered associations of male hustler and female diva intact, but a formulation that exposes the insidious ways that power divides and creates privileged positions. No one would ever claim a hustler is the male version of a diva. Beyoncé equating the two illustrates that when it comes to work, women are always defined through men, never vice versa, and she thinks it's bullshit. She creates a complicated equation that exposes the absurdity of insisting on gendered distinctions *in* work, while also reworking the overall concept of what counts *as* work. She's working to undo work. And ain't she a diva?

Beyoncé makes no differentiation between accepted, legal forms of work—like singing in exchange for money—and nontraditional and sometimes illegal labor either. A hustler is commonly known as someone who makes money dealing in stolen goods or drugs, nontraditional exchanges both inside and outside conventional capitalism. Playing off that primary definition of a hustler is also the notion of someone always *working* the scene—keeping an eye out for any available opportunity, questionable or not, to move up the social ladder. In the song, Beyoncé makes it clear that she's out to get the money or do the work by any means necessary, resisting the reduction of different kinds of work as good or bad regardless of the law. She refers repeatedly to the song as a "stickup"—she's wearing a mask and she wants that money. No one can stop her. And so necessary political work is also positioned here as a "stickup" and outside the bounds of the status quo, further mirroring Lorde. In fact, Audre Lorde repeatedly performed a similar kind of "stickup" by announcing herself into every room she entered as a speaker with the various pieces of her identity front and center—as "Black," "lesbian," "feminist," "warrior poet"—stringing together different facets of herself at different times in different orders to also indicate that she is never just one thing or the other. She confronted the audience, essentially sticking up the crowd, to claim each space uniquely as her own. Just like Sojourner Truth's imagined battle cry that continues to reverberate. "This is a stickup. This is a stickup."

Back to the term "diva" itself: it signals racial stereotypes in common parlance that can't be denied. As a negative attribute, it gets associated with Black women in music much more than white women, tacitly labeling them difficult. It should be stated that difficult, however, is almost always a matter of opinion. What appears difficult to work with from one vantage point is confident and assertive regarding one's vision and performance from another. Usually, race, gender, and sometimes sexuality are contributing factors in these distinctions. In mainstream music, women are more likely than men to be called divas, and women of color—Black women especially—are more often referred to negatively as divas than white women, whether they have worked to achieve the title or not. Multiple scenes from *Life Is But a Dream* show Beyoncé being negatively dismissed as a diva for having a clear vision for a performance and expecting it to be precisely executed. Though the word itself is not used, it's clear from facial expressions and snide comments from some of the production team that Beyoncé's assertiveness is received as bossiness when she insists on stage and lighting changes that had already been ignored by them multiple times.

The cable music network VH1 reinvigorated the concept and category of diva in the late 1990s when they launched their *Divas Live* franchise. Out of twelve concerts aired since its premiere in 1998, Black women made up a majority of the divas in nine concerts. Eleven featured a majority of women of color more broadly as divas. Only one sole *Divas Live* special featured a majority of white divas. As a question of representation and talent, these numbers seem positive and affirming, but if being a diva is implicitly seen as negative in society—something Beyoncé is trying to rewrite—then it becomes telling that women of color, and Black women specifically, are pigeonholed as the divas VH1 celebrates. It's a catch-22: celebrated and derided simultaneously. Which, unfortunately, is not a new experience for Black women in America. While challenging the negative, gendered dimensions of the diva, Beyoncé is also challenging the term's racial stereotype as a Black woman caught within that catch-22 herself.

Gender and race intersect in the category of "diva," as does class in some loose ways relating to work. But so do sexuality, gender identity, and presentation. *RuPaul's Drag Race* is another significant way the diva has been catapulted into the pop culture mainstream and reflects a certain queerness and nontraditional gender performance. The show itself is a celebration of the excess of drag divas—queens who go above and beyond to compete for the title of the next drag superstar. The portrayals on the show are often far from the most nuanced political representations of cultural resistance possible through drag, especially given various accusations of racism and transphobia against contestants, fans, RuPaul, and the show's staging and production over its run. And the visible corporate sponsorships certainly celebrate commercialization and capitalism, but for better or worse, the show remains the most visible and circulated representation of queer divas among the largest number of people.

Beyoncé plays with queerness and stereotypical rules of gender in "Diva" too by performing the song as Sasha Fierce, one of her central symbolic alter egos. The song appears on the "Sasha Fierce" side of the *I Am . . . Sasha Fierce* album—the side on which the normative categories of gender and sexuality easily recognized by mainstream American society are thrown into question. Sasha Fierce, these claims, and more are the explicit focus of chapter 7. Suffice it to say for now, though, that Sasha Fierce's eccentricity, performance of overblown confidence, and drastic makeup choices point to the likelihood that Sasha Fierce is meant to be read as a drag performance. Viewers shouldn't read Beyoncé-as-Sasha-Fierce as simply female when she appears, including during the music video for "Diva." Sasha Fierce is a complex alter ego—a cisgender female body (Beyoncé) performing feminine drag (Sasha Fierce), but funneled intermediately through society's traditional construction of masculinity (since mainstream drag queens are often cisgender, male-identified individuals still relying on the gender binary for campy humor). And that's a lot of *work*.

Beyoncé is doing the absolute most performing as Sasha Fierce, and for good reason. Alongside Sojourner Truth, Sasha Fierce appears in "Diva" to deconstruct all the above categories that inflect and inform her diva, and explode their conventionally limited notions to confront audiences with Truth's query anew. What do gender, sexuality, race, and class even mean? Who is being included and who is being excluded? Sojourner Truth phrased it "Ain't I a woman?"; Beyoncé metaphorically demands an answer to "Ain't I a diva?" while telling the audience exactly what makes a diva at the same time. Sasha Fierce is fiercely *working it* and also working to break down the exclusionary ways people get categorized in the world. A diva here is damn well politicized. A diva does her necessary political work, certainly no do-nothing bitch, and does not allow status quo gender categories, along with their racial and sexual inflections, to stand without question. A diva is not just political, but confrontational.

Where Truth's purported speech demanded the audience look at her arms and body, recognize her womanhood in conjunction with the ways she was forced to plough and plant, Beyoncé prefaces her "stickup" with, "Since fifteen in my stilettos, been strutting in this game / 'What's your age?' was the question they asked when I hit the stage / I'm a diva, best believe her, you see her, she's getting paid." Reenacting themes of work that mirror Truth (even in similar cadence and construction) but through her own experience as an entertainer, Beyoncé centers age as yet another intersectional component of her diva. She's been doing this since a young age. She's been working, in an industry that has sometimes been likened to slavery, especially by Black performers, where the reality is a disproportionate number of white men make millions off of the creative output of Black artists. And hasn't Beyoncé made it? Hasn't she achieved what most, if not all, rich white men can only even dream of, let alone bring to fruition? Ain't she a woman? Ain't she a diva? She grew up working, and now that she's grown, she's asking for some R-E-S-P-E-C-T, just like Truth and Aretha Franklin, another famous political diva who popularized the refrain. Franklin's career reinforces that a true diva is confrontationally and unapologetically political; she promised to pay Angela Davis's bail when she was arrested in the 1970s, and devoted much of her career to highlighting civil rights issues and donating money and time to the same.

In the final scene of the "Diva" video, after loitering in an abandoned warehouse and fanning herself with dollar bills, Sasha Fierce casually lights a cigar, takes a puff, and tosses her Zippo lighter into the trunk of a car stuffed full of mannequin parts. Mannequins typically represent sanitized conformity, lack of individuation. The viewer can also understand the mannequin parts as representative of the various pieces of the system, of which Beyoncé's diva has been offering commentary—the pieces that make up Truth's woman and Beyoncé's diva: race, gender, class, sexuality, age, etc. Various axes of intersectionality. Pieces of a whole, differentiated and kept separate historically through capitalism and work. As Beyoncé nonchalantly walks away, the car holding those mannequin parts explodes, as do old normative expectations and assumptions attached to all the above categories now jammed into the car's trunk. Via those mannequins, Sasha Fierce literally blows up conformity to a system that does not make space for her humanity. She doesn't run from what she knows to be a pending explosion either; she walks away slowly. When Sojourner Truth escaped slavery, she recounted in her own *Narrative of Sojourner Truth*: "I did not run off, for I thought that wicked, but I walked off, believing that to be all right." Beyoncé, as Sasha Fierce, confidently but defiantly walks off. She leaves behind the fiery remnants of various plastic pieces, burning and melting, melding together into something new as she retreats. Blended, fused together, inseparable.

Who *is* Beyoncé? She's undefinable. Something old, something new. Never one thing or the other. A blend of Sojourner Truth's woman and Sasha Fierce's diva—she connects history to the present while making history in real time. An artist and a teacher.

PAST

2
MIXING LEMONADE,
REMIXING AMERICA

I SAT DUMBFOUNDED, JAW ON THE FLOOR, FOR THE entire sixty-one minutes of *Lemonade* (including credits) and for an unknown amount of time directly following its HBO premiere on Saturday, April 23, 2016. I couldn't tear my eyes from the screen. It wasn't just the sheer majesty with which Beyoncé presented a genre-bending narrative and catchy-as-fuck collection of songs—a fully realized *visual album* unlike anything prior—but the way she expertly, cohesively retold many of the same stories and conversations I'd been having with students in classrooms for years, emanating from her other work. Of course, there was much that was new and particular to *Lemonade*. It was deeper, more complex, concisely refined and merged into one film. But there were elements of everything that came before blended into those eleven tight tracks, interspersed with British Somali poet Warsan Shire's poetry and illustrated through lush visuals based on Julie Dash's 1991 independent film *Daughters of the*

Dust (the first widely distributed feature film directed by a Black woman). A perfect recipe; a groundbreaking artistic achievement. Lemonade out of lemons in a multitude of ways.

So many incredible Black women critics, activists, thinkers, and artists quickly—with lightning speed, actually—produced scholarship geared toward a deep understanding and analysis of *Lemonade*; there are far too many to name in these pages. The speed with which critical engagement appeared spoke both to the complex artistry of the narrative and the profound desire for more nuanced Black women's stories to be featured and available in mainstream pop culture. Engagement far surpassed typical reactive think-piece fodder, intensively mining cultural references and honoring experiences that aren't typically celebrated and centered, even still. A particularly robust and comprehensive list of writing on *Lemonade* was compiled by Janell Hobson and Jessica Marie Johnson for the African American Intellectual History Society and published online only three weeks after the album's release, titled "#Lemonade: A Black Feminist Resource." Additional college courses emerged devoted fully to *Lemonade*, along with the "Lemonade Syllabus" compiled by Candice Marie Benbow. The achievement truly catapulted Beyoncé and the way the public at large viewed her work into a new critical galaxy.

As a fresh addition to the syllabus in 2016, and given its explicit focus on the experiences of Black women— more so than anything else in Beyoncé's catalog—I immediately jumped to pedagogical and personal questions about where *Lemonade* fit into "Politicizing Beyoncé." How could I carefully and honestly address and position *Lemonade* in a way that wouldn't over-step any boundaries, but still allow students from various backgrounds to respectfully grapple with this brand-new cultural touchstone as the next piece of Beyoncé's growing legacy? I'd always pushed students to look for the subtle politics layered into Beyoncé's work in the classroom, but with *Lemonade*, so many of the explicit politics were shamelessly on the sur-face. Because the entire conceit of my course is to not assign writing *about* Beyoncé, I needed to get even more creative and unconventional, as most everything possible to say was immediately and importantly said, and continues to be said, by Black women critics and scholars.

While the narrative is a deeply personal and pain-ful story of an infidelity and its aftermath, a Southern gothic love letter to Black women as a celebration of vulnerability and strength, Beyoncé also created *Lem-onade* in such a way that everyone, regardless of iden-tity, plays a role. Beyoncé invites wider participation as long as Black women are centered first, with others positioned on the margins. As a tribute to resilience in the face of a lie, the album is also an indictment of the lie itself and an exposé of a broken promise. Those who aren't lied to are the liars—only able to enter the narrative of *Lemonade* through that broken promise, as part of the culture that devalued Black women so much so that recognition and reclamation were necessary in the first place. Just like the perfect balance of sugar and lemon in the water that makes lemonade, *Lemonade* is a meticulously balanced blend of celebration and condemnation.

America as a whole broke its promise to Black women. Removed from any gossip about Beyoncé's personal life, that's the truth at the core of *Lemonade*. Some conversations about the experiential weight of that broken promise, of course, are for Black women to lead, but other conservations must be had by wider, diverse groups of people. My students have always come from many different backgrounds, so I urge them to find and investigate their places in the narrative. As with all her other work, I try to highlight aspects of *Lemonade* in class that invite everyone to talk about complicity and responsibility in critiquing the same world that devalues Black women, because everyone exists together in that world. In the aftermath of *Lemonade*, part of that impulse became connecting moments and themes from *Lemonade* back to pieces of Beyoncé's previous work—seen as historical texts themselves from the vantage point of 2016—on top of all the other works assigned. Here, I'll discuss some larger aspects of *Lemonade*, but many other moments get looped into subsequent chapters by theme. *Lemonade* itself creates a performative historical loop in Beyoncé's catalog, one that moves backward and forward in time. "Formation" is *Lemonade*'s prologue chronologically since it was released months before the album, but featured on the album as an epilogue, track twelve and not included in the film's narrative. This clever move requires the viewer look even further back into the past for prologue—to the ghosts of *B'Day* and "Déjà Vu," where some of *Lemonade*'s ingredients also first appeared. With many stops in between. A much longer story that remains the overall focus of "Politicizing Beyoncé."

Beyoncé weaves a critical tale with *Lemonade* on its own that attempts to rewrite the social contract itself, to imagine a different world. She offers instructions to repair what has been and continues to be broken by examining what the Combahee River Collective named "Black women's extremely negative relationship to the American political system" in their famous 1977 statement. In addition to all else that it is, *Lemonade* is an examination of that negative political relationship, that broken promise. It also highlights potential complicities in the system that is devaluing and lying to Black women continuously. Ultimately, *Lemonade* leads the audience on a journey that exposes freedom itself as nothing more than America's most intimate lie—a perpetually broken promise by design.

Broken Pieces

For students, I pair *Lemonade* with selections from a trio of writers: Saidiya Hartman, Claudia Rankine, and Octavia E. Butler. Together, they draw out some major overarching themes. Hartman traces the history of the Atlantic slave trade next to her personal travels in Ghana in *Lose Your Mother: A Journey Along the Atlantic Slave Route*. She writes, "As both a professor conducting research on slavery and a descendant of the enslaved, I was desperate to reclaim the dead, that is, to reckon with the lives undone and obliterated in the making of human commodities." Hartman's family lineage was lost somewhere between Africa and antebellum Alabama when records were misplaced, destroyed, or never existed and are now untraceable. To "lose your mother," as the title metaphorically suggests, is to be broken apart from history, split in two and constantly haunted by ghosts around every corner. In the introduction, she notes, "History is how the secular world attends to the dead." But when history doesn't tell the full truth, or actively erases pieces of the past, the dead come back as ghosts. And in *Lemonade*, ghosts conspire to expose traces of the past in the present. American history has tried to keep them buried, but they assemble nonetheless—watching from trees, in anachronistic moments where things appear out of time. As Beyoncé narrates in the beginning: "The past and the future merge to meet us here / What luck / What a fucking curse."

Just like Hartman, Beyoncé reaches backward through generations of women, through her own family line. The album title comes from a combination of both Beyoncé's and Jay-Z's grandmothers as referents for an older proverb. *Lemonade* features footage of Hattie White proclaiming, "I had my share of ups and downs, but I always found the inner strength to pull myself up. I was served lemons, but I made lemonade," at her ninetieth birthday party, and Beyoncé's own family lemonade recipe passed down from her maternal grandmother, Agnéz Deréon. She also reaches backward through her career in an act of artistic genealogy: the geography and aesthetic of *B'Day*; a resurrection of Sasha Fierce; the tight, focused musicality and structure of *4*; and the rich visuality of *BEYONCÉ* and its explicit Black feminist focus all reassemble.

Claudia Rankine meditates on the citizenship contract between Black women and America in her own genre-bending poetry/prose collection *Citizen: An American Lyric*, naming it a contract contingent on forgetting. Forgetting past injustice, forgetting racism, forgetting sexism, forgetting all the violent oppression from and on which America was founded, which it literally wrote into a constitution that never included Black people or women, let alone Black women.

Citizenship for Black women, according to Rankine, involves looking the other way—away from oppression, lies, and infidelity. Beyoncé plays (and very well may personally be) a Black woman scorned by a cheating spouse, and Rankine's citizenship contract is easily superimposed onto that relationship in *Lemonade*. Marriage itself is a contract between two individuals sanctioned by the state or government. *Lemonade* finds Beyoncé not only refusing to forget the lies, but foregrounding the broken promise at the heart of the citizenship contract between Black women and America. "I tried to make a home out of you / But doors lead to trapdoors / A stairway leads to nothing," she says. Tracing memories back and staring history in its face, attempting to write a new contract.

She narrates the entire process, from describing and exposing the lie to prescribing possible remedy—from intuition to redemption (each track is paired with a corresponding emotional force) and various stages/songs in between. Reconciliation only becomes ultimately possible through a reorganization of the system—one contingent on Beyoncé remembering, not forgetting. "6 Inch" provides the turning point in the narrative, but it's during "Sandcastles" (and the notion of forgiveness with which it is paired) that Beyoncé signals her specific refusal to forget—through the seemingly innocuous inclusion of a kintsugi bowl before the song's first piano chords ring out. Kintsugi is a form of ancient Japanese pottery in which broken pieces are repaired and joined together again with lacquer, often dusted with precious metals, in such a way that the cracks are featured as part of the beauty, not hidden. The bowl becomes more valuable, considered stronger because of the visible cracks—a way to focus on accountability as a constant process, not a destination. A metaphor for what America could be as opposed to what America is. A refusal to fully forgive, forget, or erase the damage of the past; rather, a conscious decision to hold them in tension. The bowl is shown fleetingly, but its importance is highlighted in *How to Make Lemonade*, Beyoncé's limited edition coffee table companion tome to the album.

Reaching back through generations, remembering history instead of forgetting in order to expose the deep cracks in America's foundation, also involves time travel. Ghosts bring the past to the present, but Beyoncé's lemonade must also quench the thirst of the past, travel backward to tell the truth about history. In *Kindred*, Octavia E. Butler's 1979 novel, Dana, a Black woman, gets called back and forth in time between the antebellum South, in order to save a particular white man from death at different points in his life, and her own 1976 California present. Over the course of the novel, she learns that her own ancestral line is violently tangled with this man's. To let him die, as much as she wishes to see him dead, would erase her own existence in the present. *Kindred* opens with Dana's confession: "I lost my arm on my last trip home. My left arm." The arm was severed from her body by a wall in the present that didn't exist in the past, and at the exact spot where her white ancestor, Rufus, aggressively grabbed her in order to hold her in that past. Where Dana's arm used to be is named an "empty place" in *Kindred*, and exists not as an absence but the presence of a physical and psychic wound, impossible to heal. After all, there is no arm to reattach in 1976. It technically no longer exists.

Time travel may be a less obvious aspect of *Lemonade*, but it does create interesting, unorthodox conversations around Beyoncé's magnum opus. Black-and-white scenes are littered throughout, the first being a simple shot of metal chains in the film's opening moments. I ask students to think of all the black-and-white scenes as marking time travel outside a linear narrative. Moments where Beyoncé and others, like Dana, are called back and forth through time. Or, from another direction, moments where Beyoncé calls the audience back and forth in time to draw further attention to the ways that this past is still alive today. Calling attention to places in the past and present where white men's hold on history inflicted life- and history-altering pain on Black women and others. Exposing the great lengths to which Black women's pain has been central to America's promise of freedom for only some. Alongside Butler, Beyoncé holds up and celebrates the empty places in *Lemonade* while also demanding change. Doreen St. Felix named *Lemonade*, at its core, "a demand for flesh" in her *MTV* review of the album, and paired with *Kindred*, it becomes a demand for the return of flesh, to fill the empty place where Dana's arm used to be. To repair broken bonds with something different, like the lacquer and precious metals used to fuse pieces of the kintsugi bowl back together.

To create the bowl, pieces first have to be broken. To rewrite the contract, the old one must be exposed and destroyed. Beyoncé has to reopen the wound. In *Lemonade*, she follows her intuition into denial and anger, and takes to the streets with a baseball bat to break what is old and not working. She throws her wedding ring at the camera and onto the cold, hard ground to wipe the slate clean. After the emotionally raw "Pray You Catch Me" and a swan dive off a skyscraper, Beyoncé emerges from a grand doorway, unleashing a flood onto a city street. She channels the Yoruba and Ifá deity Oshun, the goddess of water (and sexuality, beauty, love, and pleasure). Joan Morgan points to the mirror the goddess carries as "the tool Oshun holds up to our faces when she requires us to do the difficult work of really seeing ourselves." Though Beyoncé doesn't hold a physical mirror herself, her mirror's direction, like Oshun's, is doubled—reflecting Black women back to themselves, but also reflecting the broken promises of America back to those who refuse to look, demanding the violence of history be seen.

Oshun's mirror becomes Beyoncé's baseball bat, and she begins gleefully destroying cars, buildings, and windows, revealing America to itself through all the damage it created. Her destruction is a visual manifestation of broken promises, as well as action that turns the tables and breaks things back. The destruction is presented through sonic dissonance; viewers see explosions and shattered glass, but hear none of it. Instead, the upbeat, dancehall-inspired "Hold Up" bounces from the speakers and Beyoncé mimes blissful denial, happily destroying shit. All of this is in response to the direct question, finally asked: "Are you cheating on me?" She already knows the answer, and viewers know she already knows the answer, but she demands it be spoken. Seeing the broken promises as systemic and institutional, Beyoncé's actions can also be refigured as constructive, not just destructive. Paving the way for something new. She's neither "crazy" nor "jealous," the only options for how she can be perceived listed in the lyrics. When she proudly declares, "I'ma fuck me up a bitch," she's wielding calculated political critique of the system, not irrational emotion, through the tip of her baseball bat.

Extending that critique, Beyoncé breaks the classic fourth wall of film twice during "Hold Up" with progressive importance. Rule one of the fourth wall—traditionally known as that which separates a performer from the audience—is to not look or speak directly into the camera. First, Beyoncé walks straight up to a security camera surveilling the street as the viewer's gaze becomes funneled through its lens. The audience is watching, but she's watching back. With a smirk and sneer, she smashes the lens and the feed cuts to static. Rejecting and refusing her own surveillance. Cutting ties. At the end of "Hold Up," she walks toward the main camera with another knowing look in her eye. The one that's supposed to remain invisible in order to give a film or video the illusion of depicting actual, real-time events. After a last dramatic windup, she swings for the fences and demolishes that lens too before dropping the bat. The camera also falls to the ground, and the impact flips the shot to black-and-white. The viewer's window into the action falls with the camera. The baseball bat echoes against the ground (breaking the video's sonic dissonance) and Beyoncé walks away. She knocks the narrative into the past to return her destruction of America's original promise—now broken many times over—back to its origin. Time travel here indicts the mistakes of a system with which at least parts of the audience are no doubt complicit to varying degrees.

It's at this moment that Beyoncé poses the major question that haunts the entirety of *Lemonade*: "Why

can't you see me?" She asks it three times before adding, "Everyone else can," then moves into "Don't Hurt
Yourself." She's multiply referencing Black women
themselves as erased by the system, and the ghosts
of history, the "ghosts of black women scorned" that
Janet Mock names as ever present in *Lemonade* in
her own meditation on the visual album. Footage of
a Malcolm X speech where he calls Black women the
most disrespected, unprotected, and neglected people
in America interrupts the song after Beyoncé asks her
question about visibility to mirror her point. Beyoncé
also redirects the injury of Black women's erasure
(and other physical and psychic injury)—Dana's lost
arm—back at the system itself, exposes through the
lyrics how when America hurts Black women, it hurts
itself. Conversely, she offers a bit of advice for repair:
"When you love me, you love yourself."

Jack White, a white man well-known and lauded
for his work in rock music, is featured on "Don't
Hurt Yourself," and his inclusion subtly replicates
and replays the song's lyrical conceit through its very
musical structure. Beyoncé officially featured white
men for the first time in her career on *Lemonade*, an
album undeniably and explicitly about Black womanhood. The curious juxtaposition alone points to
deeper layers and meaning. White stands in for white
America, specifically the appropriation of rock music
by white artists. Sister Rosetta Tharpe, a queer Black

woman known to have created the electric guitar sound that has become widely recognized as today's rock music, by blending gospel and blues, still goes largely uncredited. Her 1944 single "Strange Things Happening Every Day" can easily be considered the first American rock single, but instead, white artists like Elvis Presley are usually named as the genre's originators and creative forces (the same is true of almost every genre of music). Beyoncé uses White's presence in *Lemonade* (heard but not seen) to reclaim Black women's roots in the genre while ultimately proving the dynamic in the lyrics true: what's done to Black women will be done back to the system in time. She reclaims the music stolen and reenacts what was done to Black women in the past by using white White in the song but never showing him. Literally "re-appropriates" the genre of rock according to Brittany Spanos for *Rolling Stone*, sampling a Led Zeppelin track too, which was built off an older song cowritten by Memphis Minnie. What goes around comes around.

In "Don't Hurt Yourself," Beyoncé also utters the important line, "I'm just too much for you," before pitching her wedding ring to the ground. The humanity of Black women is literally *too much* for a system grounded in racism, sexism, homophobia, and other forms of intersecting oppressions, which is why the system attempts to erase Black women's experiences at every turn. Black women threaten a system in which they "were never meant to survive," in Audre Lorde's words, because listening to Black women and their experiences exposes what the system cannot contain. And that's why the citizenship contract between Black women and America relies on a perpetual forgetting, why America's promises were always disingenuous. Beyoncé knows and names it. And to further reinforce it, she plaintively asks, "So what are you gonna say at my funeral now that you've killed me?" Once the lies of past and present are brought to light, America can't have it both ways any longer. Is it going to be eulogy or accountability?

"Sorry" continues to foreground all the broken promises between Black women and America by returning the action to a plantation house. It's also the only full segment of *Lemonade* filmed entirely in black-and-white. Apathy, with which the song is paired, is not just simple disregard. The word has etymological roots in "freedom from suffering," and the lyrics name a refusal to apologize for demanding a freedom from suffering. The repeated call of "sorry" hauntingly bleeds into the rebuttal "I ain't sorry" in the background throughout. Serena Williams, prominently featured on "Sorry," is discussed in more detail alongside Sasha Fierce (see chapter 7), and the plantation house setting is obviously tied to the ways American history used slavery to secure profit, to bolster capitalism. All at the expense of Black humanity. As

Beyoncé and Serena Williams move through a plantation house, they slyly work magic while opening up a critique of capitalism itself—one foregrounded in the emptiness of "6 Inch"—to further unravel lies of the past (see chapter 8). Beyoncé nods to capitalism as the overarching reason suffering thrives in America, especially along lines of race, gender, sexuality, and class. Or, more strongly, that capitalism itself necessarily produces suffering along those lines—the very suffering from which she wants to be free—to insidiously ensure that the most privileged few straight white men can thrive.

Freedom *from* suffering also redirects the audience toward freedom itself in American history as a concept never equally applied or distributed. In American ideology, freedom references the absence of ties and bonds. But one can only be defined as free when bonds exist for others. If freedom were ubiquitous, the concept would undo itself. And so the idea of freedom lies at the heart of all America's broken promises. The bonds of Black women and Black people in general (among various other marginalized groups) have been used to define freedom for white Americans as the norm. Consequently, the "freedom from suffering" inherent to the apathy that white Americans can indulge in continually highlights how freedom is contingent on the previous bonds, and ongoing suffering, of the oppressed, even when freedom is eventually granted. The promise of freedom for anyone but the most privileged straight white men in America—whose freedom was never in question, who have always been free from suffering—is conspicuously just another door leading to trap doors, a stairway leading to nothing. So freedom itself emerges in *Lemonade* too as just another lie—as the foundational lie—that needs to be reimagined.

Forward . . .

"Forward" is the bridge between "Sandcastles" and "Freedom" on *Lemonade*; resurrection is the bridge between the (complex) forgiveness and hope the other songs are tied to respectively. After Beyoncé names reconciliation as finally possible, "Forward" coaxes the narrative to its climax in a dissonant prayer. More of an interlude, the track is often overlooked, but the name itself marks its centrality and importance to the *Lemonade* journey. While black-and-white scenes have been shuttling between past and present, caught in a historical loop, "Forward" names its own direction and breaks out of the loop while resurrecting more ghosts simultaneously. James Blake sings the majority of the lyrics alone during the seventy-nine-second track. Beyoncé, in an unusual move, only joins him for harmony on one line at the end. Musically, it's the darkest, most sonically discordant moment on *Lemonade*; visually and conceptually, it exists as artistic bridge between life and death, while a storm gathers on the horizon.

Beyoncé uses James Blake on *Lemonade* similarly to how she already used Jack White. He stands in for America, for the system. And as a white male alternative soul artist, and British to boot, his presence—again, heard but not seen—is another one of Beyoncé's careful manipulations and reclamations. She presents a white voice that reenacts the violence of the British settling America; the white male power that represents America's so-called original founders. The voice of genocide and displacement of indigenous peoples in the creation of a country, the voice of slavery as a foundational American institution. Blake-as-the-system sings about moving "forward" and acknowledges it's "time to listen" in an ultimate confession of wrongdoing. Though much too brief to fully atone for America's original sins (as if anything ever fully could), it's symbolic release. It serves as a new point of departure from which Beyoncé resurrects Black women and Black women's children prematurely killed, brings back previous generations—lost mothers and grandmothers and family lines. To clearly illustrate the resurrection, Beyoncé features some of the Mothers of the Movement, Black women who have lost children to police brutality or gun violence, during "Forward." Gwen Carr, Sybrina Fulton, and Lezley McSpadden—the mothers of Eric Garner, Trayvon Martin, and Michael Brown, respectively—all stare directly into the camera while holding photos of their children, as both celebration of their lives and condemnation of America for killing them too soon. These few stand in for millions more.

Beyoncé sings only, "Go back to your sleep in your favorite spot just next to me," and the word "forward" once. The word repeats in Blake's voice, though, hauntingly modulated and remixed. The sounds of the past and future merging. The sounds of Beyoncé taking control, old bonds being broken. *Lemonade* moves forward through old slave quarters, plantation houses, and various other settings only to arrive at its ultimate celebration/confrontation on an outdoor wooden stage. Beyoncé stands motionless in front of an audience exclusively comprised of Black women and girls. The clouds that have been gathering throughout the film begin to part. Rolling drums, horns, and lush orchestration cut to deafening silence as Beyoncé starts to sing "Freedom" a cappella. As already noted, freedom operates in a binary with slavery. There's no understanding one *without* the other. Freedom depends on the bonds of slavery, which also means freedom can only be bestowed by previous oppressors. That foundation has never been, and can never be, equal. Beyoncé sings for her life, not to beg for freedom, but to undo the very idea of it, along with its attendant unequal distribution, in order to move forward.

Sherley Anne Williams's novel *Dessa Rose* follows Dessa, a Black woman who has taken part in a violent uprising and escaped from slavery, and a white woman, Rufel, as the two form an unlikely and often uncomfortable friendship in an elusive search to secure Dessa's, and some of her friends', freedom. Because Dessa is never truly free, no matter how many times she escapes the bonds of slavery. The novel highlights just how precarious and contingent freedom is, how Dessa and her friends need to ultimately rely on and trust Rufel to help them make their way north and west. Protection and hiding is contingent on benevolent white people willing to actively collude, take risks, or simply look the other way. As one character, Harker, says to Dessa, "Maybe there is some islands out there where black peoples is free, but we got to depend on strange whites to get us there." She agrees, knowing from her own experience inside and outside a plantation and coffle, that there is no legitimate outside to the institution. "You could scape from a master, run away, but that didn't mean you'd scaped from slavery. I knew myself how hard it was to find someplace to go." Even once slavery was abolished, the control of the system merely shifted: the backlash to Reconstruction, segregation, the epidemic of lynching, Jim Crow laws, mass incarceration—and the list continues to grow.

What Dessa comes to describe is the overarching

impossibility of freedom in a system that was founded on the practice of slavery. There is no truth in the promise of freedom. Yes, some could and did escape, and slavery was eventually abolished, but the very concept still festers at the core of America. Those who have been enslaved, either individually or collectively, are kept just shy of truly *feeling* free perpetually. Nina Simone, in a 1968 interview, named freedom as the near-impossible feeling of simply "no fear." An absence of fear, an absence of the fear of suffering. Dessa testified to fear never going away, never dissipating, even while one is theoretically and technically free. The possibility for an absence of fear connects back to the apathy of "Sorry," not referencing the "freedom from suffering" root this time, but its initial indifference, the complete absence of any feeling for something that feels nothing for you. No fear. A kind of critical disregard and contempt of the current system, in which freedom has never been free. Beyoncé's "Freedom" echoes Dessa's realization and instead tries to imagine a new social contract stemming from a different center, one that didn't and doesn't rely on the binary of slavery and freedom. That's why she's been resurrecting ghosts, that's why she's moved back and forth in time trying to reorganize the present. The promise of freedom itself is the fucking curse, already broken but not destroyed, and thus preventing forward movement.

Beyoncé's not asking to be set free in the lyrics of "Freedom," either; the actual grammatical construction of the lines in the chorus directs critique *at* the concept of freedom, doesn't name a desire or hope for it: "Freedom, freedom, I can't move / Freedom, cut me loose." It can be read as direct address. She's naming freedom as that which renders her immobile, captures her in a web of control. She's asking to be cut free of freedom itself. The verses find Beyoncé taking deliberate action, crying out to defy freedom despite its constraints. She demands an uninhibited ability to walk, dance, cross borders; to move through the world without being stopped, profiled, searched, suspected, arrested, killed. She warns the listener that she plans to wade through water, riot at borders, march, run, challenge the status quo. She delivers the guttural and impassioned lines as a sermon and, invoking more of Audre Lorde's words, forges on, "deliberate / and afraid / of nothing." No fear, joining her voice to Nina Simone's unique contralto that wafted across shots of a hallway during a pivotal interlude earlier in the *Lemonade* film, during the moments the kintsugi bowl first appeared. Simone said during that same 1968 interview that she had experienced a few fleeting moments of true freedom on stage in the past, but longed for more. Perhaps Beyoncé, from her stage in *Lemonade*, which is both future and past, is seeking to offer some of that fleeting feeling back to Simone, especially because Simone has become a consistent guide and inspiration for Beyoncé since she first referenced the older performer in 2013's *Life Is But a Dream*.

The actual force Beyoncé's singing about in "Freedom" is, more correctly, liberation. Taken, not given. But it also demands an entire reorganization of the way the history of America is seen and understood. It's about foregrounding the lies in the cracks of the kintsugi bowl, not sweeping them under the rug and turning away. It's looking to the experiences of Black women to better understand the ways power insulates itself through misdirection and manipulation. And smack in the middle of "Freedom," when the lie of freedom itself begins to become undeniable, the Black ballerina Michaela DePrince takes center stage to perform liberation—she improvises without restriction or fear. DePrince herself endured horrors akin to slavery in her native Sierra Leone before coming to America at age four. As DePrince dances, the camera cuts to other scenes where the ghosts of slavery glare into the camera confrontationally, indicting at least part of the viewing audience as complicit with a violent system that has found too many deceptive ways to disguise itself. In "Freedom," the critique is about bringing back and seeing the ghosts as an example of finally breaking the chains and constraints of freedom itself—the very chains featured in the first black-and-white scene of the entire visual album. Emptying freedom of its previous meaning. Freedom itself is a lie. Fuck freedom.

Finally, Beyoncé shares her own secret family lemonade recipe and Hattie White's speech, now that she's mapped the journey—described and prescribed—to a new social contract contingent on liberation of and through generations of Black women. A revised citizenship contract that refuses the forgetting Claudia Rankine named, and places the burden of the recovered painful memories back on America and all those that have devalued Black women, urged or required they forget simply to survive—whether intentionally or by default. Accountability as perpetual living memory. The last force Beyoncé calls forth in *Lemonade* is redemption with the song "All Night," and not her own, because she never needed to be redeemed. She's nodding to a wider redemption as possible, if her directions and example are followed. If America chooses to remember. Ensuring the exposure, destruction, and rewriting of the social contract becomes impossible to forget allows Beyoncé to turn her torturer into remedy, as she references in the lyrics. The final scenes of *Lemonade* all exist in color, and feature a diverse collection of faces and couples in an extended joyful photo montage, promoting love and new connection, whether through friendship, romance, or family.

"So we're gonna heal / We're gonna start again,"

she says, having found and exposed the truth beneath the lies. When Beyoncé exclaims, "I've missed you, my love" at the end of "All Night," it's not a reembrace of what came before. It's an embrace, for the first time, of an entirely new system for which she just laid a different foundation, along with Black women across time, along with those who became casualties of a violent system in one way or another. A love she'd hoped for, but that hadn't yet existed. She's standing alongside innumerable Black women who have written, spoken, theorized, performed, or simply survived. And the journey of *Lemonade* then throws itself forward into the future, "all night long." The screen cuts to black, and "Formation" plays as the credits roll. Reaching back one more time. "Formation" prepared the world for *Lemonade*, but also provides additional instruction and directive as a newly situated epilogue to the visual album. It anticipates, extends, and lacquers it all together while highlighting the cracks. The time travel and historical loop of *Lemonade* performatively spin out from the album's center to follow more ghosts and instruct the audience to cultivate a political lens that further and completely critiques America's normative core. Now, Beyoncé implores, get in formation.

3
GET IN/FORMATION

"FORMATION" IS OFFICIALLY THE TWELFTH AND FINAL track on *Lemonade*—it plays during the film's end credits—but it transports the listener back two-and-a-half months into the past, to the song's own February 6, 2016, surprise premiere alongside its stand-alone video, not part of *Lemonade*'s official action. Through this strategy, Beyoncé captures the audience in a viewing/listening loop that turns endlessly back on itself, emblematic of history repeating. And the anthemic call to action of "Formation" is twofold: get in formation and get information. Make a damn movement. Together, collectively, but through taking into account the example she's modeled in her music, in *Lemonade* especially. Dismantle power by paying attention to the politics and experience she's shared. Listen to Black women. Listen to those at the margins.

"Formation" maps those margins in ways that illustrate Kimberlé Crenshaw's theory of intersectionality perfectly. In her first foundational piece,

"Demarginalizing the Intersection of Race and Sex,"
Crenshaw contends that Black women must be centered for any progressive social change, any endeavor
that hopes to dismantle the status quo. "With Black
women as the starting point, it becomes more apparent how dominant conceptions of discrimination
condition us to think about subordination as disad-
vantage occurring along a single categorical axis," and
simply focusing on the most privileged members of a
group when interrogating discrimination, as opposed
to those who are multiply oppressed, "creates a distorted analysis of racism and sexism because the oper-
ative conceptions of race and sex become grounded in
experiences that actually represent only a subset of a
much more complex phenomenon." Progress is only
an illusion until that complex phenomenon gets truly
seen and disentangled.

Not to be confused with a simpler politics of identity
or an additive model of oppression, Crenshaw names
intersectionality rather as "an analytic sensibility, a
way of thinking about identity and its relationship
to power" in her more recent "Why Intersectionality Can't Wait" for the *Washington Post*. Of course, a
multitude of additional intersections exist and must
be attended to in order to prevent the erasure of the
most vulnerable lives. Intersectionality is not exclusive
to Black women, but Black women's experiences are
at the theory's center. From that center, it becomes

a way to further map "the intersections of racism, sexism, class oppression, transphobia, able-ism and more. Intersectionality has given many advocates a way to frame their circumstances and to fight for their visibility and inclusion." More than just a call for visibility and inclusion, intersectionality also highlights a critique of power in a society where that power has rendered some invisible and excluded to begin with. Intersectionality as a lens allows those not experiencing the same oppressions the ability to see power in critical new ways by shifting focus away from the most privileged experiences within any one group.

Once "Formation" was released, it proved a useful companion to both new and old writing by Crenshaw. The pairing is a productive way to investigate that older, foundational Black feminist formation, which in turn helped form Black feminist theory as a field of academic study. I also want students to think about "Formation" and its larger cultural implications and indictments as a form of public education, a new way of seeing. Beyoncé's own master class on Crenshaw's theories. Crenshaw admits, "Intersectionality alone cannot bring invisible bodies into view"; even when it centers previously erased or ignored experiences, further action is always required to change the system. But learning, becoming aware, is still the first step. Invisible bodies stay invisible in "Formation," to mirror Crenshaw's assertion, but they speak in other ways and assemble at Beyoncé's direction. The trap- and bounce-influenced track opens in Crenshaw's margins, with a ghost—the first of many ghosts haunting "Formation"—and a warning. It ends with Beyoncé drowning herself in New Orleans floodwaters atop a police car. Again, warning and ghost. Past and future meeting. To paraphrase the Big Freedia voice-over that plays throughout, Beyoncé did not come here to play with you hoes. She came to slay, bitch. And she came to teach. She came to breathe new life into intersectionality and underscore why invisible bodies are rendered invisible in the first place. Fuck the reactions. Middle fingers up.

Back . . . by Popular Demand

Beyoncé attempts to resurrect ghosts in "Formation," as she did in *Lemonade*. In "Formation" specifically, she's conjuring. Art is always creation, but here, perhaps more than anywhere else in her entire catalog, she invokes the role of conjure woman. Janell Hobson explored the various allusions to conjure women in the "Formation" visuals for *Ms.* magazine, noting that Beyoncé positions herself "at the crossroads between life and death" from the very beginning. She crouches defiantly on the roof of a New Orleans Police Department cruiser in head-to-toe red and white Gucci and combat boots, summoning ghosts from the water flooding the streets. In *Lose Your Mother*, Saidiya Hartman said history was how the secular world attended to (or refused to attend to) the dead; in "Formation," Beyoncé gathers ghosts to attend to history and the present, standing in for a myriad possible conjure women from various Black spiritual traditions—one of the most famous being Voodoo priestess Marie Laveau, herself tied to New Orleans. Legend holds that both Laveau and her daughter, who shared the same name, were prominent priestesses in Louisiana during the 1800s—the elder known for practicing syncretic Haitian Voodoo while the younger blended elements of her mother's religion with local Roman Catholicism. The two often get conflated with each other in retellings, making it difficult to assign specific actions to either particular Laveau. Like Sojourner Truth's "Ain't I a Woman?" speech, the Laveau women also exist as important symbols in the public imagination. As powerful, free Black Creole women during slavery, they also challenged the racist social order of the day and share similarities with Beyoncé herself.

In Jewell Parker Rhodes's fictionalized account of the elder Marie Laveau, *Voodoo Dreams*, she notes, "A story should begin at the beginning. But in this story, the middle is the beginning. Everything spirals outward from the center." "Formation" is part of that spiral outward from the new narrative center Beyoncé created in *Lemonade*, itself occurring at a presumed center of Beyoncé's career. Beyoncé embodies both Maries and is swept up in the additional spiral, backward and forward, of "Formation." In later scenes, she appears next to tall white Southern gothic columns on the front porch of a plantation house, with ceremonial attendants at either side. She wears a black, oversize flat top hat pulled low, the brim shadowing her eyes and facial expressions. Thanks to conversations with scholar Kinitra Brooks, Hobson identifies those scenes as additional invocation of the loa Maman Brigitte, "guardian of the souls of the dead who loves to curse and drink rum with hot peppers." Beyoncé's movement in these scenes is especially erratic, disjointed, otherworldly, possessed as is characteristic of many Voodoo ceremonies—she performs as the vessel spirits will inhabit, having been summoned from the realm of the dead. The lyrics that begin "Formation" also exist as ceremonial incantation, monotone but hauntingly doubled in different harmonic registers. The dead returning.

Messy Mya's voice opens the video as ghost, even before what sounds like distorted and bent electronic sitar notes echo, sonically mirroring Beyoncé's attempt to bend time and history. Born Anthony Barre, Messy Mya was a comedian, rapper, and local YouTube celebrity from New Orleans, known for the biting wit he used to lovingly mock and critique his surroundings. While his queerness was debated on social media, Messy Mya's aesthetic was certainly larger than life and decidedly queer, in the sense that he defiantly differed from the norm, regardless of any publicly claimed or unclaimed identity. He was murdered on November 14, 2010, and the case remains unsolved. His voice beckons and demands answers, not just to "What happened at the New Wil'ins [New Orleans]?" in the sampled audio but "What happened to me?" Mya's question even anticipates Beyoncé's own "What are you doing, my love?" from *Lemonade*. The track then positions him to answer: "Bitch, I'm back . . . by popular demand." A sonic resurrection in the center of New Orleans, the site of the devastating Hurricane Katrina eleven years prior. Mya's question is easily alternately heard as "What happened *after* New Orleans?" (i.e., Katrina). The answer is clearly nothing, as Beyoncé shows the streets still flooded. The ghosts of Katrina's victims also enter the video through the water and another audio sample at the end of the song. Kimberly Rivers Roberts's voice reinvokes flood waters rising in a snippet from the 2008 Katrina documentary *Trouble the Water*.

More ghosts quickly assemble between the intro and outro of "Formation." Queer bounce artist Big Freedia's voice joins Mya's and Roberts's in the sonic landscape, recorded specifically for Beyoncé. As the noted queen of bounce music, Freedia's presence amps up the queerness at the song's core exponentially, and intensifies a sense of gender nonconformity. Adding to the already considerably queer elements, "Formation" also incorporates flashes of Abteen Bagheri's 2014 documentary *That B.E.A.T.*, a short film celebrating New Orleans bounce music, itself a queer subculture. Following all these references, the ghost of someone like Penny Proud then also falls explicitly into formation. Proud was a twenty-one-year-old Black trans woman murdered in 2015 in the Treme district of New Orleans. Police say she was killed during a robbery, but her murder, like Messy Mya's, remains unsolved. As with so many trans women—especially Black trans women and other trans women of color—police don't allocate the necessary resources to apprehending those responsible. Black trans women are marginalized in life and further marginalized in death. Though Penny Proud isn't mentioned or sampled specifically in the song, her ghost, too, rises from the waters, as do those of the other Black trans women and trans women of color murdered in New Orleans (which sadly boasts an alarmingly high number of such reported murders) and elsewhere. What happened after New Orleans? And what is still happening in, and to, New Orleans?

Add to the ghosts of "Formation" all those lost to police brutality and racist violence committed at the hands of the state, intentionally and unintentionally. Beyoncé calls out police brutality and the premature deaths of Black bodies specifically, not only through the use of a submerged police car as her conjuring stage, but also in a memorable scene toward the end of the video. A line of police officers in riot gear stand opposite one young Black boy. Noticeably, the police are white. In fact, the police are the only white faces in the "Formation" video. Of course, it's not an indictment of every individual white person; it's a visual indicator that white supremacy and whiteness are synonymous with the state. The young boy dancing blends the cases of Trayvon Martin (via a hooded sweatshirt), murdered by a neighborhood watchman in Sanford, Florida, in 2012, and twelve-year-old Tamir Rice in 2014, murdered by police in Cleveland, Ohio. Both made national headlines and sparked extensive protest. The boy breakdances in front of the police line. He dances for his life while police stare him down, weapons at the ready. Through invoking the ghosts of those killed by police and other authorities, Beyoncé is also trying to rewrite the story—to illustrate undeniably that the threat lies with the police and the system, not with any individual Black child, nor, by extension, any adult.

The camera then cuts to graffiti on a wall that reads, "Stop Shooting Us." Another incantation, a plea, and one connected to the Mothers of the Movement featured in *Lemonade*. In exaggerated contradiction to what manifests in the world and news so often, the line of white police officers raise their arms in surrender. While the police's surrender is something that rarely—if ever—happens in life, it serves as a powerful pop culture salve to raw, real wounds. A moment to breathe and imagine things differently. A moment to honor the ghosts. During the Formation World Tour show in Glasgow, Scotland—the very week both Alton Sterling and Philando Castile were killed by police for no reason in Louisiana and Minnesota, respectively—Beyoncé took a moment of silence to honor them, and many more, by displaying a list of names on the seven-story monolith video screen at center stage, followed by ". . . and countless others." Though she doesn't speak each name as part of "Formation," they are all present. All the ghosts Beyoncé has assembled stand in formation, as warning to the audience of the toxicity and violent inequality of the system, and also as warning and threat *to* the system. After all, to slay is to kill—ideologies, politics, structural inequalities. Voices from the margins, standing in formation, poised to slay the system: a movement the audience can also be part of by recognizing their own place and falling into formation—by proving they, too, have some coordination, through recognizing individual privileges and complicities.

Though Beyoncé conjures ghosts surrounded by water, the absence of water in another particular scene is significant. Floodwaters on New Orleans streets are juxtaposed with an empty, subterranean swimming pool, inside which Beyoncé and a group of exclusively

Black female dancers fall into formation to slay killer choreography. And the empty swimming pool that Beyoncé reclaims in "Formation" carries with it the specter of intense racial anxiety. The integration of public swimming pools routinely sparked riots, violence, and racist reactions from whites hell-bent against it. A postwar rise in suburban private swimming pools as a (white) American ideal should also be seen as a direct response to the push to integrate public pools. The proliferation of membership-based, whites-only clubs and organizations boasting swimming pools was an attempt to keep segregation in swimming alive and kicking in the private sector, against the demands of public integration.

Unashamed racist reactions and contempt persisted in public too. Urban legend holds a Las Vegas pool was drained in the 1950s before white patrons would continue swimming after film legend Dorothy Dandridge simply dipped her toe in the water. In 1964 a Florida motel manager poured acid into a whites-only swimming pool when Black people took to the water as part of a swim-in protest planned in part by Dr. Martin Luther King Jr. The aftermath was caught in now-infamous photos by Horace Cort. Countless similar incidents routinely transpired, some passed down by word of mouth, others largely forgotten or ignored, having not been officially recorded.

Beyoncé highlights the absurdity of America's

racist history while exerting power over the empty swimming pool as a space she now controls, just as she does the water itself in the other scenes. The swimming pool invokes additional recent anxiety over water, pools, and police brutality, given that Dajerria Becton, a young Black girl, was violently tackled and held to the ground by a police officer at a pool party in McKinney, Texas, in 2015 for absolutely no reason. She was attending a birthday party at a public community pool when neighbors called police over noise and possible fighting, reflecting and extending a history of racist conflicts over swimming pools. Upon arrival, police violently targeted Black children almost exclusively as problems to be removed from the situation, never considering them innocent partygoers. Becton's assault and arrest were caught on film as she repeatedly screamed for someone to call her mother while pinned down. The video went viral, drawing national attention and derision. Becton and her family sued for damages, ultimately accepting a settlement from the city. Beyoncé's empty swimming pool in "Formation" joins the police car's roof and plantation front porch as stage and cauldron, mixing and blending ghosts from the past, lives in the present, and possibilities for the future. Ongoing conjuring.

Finally, Beyoncé's conjuring is referenced linguistically through the song's title. The suffix "-ation" denotes an "action or process of doing something." In all the above instances, Beyoncé performs the action of giving form: to ghosts, to history, to ideas, and to politics. She brings the marginalized to the center, even beyond, across, and around the boundaries of death. Harkening back to the origins of intersectionality, she recalibrates the specific intersections of Black women's and queer folks' oppression as necessarily more informative than the single-issue politics that only gradually, and painstakingly slowly, include those always already closer to what is stereotypically normative to begin with. She gives form to a new version of politics with an army of ghosts that also symbolically remains invisible, because invisible bodies are impossible to bring into view by the system's design. It's only through wielding an intersectional lens and mapping the margins that the army of ghosts, later given further form in *Lemonade*, becomes possible.

"Formation" opens with a parental advisory warning of explicit content typed in retro computer font. But it's ironically disingenuous. Nothing in the lyrics or visuals requires it. Beyoncé does say "fuck" in the infamous Red Lobster line, which repeats twice, but the same can happen in a PG-13 movie. Countering the very assumptions of the warning, the lyrics and images in the video unapologetically and necessarily celebrate Black women, girls, and queer folks unlike anything heretofore seen in mainstream pop culture. And Black girls, young queer people, those typically positioned in the margins, desperately need the specific affirmations Beyoncé offers. The presence of the advisory further exposes a system attempting to label the empowerment of those never meant to be empowered within that system as the *real* threat necessitating the warning. Beyoncé's reminding viewers to stay cautious and alert, not for explicit language, but for the forces always at work that seek to render invisible those whom "Formation" attempts to strengthen and resurrect. Subverted, the warning becomes a ghost, and the ghosts of "Formation" become real. Beyoncé stands defiantly at the threshold of life and death, transforming margins into center. She drowns in those floodwaters, becomes a ghost while splayed against that police car, in order to firmly link the erasure of Black women to the state, state violence, discrimination, oppression—all the things Crenshaw's intersectionality aims to make visible. Ultimately, Beyoncé herself speaks back as a ghost in "Formation," cleverly cautioning the audience not to heed or trust the system's own antiquated and unjust warnings.

Get Information

"Formation" is a conjuring and a celebration of those at the margins, but it's also, in part, a public education project. Much of Beyoncé's music and art has been, but never as explicitly as during the major public performances of the *Lemonade* era, stemming from the release of "Formation." Each sought to impart knowledge, direct some viewers to information they might not otherwise know or want to take in. Beginning with the performance of "Formation" at Super Bowl 50, they attempted substantial paradigm shifts to unsettle the status quo—Beyoncé critiquing power from within power's center, after having amassed such a huge platform and following by 2016 that her own influence gave her access to those typically exclusive spaces. Public reaction to certain performances from this era, much more vitriolic than in the past, also exhibited just what was at stake by exposing a widespread resistance to taking Beyoncé seriously and a festering anger at the performances' content. She infiltrated spaces that reflected the very systems being critiqued, with her army of ghosts in formation, to destroy the center from within, just as she smashed up the streets in "Hold Up." Intersectionality highlights bodies rendered invisible by design as one step in demanding change to the very ways the world is organized—making essential a lens that exposes "where power comes and collides, where it interlocks and intersects," in more of Kimberlé Crenshaw's words. Judging by the backlash, Beyoncé forcing the world at large to see through that lens made a lot of people, the very people that most need to alter their perspective, damn uncomfortable.

As a teaching strategy, bell hooks talks about honoring discomfort, even necessarily producing discomfort, in *Teaching to Transgress*. Though she's already shown the concept of freedom to be a fiction in *Lemonade*, Beyoncé is certainly trying to empower those at the margins and, in doing so, consequently educate all people of the limitations and biases internalized from an unequal system. It's not her duty or burden to do so, but she incorporates these educational aspects into her performances and platform all the same, despite the backlash doing so inevitably produces. hooks acknowledges, "There can be, and usually is, some degree of pain involved in giving up old ways of thinking and knowing and learning new approaches." So, education necessarily includes discomfort, and the backlash to Beyoncé's performances exposes the productive pain involved in learning, or, perhaps more correctly labeled, unlearning. The refusal by many to hear and engage with what her performances exposed is just as important for what it says about the current state of the world, and how much still needs to be done. In its own way, the public education aspect of these performances is also Beyoncé conjuring—coaxing the public at large through another threshold, one between ignorance and responsible awareness.

An April 16, 2018, Instagram post by Beyoncé's mother, Tina Knowles Lawson, testifies that Beyoncé had been actively and intentionally teaching to transgress by fusing celebration, education, and discomfort, much as she fused celebration to indictment on *Lemonade*. Following her epic Coachella performance centered around HBCU (historically Black colleges and universities) culture, which resulted in the entire festival being jokingly renamed #Beychella, Lawson admitted that she was nervous Beyoncé's vision would confuse Coachella's primarily white audience. But Beyoncé didn't care. In fact, Beyoncé alluded to Nina Simone's quote that "an artist's duty . . . is to reflect the times," as uncomfortable as they might be, and told Lawson, "I have worked very hard to get to the point where I have a true voice and at this point in my life and my career I have a responsibility to do what's best for the world and not what is most popular." Lawson also shared that Beyoncé's hope for the performance was that young people would research anything they didn't understand or weren't immediately familiar with—get information—and work to bridge differences. Beyoncé's insistence on the absolute Blackness of the performance also highlighted a new center from previous margins, not the traditional center part of the status quo. She relied on confusion and possible uneasiness from one direction as an additional tool to encourage people to learn and come together.

With "Formation" and the work and performances that followed, the Blackness and intersectional focus of her music became truly impossible to overlook or deny. It wasn't ever not there, but there were usually other aspects or avenues to explore, examine, and engage. When it came to "Formation," the music couldn't be construed or explained in any other way. And the day after the release of the video, already her most specifically Black and intersectional piece of work, she doubled down. She performed "Formation" as part of the Super Bowl 50 halftime show, and criticism against her reached a fever pitch. As invited guest of Coldplay (the white headlining act), and at *the* pinnacle event for American sports, anticipated and celebrated across the nation—reaching into the households of large swaths of conservative, white Middle America that wouldn't otherwise be listening to Beyoncé—she planted her heels directly into the football field and performed a song full of undeniable lyrical references to Blackness, with dancers styled as members of the Black Panther Party (which was also celebrating a fiftieth anniversary, along with the Super Bowl itself). Talk about confrontation. Talk about paradigm shift.

But Beyoncé was directing the audience back to information, if they cared to listen. Though the Black Panther Party is often misrepresented in American history as a violent antagonist of police, even a domestic terrorist organization advocating armed insurrection, the reality is that they were a community-centered activist organization with a ten-point program championing the self-determination of Black people: equality in education and employment, the eradication of poverty, and the end of police brutality, among other noble pursuits. They often insisted on arming themselves against already armed police who targeted them for violence and harassment—but as a way to prevent the violence enacted by so-called law enforcement before it began, not exacerbate it. The invocation of the Black Panthers at the Super Bowl (though no weapons or references to violence were included) alongside the police car, and the "Stop Shooting Us" plea in the "Formation" video, quickly devolved into accusations that Beyoncé was anti-police. A refusal to actually engage with and see through the lens she was offering, a refusal to even consider unlearning incorrect information from the past. The discomfort even sparked a "Boycott Beyoncé" campaign that quickly fell flat on its face with no sub-stantive evidence or goal. And without any actual proof as referent, it became clear that what really upset fac-tions of the conservative public so intensely was simply a Black woman asserting her own power from within a space right-wing white America thought was theirs to control.

Saturday Night Live (*SNL*) parodied the controversy and ridiculous public outrage after the Super Bowl by creating a fake movie trailer called "The Day Beyoncé Turned Black." Obviously, the joke is that for a very long time, the public was able to imagine Beyoncé as not Black, as aspiring to whiteness, as not holding any progressive politics that would seek freedom for Black people in America. They saw her as transcending race, buying into a colorblind version of society. Despite her long-term strategy of appealing to whiteness in order to build the platform from which she could finally launch this critique—one she likely knew would take at least an implicit adherence to whiteness (as a system of control) to create—she'd always been Black. Only willful ignorance allowed some to understand Beyoncé as anything but. Her sister Solange indicted the same disconnect and ignorance in a September 2016 interview with *The Fader*: "As far as I'm concerned, she's always been an activist from the beginning of her career and she's always been very, very black," she stated. People had chosen to dismiss or ignore Beyoncé's unapologetic Black womanhood in the past, but Beyoncé refused any other lenses through which the public could see her and understand "Formation" beginning in 2016. She exposed widespread public ignorance through her refusal to be anything but exactly who she was, and always had been.

In the *SNL* sketch, one of the white actors, while listening to the song, tepidly and uneasily wonders, "Maybe this song isn't for us." Another white actor in the skit, horrified at that prospect, screams, "But usually everything is!" The truth at the heart of this brutally effective joke is that white people can't understand being a part of something without also being immediately visually referenced and represented. Yet it's exactly what white people have demanded that any and all marginalized groups do for centuries: see their experience as acted out through the universality of whiteness. The only thing new or different about Beyoncé's Blackness in the video or performances of "Formation" was the way she refused any other viewer identification. By playing with gaze and content, by layering in blatantly Black historical references and foregrounding her own experience as a Black woman, she made it impossible for anyone to enter the narrative without first honoring her Blackness—without first seeing through the lens of Crenshaw's intersectionality, and working outward from there. White audiences got just a tiny taste of their own medicine and were thoroughly confused.

Other awards show performances followed Super Bowl 50, but Beyoncé's unexpected November 2016 appearance at the Country Music Association Awards (CMAs) alongside the Dixie Chicks for a performance of "Daddy Lessons" ratcheted up public discomfort with her music and presence even higher. The CMAs appeal to a largely white, conservative audience each year, as does the current genre of country music in general. It's no surprise that Beyoncé's appearance at the CMAs was met with racist disdain, vitriol, and backlash equal to or perhaps greater than that toward her performance at the Super Bowl. But there were no actual explicit political statements made from the stage that night—just a damn good performance of a damn good country song. Which was exactly the point. Beyoncé organized the simple performance, packed it with additional information, knowing anything she did in that space would unsettle the status quo. The status quo at the CMAs, as in society in general, is most certainly conservative, white, and male. So she turned "Daddy Lessons" into another public lesson.

First, the Dixie Chicks are not just any random country band, and Beyoncé strategically aligned them in formation for this performance. When lead singer Natalie Maines openly criticized then-president George W. Bush in 2003, denouncing the Iraq war and simply stating she was ashamed he was from her own home state of Texas, all hell broke loose. Country music fans, other artists, and industry and radio executives joined together in a multipronged campaign to end the Dixie Chicks' career. They burned the group's CDs en masse, banned them from radio stations, and protested concerts. Though the group recorded another critically acclaimed album after the incident, the Dixie Chicks remain largely shut out of country music to this day; conservative country fans have held a grudge for over a decade. But Maines never backed down, even in the face of death threats. She vowed never to return to the

CMAs stage again after the country music communi-ty's despicable treatment of the Dixie Chicks. Maines noted on Twitter that *only* her love and respect for Beyoncé brought the group back to that show. During their performance, "Daddy Lessons" segues briefly into the Dixie Chicks' own "Long Time Gone," from the album they were performing on tour when Maines voiced her political dissent. Beyoncé and the group collectively and unapologetically reanimated Maines's 2003 political statements. Together, Beyoncé and the Dixie Chicks proved they were still not ready to make nice, nor back down.

It's not just the appearance with the Dixie Chicks that created controversy, though. Explicitly racist backlash to the performance disguised as criticism of Beyoncé not being a traditional country artist spoke to other information to which she wanted the public directed. There's no way she hadn't foreseen the racist reaction her very appearance as a Black woman on that stage would elicit. Country fans and artists alike asserted that Beyoncé had no place at the awards, incorrectly assuming and citing the origins and history of country music as conservative and white and male. Country music actually comes out of the artistic creations of Black women—as does nearly every aspect of popular American music. Stereotypical country instruments like the banjo, fiddle, and harmonica were essential facets of Black culture in the antebellum South, with ties to Africa. New Orleans jazz horns begin what turns into the acoustic-guitar-driven "Daddy Lessons" on *Lemonade*, highlighting the interplay between jazz, Black culture, and contemporary country. The CMAs performance did the same by featuring an ostentatious New Orleans–style brass trio, Too Many Zooz, on stage as well. With "Daddy Lessons," Beyoncé hearkens back to the original Black women pioneers of country music like Elizabeth Cotten, Memphis Minnie, and Jessie Mae Hemphill, among many others, and returns them to the CMAs stage where they rightfully belong. A seemingly straightforward performance sought to challenge Black women's historical erasure in country music and get audiences to see the past and present differently.

Beyoncé embraced a similar strategy alongside Jay-Z for the 2018 video "Apeshit" from The Carters' *Everything Is Love*, taking her tactic of commandeering traditionally white spaces for her own purposes to new heights. The couple rented the Louvre Museum in Paris, going apeshit with some of the world's most prestigious and revered works of art at their backs. Rewriting history from the football field to the Country Music Association stage to Coachella to the Louvre and the entire notion of Western art. Not only did the "Apeshit" video infuse Blackness into that space, it encouraged a disrespect for the traditional rules and norms that exalt whiteness at the expense of all else.

What, for instance, is the inherent value of the *Mona Lisa* that the painting deserves so much more reverence than innovative works by Black artists or even the trap beat of "Apeshit" for that matter? The video confronts the viewer with these contradictions. Museums are usually quiet, reverent spaces, but Beyoncé repeatedly goes apeshit, dances wildly and frantically to break the stillness of most of the scenes—while also diverting the viewer's gaze away from the highly prized works, almost mocking them, and onto the Carters themselves, their own music, and other quintessential symbols of Black experience.

Beyoncé serves as teacher (posed to transgress) during all these performances and many others, but a formation, technically speaking, is ultimately a leaderless configuration. The word is commonly used to reference a disposition of military troops or the assembling of soldiers to attack in unison. It's alternately used to allude to dancers moving in synchronicity. Collectivity with no clear center of power. Individuals may perform their own unique movements not mirrored by the entire group, but the choreography as a whole creates a seamless coalition. Falling into formation, whether military, a member of a dance troupe, or just part of Beyoncé's audience, consists of learning the steps modeled by a leader and then quickly re-creating them so the subsequent movements become uniform. The leader becomes subsumed into the collective, and the ensuing formation becomes a leaderless movement. Carrying the skills and lessons forward together.

Beyoncé demands this coordination from audiences at every turn, too, or at the very least evidence of good faith attempts. "Prove to me you've got some coordination." Not just in movement, not just by dancing to "Formation" or any of her other music, but coordination in hearts and minds and approach to the world. "Formation" also served as namesake to the Formation World Tour—announced immediately after her Super Bowl 50 halftime performance—as an additional way to coordinate information, build a collaborative movement through music, if people were willing to listen and reflect. If an audience approached the music from the angle, positionality, and perspective Beyoncé had already foregrounded. In that impulse, the roots of "Formation" are planted squarely within Janet Jackson's *Rhythm Nation 1814* pop political movement building and coalitional politics ("It's time to give a damn / Let's work together," Jackson demands of those who share her vision for a better world), as well as Kimberlé Crenshaw's intersectionality and larger Black feminist history. Beyoncé lays out precise steps necessary to fall into formation, steps explored earlier in her work and steps hidden within her larger oeuvre, especially when considered with post-2016 hindsight. The steps themselves may be uncomfortable or downright painful for those afforded any number of privileges in society, but they model what it takes to learn. Or rather, to unlearn, to coordinate.

Will audiences get in formation? Will they get information? Will they listen—to Beyoncé or to Kimberlé Crenshaw and so many others? Will they assemble in formation to prevent and/or protest the violence against those most vulnerable and marginalized in society? Will they reform their understanding and ways of seeing the world to center those most vulnerable and marginalized in both life and death? Will they coordinate efforts to break the tie between state violence and Black bodies, especially Black women's bodies? Will they map these connections, not erase or ignore them? "Okay, ladies, now let's get in formation." (And "ladies" is already more complicated and nuanced than a heteronormative cisgender category; see chapters 7 and 9). Okay, ladies, now let's get information. "Slay trick, or you get eliminated." You're either part of the solution or part of the problem. No more middle ground, and the lines are clearly drawn. So choose.

The final lines of "Formation," "Always stay gracious / Best revenge is your paper," coyly reference money, and yes, money can provide wonderful revenge when rubbed in others' faces, even as capitalism creates a host of other problems. But paper also alludes to the pages of books containing information—like

Crenshaw's intersectionality—that Beyoncé has fore-grounded as precondition for coordination. Read, study, learn. The waters at the end of "Formation" continue to rise, emergency sirens blare, clouds burst, thunder rolls, more rain falls. And I ask students to follow the information, the ghosts of "Formation" and the subsequent *Lemonade*, back even further to *B'Day* in 2006, where Beyoncé invoked a similar Gulf Coast geography and sonic landscape. And so that historical loop, that spiral out from an (always shifting) center, widens again.

4
GHOSTS OF SLAVERY ~~PAST~~

THE FADE-OUT ON BEYONCÉ SUBMERGED IN FLOOD-waters at the end of "Formation" conjures another famous literary scene as its opposite. Toni Morrison introduces Beloved in her novel of the same name by simply stating: "A fully dressed woman walked out of the water. She barely gained the dry bank of the stream before she sat down and leaned against a mulberry tree." Beloved is a ghost, resurrected from water in Morrison's brutal interrogation of slavery's endless intensity. *Beloved*, in razor-sharp prose, recounts the murder of Beloved at the hands of Sethe, her own mother. Having escaped slavery with her two children, and upon being tracked down by her former owner and overseer, Sethe frantically slices Beloved's throat open with a handsaw and tries to smother her other daughter, Denver, in order to spare them enslaved futures. Denver survives. Beloved does not, though she returns. This is what slavery did to a people: the institution was so violent, so dehumanizing, so incomprehensible and confounding, that it transformed an act of murder—infanticide, even—into one of love in Sethe's head.

Such a gruesome transmuted truth is almost impossible to grasp in contemporary society, even though 2019 isn't that far removed from slavery, as an institution, being legal. And its racist afterlife is far from over. That merciless reality is a fact from which Morrison refuses to flinch. She demands the reader consider an impossible question: Which fate does less damage? Is it better to survive enslaved or be free in death? The questions themselves return to the impossibility of freedom investigated in *Lemonade* and Sherley Anne Williams's *Dessa Rose*. Not just a fictional meditation, Sethe's actions are loosely based on the real-life case of Margaret Garner. Garner escaped slavery in 1856, and, before being captured by US Marshals shortly thereafter, infamously killed one of her daughters rather than have her forced back into slavery. After weeks in jail, she was ordered back to a slave state under the Fugitive Slave Law, and, according to her husband, she died two years later.

Ghosts, water, and the New Orleans locale fuse "Formation" to Beyoncé's earlier *B'Day*, where all the same appear. But another major literary and critical intervention by Morrison also points back to that earlier work: the concept of "rememory." Rememory is the process by which memories come to life, the phenomenon through which Beloved walks out of the water. Rememory resurrects past events, perpetually replays what has happened there, in the place where the thing rememorialized originally occurred.

"Someday you be walking down the road and you hear something or see something going on. So clear. And you think it's you thinking it up. A thought picture. But no. It's when you bump into a rememory that belongs to somebody else," Sethe counsels Denver. Past actions and events continue to exist temporally, able to wreak havoc all over again—psychological havoc, certainly, if not also physical calamity. Sethe is constantly terrified of bumping into one of the thought pictures that linger everywhere. Either her own or a rememory stemming from someone else's experience. Ignoring the pervasiveness of rememory, refusing to attend to the dead even when they materialize, is integral to maintaining slavery's perpetual afterlife. Building on a similar suggestion that slavery was not a singular event, but an ongoing singularity, scholar Christina Sharpe warns in her book *In the Wake: On Blackness and Being*: "In the wake, the past that is not past reappears, always, to rupture the present." Both Beloved and *Beloved* exist as examples of such rupture; *Lemonade* might even be considered one of Sethe's thought pictures come to life. But the *fear* of rememory and rupture—Sethe's terror—can be located in Beyoncé's earlier work.

In the introduction to *Beloved*, Morrison writes, "To invite readers (and myself) into the repellent landscape (hidden, but not completely; deliberately buried, but not forgotten) was to pitch a tent in a cemetery inhabited by highly vocal ghosts." But the fact of the matter is this: to live in America today is to camp in that same cemetery. The repellent landscape in which slavery is forever entangled remains covertly hidden just beneath the surface. Painting over graffiti on a wall doesn't erase it—slavery is a repellent palimpsest, always lurking. As in her earlier work highlighting intersectionality, Beyoncé also demands that her audience uncover the hidden writing that has always been and is still on the wall, to paraphrase Destiny's Child's sophomore album. Looking at Beyoncé's "Déjà Vu" through the lens of rememory and Morrison's ghost of Beloved positions *B'Day* as a necessary prologue in the historical loop of *Lemonade* and "Formation." And it returns to another beginning, since it was Daphne Brooks's article "Suga Mama, Politicized," and particularly her own analysis of "Déjà Vu," that sparked my interest in designing an entire course around Beyoncé's work years ago. Beyoncé has long been sitting in the same cemetery as Morrison, attempting to listen to highly vocal ghosts. The ghost of Beloved herself, actually, might be hiding in the repellent landscape of "Déjà Vu," and déjà vu as a phenomenon is just another form of rememory.

Gulf Coast Ghosts

"Déjà Vu" was the lead single from Beyoncé's second solo album, *B'Day*, in the summer of 2006. The video opens with an unlikely close-up shot of Beyoncé's sweaty back. The heat must be stifling, but the beads of sweat also immediately bring to mind hard work, backbreaking work. As the beads of sweat run down the curve of Beyoncé's neck and spine, she begins to call in each instrument and pound the bass line against the wall with her raised fist. *B'Day* was a fierce, empowered rebranding after playing Deena Jones in *Dreamgirls*, so focus on her back, not face, was an unusually conspicuous marketing strategy to introduce a new look and sound. Seen another way, it was Beyoncé exerting her own power over her audience and the video's frame by refusing to turn and address the camera until she was ready; she made viewers wait. "Déjà Vu" was also built at Beyoncé's specific instruction. It's not until she called in each instrument and Jay himself that she turned to face the camera with the command of "Let's go get 'em." Assembling the song not only exhibited explicit control, but performed the literal construction of musical layers which mirror the complex visual layers central to her music from 2006 forward. This was a new and newly seen Beyoncé, literally and figuratively, and she was in charge.

A focus on a Black woman's back as an introductory image also invokes slavery insomuch as the back was often the site of punishment, lashes from a whip. Sethe's own back is brutally scarred in *Beloved* with the shape of a chokecherry tree. In 1981 the backs of Black women and women of color, and the various burdens they are forced to carry, were canonized as metaphorical bridges in the classic feminist anthology *This Bridge Called My Back: Writings by Radical Women of Color*. Bridges serve the positive and necessary function of connection, but the fact that already marginalized women have to function as intermediaries between single-issue groups is decidedly negative and harmful. Bridges must also bear the weight of being traveled over, walked on, paved, while not truly part of either side. Bridges are liminal spaces—Crenshaw's margins. The bridge called Beyoncé's back in the "Déjà Vu" video immediately invokes the underappreciated work Black women have been doing and continue to be forced into literally, emotionally, politically, metaphorically. Beyoncé reclaimed and redeployed imagery of her own back as a confrontation and rejection of those burdens. As singer, songwriter, and activist Doria Roberts asserts in the song "Because" from her 2011 album *Blackeyed Susan* (itself a historical reclaiming—a tribute record to trailblazing folk singer Odetta), "This bridge called my back is no longer for hire."

Beyoncé's refusal to turn, her decision to instead foreground her own back as prolonged introductory image, anticipated and extended Roberts's lyric, and "Déjà Vu," along with *B'Day* generally, demands that Black women's backs no longer serve as bridge. Society must build its own bridge to meet Beyoncé where she is. And *where* she is, geographically and historically, is referenced through a number of context clues. The entire artwork of *B'Day* is based off of the "Déjà Vu" video (or vice versa), and the only other prevalent actor in the video is the expansive (repellent) landscape. While it proves lush and gorgeous on film, there's something dangerous lurking beneath, as Morrison indicated. And this particular landscape ties Beyoncé's performance and viewers specifically to the Gulf Coast. Coincidentally (or quite intentionally), *B'Day* was released almost a year to the date after Hurricane Katrina hit that same coast. The kitsch of *B'Day*'s release was that it dropped to coincide with Beyoncé's own twenty-fifth birthday—birthday, b'day, Beyoncé day. She speaks that date slowly on the album's second track, "Get Me Bodied," right after "Déjà Vu." Including "Déjà Vu" first, though, redirects attention to the repellent landscape lurking beneath the surface through her invocation of the Gulf Coast on the almost exact first anniversary of Katrina.

Of course, analysis of "Déjà Vu" and some other aspects of *B'Day*, following Daphne Brooks, were the earliest kernels of what eventually became an entire Beyoncé course. And Brooks herself thinks the timing of *B'Day* is politically significant. She called the record "one of the oddest, most urgent, dissonant and disruptive R&B releases in recent memory" in "Suga Mama, Politicized." She went further to say Beyoncé defied all expectations and deserved to be seen as part of a longer history of Black female protest singing, a tradition much deeper and intense than a silly, surface-level birthday theme for a record comprised mostly of up-tempo bangers. Brooks named a number of other major parallels between *B'Day*, with its lead single "Déjà Vu," and public memory of Hurricane Katrina too. The release date being only one of the most explicit. She noted the aesthetic similarities between the "Déjà Vu" video and the overall album imagery, both directing attention to the Gulf Coast. Beyoncé has familial ties to the area as well, so it serves as a personal connection and homage. Brooks named the location a "rural American South that the world confronted in new and unsettling ways over the past year." She pushed understanding further, claiming the "Déjà Vu" video also "recycles an historical déjà vu of the creepiest sort—a tricked out plantation setting with Knowles alternately draped across ornate Victorian furniture and dashing haltingly through everglades and (cotton?) fields looking like a deer in headlights or, perhaps more accurately, like a fugitive house slave on the run." Indeed, Beyoncé does appear to play the part of runaway slave in one scene, fleeing from the plantation house itself, while in others she runs frantically through fields, constantly looking over her shoulder. The video in no way follows the surface-level lyric story—an inability to forget a past lover or partner and intense desire to be reunited with that ex. Something repellent, abhorrent, aberrant is lurking beneath.

No one seems to be chasing Beyoncé as she flees in "Déjà Vu," but simultaneously, all of history is on her trail. Her face contorts with fear and urgency. She appears terrified, just like Sethe fearing her old overseer around every corner. When Sethe tells Denver about the plantation where she was formerly enslaved and abused, she warns, "If you go there and stand in the place where it was, it will happen again; it will be there for you, waiting for you." Watching Beyoncé react throughout "Déjà Vu," it's easy to imagine that she's standing in "the place where it was," and the violence of history is chasing her. It's happening again. The past is poised to rupture the present and only Beyoncé sees it. Not only does "Déjà Vu" invoke the (deserted) antebellum South, there are additional, distinct time periods and moments referenced repeatedly. I ask students to search for other associations, whether invoked through costume, set, styling, or even choreography, and tie them to historical moments. What time period does a particular dress Beyoncé is wearing conjure up? Do any of the shots appear to mimic specific historical moments? A handful of examples in particular generate even more of Daphne Brooks's historical déjà vu to mirror the song's title.

While images of the antebellum South occupy the majority of the video's screen time, the post–Civil War South is invoked too, given the emptiness of the plantation itself. Beyoncé is alone for most of the video, dancing around ornate Victorian furniture in an empty mansion. In Margaret Walker's epic novel *Jubilee*, Vyry Brown stays on for a time at the near-deserted plantation where she was formerly enslaved after Union soldiers arrive to announce the end of the Civil War and emancipation. Beyoncé embodies Vyry after the Civil War in much of "Déjà Vu," both tied to the isolated plantation house, even taking comfort in it at times, while simultaneously desperate to leave. At other moments, Beyoncé stands close to water, on the banks of the bayou. In these scenes, the costuming seems to reference a 1920s flapper. The music of "Déjà Vu" also brings to mind the 1920s jazz heyday of New Orleans through its use of horns and syncopated, swing-influenced cadences and phrasing, even more evident in some live performances of the song. So, in addition to the antebellum South, the viewer catches glimpses of both Reconstruction and the Jim Crow South. Obviously, 2005 Katrina-ravaged New Orleans haunts every scene of the video, too, but unlike the flooded streets of "Formation," the water doesn't over-run its banks.

Another historical moment and additional refer-ences get added to the mix later in the song. The cam-era cuts to Beyoncé dancing on what appears to be a sandy desert or beach, kicking up dust in an aggressive shift in choreography. The costuming changes dra-matically too. She dances percussively in a halter top and green skirt, reminiscent of a grass skirt and stereotypical notions of a supposedly primitive African coast, predating the enslavement of Africans in the United States. At the same time, it invokes a notorious Josephine Baker dance in which she donned a banana skirt to reference, mock, and critique stereotypical notions of Africans as uncivilized. Beyoncé performed her own version of Baker's banana dance, complete with infamous skirt, on Fashion Rocks in 2006 as a tie-in to "Déjà Vu" and *B'Day*'s release. In her article "What Does Beyoncé See in Josephine Baker?," Terri Francis marks Beyoncé's explicit embrace of Baker, via multiple mentions during a 2006 *Good Morning America* interview with Diane Sawyer and the Fashion Rocks performance, as integral to the independence central to her *B'Day* rebranding. Though the "Déjà Vu" dance isn't a literal Baker quotation, it certainly builds on Baker's choreography; it "strategically samples Baker's famous costume and dance practice (speed, Africanisms mixed with older and new American dance) as [Beyoncé] remixes [Baker's] 1920s aesthetics for contemporary audiences." Josephine Baker herself serves as rupture and rememory in "Déjà Vu," as well as an important influence Beyoncé returns to many times over in her work.

Toward the end of the video, the camera zooms in on Beyoncé outdoors at night. More than any other moment in "Déjà Vu," Beyoncé appears as the contemporary performer on stage viewers know her to be in 2006 and beyond; Beyoncé's current time through which all the previous moments then begin to rupture and remix. With Beyoncé donned in a modern sparkling black short set, mid-backbend in the choreography, the scenes jump-cut erratically back and forth with no linear consistency. An early bit of the time travel that returns in *Lemonade*, and while Beyoncé literally bends over backward to impart her message and force viewers to look beneath the surface. These cuts create the titular feeling of déjà vu for the viewer, and speak to the fact that Black women have been living and reliving a feeling of déjà vu historically. Déjà vu literally translates from the French as "already seen," and has commonly become understood as a person having the strong sensation that an experience or feeling in the present has been previously felt or lived, whether or not verifiable facts back up the assumption. Here, the facts certainly do back up the déjà vu of the present—from Africa, to treatment under slavery in the

US, and various points in history up to 2006 (album release) and today (whenever one views "Déjà Vu"). Slavery. Reconstruction. Jim Crow. Hurricane Katrina. Add the ghosts of "Formation." Add *Lemonade*. Stir and repeat.

The déjà vu is not only symbolically disorienting; it exposes the failure of America to value Black women and address their concerns, and it anticipates the broken promises of *Lemonade*. The force of Beyoncé's déjà vu is connected to specific additional burdens Black women are then forced to bear for the nation, a prime example being that Black women and Black women's pain are often disingenuously and counter-intuitively used to assuage national guilt for having created historical pain, while those in power simultaneously continue to ignore Black women's concerns in the present and deflect responsibility. The dynamic was especially apt in the aftermath of Katrina, as Melissa Harris-Perry notes in her book *Sister Citizen: Shame, Stereotypes, and Black Women in America*. "As the disaster unfolded, Black women became the main characters through whose suffering and resilience the media told the story." Harris-Perry argues that Black women were not only struggling for their lives but were also used by the media to bear the brunt of the nation's pain. What was disguised as a "natural" disaster actually exposed long histories of racism, discrimination, and inequality, and whom the US government deems worthy of protection. Harris-Perry concludes that Black women "were the bridge over the deadly waters that allowed the rest of America to cross into the agonizing realization of how unequal the country remained at the dawn of the twenty-first century" while still not enacting substantive change. Another bridge on another back. Beyoncé returns to these same issues in the video for "Formation," showing how an additional decade passed with floodwaters still rising.

So it's precisely the paradox that Black women have been ignored, neglected, *and* expected to hypervisibly bear and represent national pain, over the course of multiple historical time periods that fuels Beyoncé's performance; and the absurdity that Black women must simultaneously represent conflicting positions, always caught in a catch-22, is driven home explicitly when Jay ignores Beyoncé in the one scene where they appear together. They aren't Jay and Bey in this video—they're playing parts, much like they do as characters in their duo of On the Run tours; they're political actors. Given the other layers of the video, it's not hard to imagine Jay as representative of power and the system. The United States government, and then-president George W. Bush, were rightfully ruthlessly critiqued for their slow response to the devastation Katrina unleashed on New Orleans. Those in power did not adequately prepare, respond, or actively assist those most affected by the storm. They broke that implicit promise embedded in the citizenship contract: that a government will take care of its citizens in times of need. Those most affected and disenfranchised by the storm were poor and disproportionately Black, and the fact that Black women in particular became associated with the storm through the media further exposed America's lie along gender, race, and class lines at once. It was Black women again being asked to forget the broken promise, like Claudia Rankine described, and take on additional pain. Lies are highlighted in the very beginning, too, because despite Jay's boast that he "runs the bass, hi-hat, and the snare" in his intro verse, listeners hear Beyoncé prove that she's actually the one at the helm as she calls each in.

Though she expresses power as an artist and slyly and symbolically counters the lie, there's one thing she's still not able to fully capture: attention or recognition from Jay. The aloof character Jay-Z plays during the video is not completely contrary to his own performance persona, but it invokes an altogether different feel in this video. Beyoncé is doing the absolute most to get noticed, wildly dancing directly in front of him, at times dropping to her knees sexually, tugging on his belt. He looks anywhere but directly at her. She shakes her chest at him. When she shoves her face up next to his, in the direction he's looking, he immediately averts his gaze and looks in the opposite direction. Jay-Z is also doing the most to refuse attention intentionally. He represents power and the government response to Katrina, and the scene replays indictment of the state's failure to swiftly act despite every plea to do just that.

As Beyoncé runs through the otherwise empty landscape, or the repellent landscape densely populated by ghosts, she may not only be invoking Sethe's fear of rememory, but, alternately, the actual ghost of Beloved risen again. No one sees Beyoncé emerge from water (at least in the context of *B'Day*). No one saw Beloved walk out of the water either. The reader knows because of Morison's omniscient narration, but there are no witnesses. Beloved lost her life to a violent nation, not simply to Sethe's hand. That ruthless action was meant to save Beloved from further violence, from slavery, even though the nation seeks to continually hide its own violence, its neglect, and place pain and responsibility back on individual Black women like Sethe as distraction. Beyoncé dancing around Jay, trying to attract attention and gain recognition of the unequal truth at the heart of the government's response to Katrina, mirrors Beloved's return. Her appearance indicts the overall brutality of slavery as an institution, doesn't just demand retribution for

Sethe's individual choice. It was already an extension of a more original violence.

Beloved is still a vindictive ghost though—she wants revenge and redress. She refuses to forgive or forget overall. Not just in relation to Sethe; she refuses to forgive an entire system that produced the conditions under which Sethe was able to consider the murder of her own daughter an act of love. Beyoncé embodies these aspects of Beloved in *B'Day*'s second single, "Ring the Alarm," as she threatens (and perhaps succeeds) to burn down a house, along with everything she owns, rather than relinquish it to someone else. That justified anger also returns on *Lemonade*. Beloved was never just the ghost of Sethe's dead child, either, but an elusive something more, something much bigger, as Denver describes late in the novel. Perhaps representative of the "sixty million and more" Morrison dedicated the book to, a guess as to how many lost their lives to the slave trade, though no number can ever be truly corroborated. In naming those sixty million and more, Morrison is also refusing to forget. And it connects back to the "countless others" Beyoncé named during the Formation World Tour. Though Beloved simply turns into nothingness after making her grievances known and wreaking havoc, Beyoncé's version of Beloved returns to water many times over.

Hold On to Me

In "Formation," Beyoncé drowns. She is again submerged in water at the beginning of *Lemonade* and notably walks back into water later. During "Love Drought," Beyoncé and a group of women march—backs straight, heads held high—into the waters of Lake Pontchartrain, in a historical reenactment connected in part back to Morrison's "sixty million and more." In 1803 a mass suicide took place at Igbo Landing in Georgia. Enslaved individuals being transported to America gained control of their ship, ran it ashore, and marched back into the ocean, choosing suicide over slavery. Again, an impossible choice. As the visual reaches backward in time, the conditional future tense of the lyrics of "Love Drought" reaches forward to posit a future possible only if the past is attended to differently, as part of Beyoncé's overall refigured citizenship contract. "You and me could calm a war down / You and me could make it rain now"—could, but haven't yet. She's rupturing the present with rememory intentionally, replaying what previously happened, trying to use the mistakes of the past to change the future as the second, prescriptive half of *Lemonade* gains momentum. At another point in "Love Drought," black-and-white shots show her lying on a sandy shore, arms stretched to either side. A piece of tulle resembling a fishing net covers her, tangled. Suddenly, she blinks life into her eyes. A resurrection, just like Beloved's return, but tied directly to that suicide at Igbo Landing.

Directly following "Love Drought," Beyoncé speaks the matter-of-fact words, "There is a curse that will be broken," and that curse may very well also include the historical loop explored and reenacted in these works across time. She does seek to break the curse with a new version of a citizenship contract, and by teaching her audience to see the past and present differently in *Lemonade* and "Formation." But she also recenters the very same generational bonds dissolved throughout history and named in Saidiya Hartman's *Lose Your Mother*, the bonds severed between Sethe and Beloved, to offer an unlikely addendum to the violent historical repetition infused into her music. One that looks forward, to her own daughter. Blue Ivy appears in *Lemonade*, but it's "Blue," the final track from *BEYONCÉ*, that most fully attempts to redirect Morrison's rememory in a new, hopeful direction, to transform a ghost into unforeseen possibility. In a poem that commemorated protests against apartheid by over forty thousand women and children, June Jordan named an irreversible, moving force with the power to shake the mountains and sea—the very landscape—uniquely possible through the sustained action of mothers and children in particular, recognizing their own strength and standing up together.

She cited something intrinsically powerful in that generational bond, closing her "Poem for South African Women" with, "We are the ones we have been waiting for." It sounds simple, but Jordan's words exist as powerful affirmation and command; "Blue" casts that same powerful bond and force Jordan names into a possible future. And the video for "Blue" begins, again, at water's edge.

In class, I always replay assigned videos to spark that day's discussion. Watching together grounds conversations in a common experience and jogs memory. Rather than jumping directly to some major point, I first ask for general reactions and thoughts—a useful way to name and honor personal opinions before moving into more critical territory, to gauge where any group of students is coming from. With "Blue" especially, students gravitate toward the personal aspects of the video, gush over the cuteness, and revel in some of the first, more extensive footage audiences were ever allowed to see of Blue Ivy. Plus, there is always near endless adoring chatter over the vocal sample of Blue herself that closes the song. Coming after *Lemonade*, "Déjà Vu," *Beloved*, and lots of talk of ghosts, "Blue" might seem like an abrupt turn in a different direction. So I ask questions that nudge students, when necessary, to keep looking beneath the surface of the lyrics and visuals. Because nothing Beyoncé ever does is purely personal or coincidental. How does the use of water in "Blue" compare or contrast with that in other Beyoncé videos? What story do the lyrics tell when setting aside the fact that Blue is Beyoncé's daughter? What connections to the readings come to mind? I remind students to consider alternative contexts, as well as any and all possible interpretations of different camera shots, moments, and sounds—even when they don't seem to make immediate sense. They can be placed into a larger narrative later. A charming, simple song sung from a mother to a daughter on one hand can become something else entirely following Toni Morrison and June Jordan. When all else fails, it's useful to start with the chorus.

In "Blue," the chorus repeats the command to "hold on to me," a plea that seeks to sing a connection into being and "make it last forever." Repair and reorganize the past. The lyrics reference the concept and passage of time, but in ways that counter Sethe's warnings to Denver about rememory. Beyoncé's not afraid, despite naming walls caving in on her as clear and present danger in the first verse. Though the present contains vestiges of the past, ready to happen again, Beyoncé looks to her daughter and still feels alive. Fortified. She's singing from a place of hope, not terrified of rememory but alive and joyful in spite of it. Approaching time this way, the lyrics also speak not of history bound to repeat, but a trajectory that contains the possibility of breaking the cycle. Make this feeling, this connection, last forever, she sings. A command that seeks to determine the future, invoking her own daughter, the next generation. A gathering of blue water. Though the synthesized piano chords of the song have been bent and lightly distorted throughout, slightly transfigured like the opening notes of "Formation"—vacillating on either side of perfect pitch—it becomes most overt and noticeable the very first time Beyoncé calls Blue's name at the end of the first chorus. Even through the soundtrack, Beyoncé is performing the bending of time and history to serve her purpose, unsettling past, present, and future through a strategy that mirrors the way the moon pulls tides, all while the video shows water intermittently lapping at a sandy shore.

The lyrics also metaphorically build a bridge with the future through physical touch. A new bridge that reconstitutes earlier unequal, historical iterations of that bridge called Beyoncé's back; turning the previous burdensome expectation that Black women build, sustain, and *be* the bridge between single-issue groups and politics on its head. Manifesting a different, self-directed, bridge. Declaring again, more forcefully, "This bridge called my back is no longer for hire," following Doria Roberts. "Hold on to me," Beyoncé croons to the water and to her own daughter. Join hands. Reach forward, while another reaches back. Hold on to one another. In light of the ghosts of slavery, its legacy and reverberations for society in general, this simple plea is actually a rejection of a violent history that ripped families apart, tore enslaved women from their children and sold them to locations unknown without batting an eye. Beyoncé's chorus seeks to address and redress Sethe's impossible choice; to undo the gruesome, yet love-filled murder of Beloved, to reunite mothers and daughters cut from one another, whether through handsaws or history. Holding on to Blue, with Blue holding back, is a projection of Black womanhood into the future, something that was never guaranteed to Black women of the past. Often, that future is still not guaranteed to Black women in today's present.

The bridge of the song finds Beyoncé repeatedly singing a hard and impassioned demand to keep holding on, her voice a beacon and the only unmodulated layer of the soundtrack. But the chords quickly take an urgent, minor turn. The vocal line becomes a battle with all the historical forces that continue to devalue Black women in the present. As rememory attempts to surface, Beyoncé still doesn't cave to fear. She doubles down on pleading louder than before that "we," "I," and "you" all must hold tighter. She builds a bond through sound, though imperfect, to reconnect bonds that have been broken, time after time, through violence, ignorance, inequality, discrimination, even death. It's no coincidence that "Blue" directly follows "Heaven," a song focused on a broken bond through untimely death, the video for which shows Beyoncé mourning a friend, another Black woman. There, she consoles herself by justifying, "Heaven couldn't wait for you," but through "Blue" and the bonds she sings into being, she's showing that these kinds of premature death should never happen to begin with—and, through its proximity to "Heaven," that Black womanhood has been, and is too often, associated with a kind of premature death.

The video for "Blue" is shot to look like Beyoncé's own home-video footage of favelas in Brazil, celebrating the local residents. The ghosts of slavery certainly exist outside the United States, but it's important that Beyoncé chose an external setting to highlight an alternative landscape apart from the explicit ways the ghosts of slavery exist for Black women in America. Beyoncé is uncharacteristically out of the frame for the majority of the video, instead turning the camera on the people of Brazil and occasionally on Blue Ivy herself. Youth and innocence are highlighted alongside regular, ordinary people celebrating life. The visuals are relatively straightforward, lovely, joyful. But the final moments, above all else, hold significant weight, especially as "Blue" is the final track of the *BEYONCÉ* album proper. Blue Ivy's featured vocals on the track come at the very end of the song—the last moments that reverberate with the listener as audio and video fade out.

During her feature, Blue returns the lyric Beyoncé has been singing throughout, calling out, "Hold on to me, Mommy, hold on." Apart from eliciting emotional outbursts, maybe even happy tears, from the audience, Blue's words do something more important—something magical, actually. Beyoncé wouldn't include this snippet without important reason, as it's clear how closely she guards her and her family's privacy. But it is included and featured prominently. Blue's voice signifies the bond taking form in multiple directions, backward and forward. And her words echo, performing their own projection into the future. The last thing audible is Blue's voice literally reverberating outward. It's unknown how long the echo lasts because the track fades to silence while the echo continues to bounce, captured in perpetuity.

And that's where "Blue," finally, connects back to chasing ghosts through Beyoncé's work. What, after all, is the temporality of a ghost? From the vantage point of the present which it haunts, a ghost brings back a piece of the past, unresolved or unexamined, perhaps, but important nonetheless. Beloved walking out of the water and carrying the legacy of slavery with her; Messy Mya speaking from beyond the grave on "Formation." Ghosts affect present moments, even if others don't see or recognize the evidence of their presence. Rememory, the past returning, déjà vu. What about an echo? While standing in the present, an echo extends or projects a sound from that present into an unknown future. A plea thrown into an empty place so that it might powerfully bounce back, make an impact, although it can't be fully directed or anticipated. An echo, then, might be just what hope sounds like. And it's the temporal opposite of a ghost. One brings the past to the present. The other takes the present (with its attendant past) and throws it into an open, undetermined future continuously. It might very well be that a simple echo, and all it represents, can effectively escape and alter the historical loop Beyoncé painstakingly re-created and performed from *Lemonade* into "Formation," back to *B'Day* and forward again.

In those fading last moments of "Blue," while Blue Ivy's voice echoes, the sound of water, the tide rushing back, is also heard. And seen—the last scene shows Beyoncé, holding Blue in her arms on the beach, walking away from the camera and the viewer's gaze. Feet slowly sinking into the sand, moving back toward the water. Walking into a new future that the water now holds while simultaneously reimagining the past that same water represented and defined. Returning to the water, finally, in a new way. She's enacting reconciliation between Sethe and Beloved, an alternate timeline where the two escaped the repellent landscape of slavery together, or where there was never a slavery to escape. Where no one's freedom was ever in question.

She's also envisioning a future where that same repellent landscape and ghost-filled waters don't hold the present in limbo, don't determine the future. Water echoes, waves crash, the last sounds of *BEYONCÉ* reverberate. From water to water, sea to shining sea. "The past and the future merge to meet us here," and maybe Beyoncé has generated some hope that the curse will finally, truly be broken. Destroyed. The ending of "Blue" creates some hope that moving in other directions, outside the sweep of history's arduous loop, is possible. And so the syllabus, too, moves in new critical directions, while never letting go of the past.

PRESENT

5
A CROOKED ROOM OF ONE'S OWN

PICTURE IT: YOU WALK INTO A ROOM AND EVERYTHING is tilted. Things look off, wrong. You might even get dizzy. Vertigo. In order to make sense of what you're seeing, do you tilt your body to align with the room's slant, or do you stand upright, continue forward with arms outstretched, trying not to bump into anything despite the disorienting angles? What kind of toll do either of these strategies take on an individual body and psyche? Students have already approached pieces of Melissa Harris-Perry's work alongside Katrina and "Déjà Vu," but it's her metaphor of the crooked room from *Sister Citizen* that becomes foundational to the rest of "Politicizing Beyoncé." It's a particularly engaging, compelling, easily understood way to think about stereotypes, important especially because it returns the burden of stereotypes back to the system that creates and perpetuates them, rather than blaming any individual for adhering to them, intentionally or unintentionally. She uses the notion of a crooked room to describe the way Black women experience America, given the pervasive stereotypes of Black women that exist. Of course, the metaphor can be applied more widely to other marginalized groups, but the distinct stereotypes encountered—or the particular crooked-ness of the room—change in each scenario.

To be safe, to be acknowledged, to be understood—to be *seen* and survive—Black women, understand-ably, might sometimes bend themselves so that the room makes more sense, according to Harris-Perry, conforming to a stereotype for lack of any other options for recognition. Why wouldn't they? It's not the individual's fault; the blame lies with the room itself. Harris-Perry writes, "Bombarded with warped images of their humanity, some black women tilt and bend themselves to the distortion. . . . To understand why black women's public actions and political strate-gies sometimes seem tilted in ways that accommodate the degrading stereotypes about them, it is important to appreciate the structural constraints that influence their behavior." Who is anyone to judge the various ways some cultivate to survive in a hostile, violent world? Oppressive systems can't always be directly and actively challenged—that takes a lot of privilege, power, and relative security in other aspects of life. In other words, taking part in the same systems that oppress in some ways, or bending to meet the crooked room to some degree, even while simultaneously resisting, is almost inevitable.

Beyoncé has been accused of reproducing various stereotypes in her career to court a mainstream audience. But placed inside the crooked room, Beyoncé's actions might be understood more subversively. It's been mentioned earlier how, once she had achieved an enormous amount of power, Beyoncé strategically commandeered white spaces to make major public statements about who is seen at the center and who is relegated to the margins. She was, in effect, exposing the crooked room and the constraints some experience when trying to stand up straight. That same theme appears in much of her other music more subtly, and once students begin to think about the crooked room, they seem to find examples everywhere. Even Beyoncé asking "Why can't you see me?" in *Lemonade* is an attempt to break out of the crooked room. Though Harris-Perry names three specific stereotypes built into the room (featured more specifically in the next chapter alongside "Partition"), I've found it useful to also name Western (white) beauty standards as their own overarching element of the architecture—an area where Beyoncé has received particularly intense and cruel criticism.

Controlling images construct and uphold the crooked room in today's highly visual culture. Sociologist Patricia Hill Collins describes the way Western beauty standards create a form of control and hierarchy for Black women and girls. In *Black Feminist Thought: Knowledge, Consciousness, and the Politics of Empowerment*, Collins notes that "controlling images of Black women are not simply grafted onto existing social institutions but are so pervasive that even though the images themselves change in the popular imagination, Black women's portrayal as the Other persists. Particular meanings, stereotypes, and myths can change," Collins explains, but the thrust of the images stays the same. The goal is a subtle but swift internalization of an unattainable aspiration toward whiteness. To mix Harris-Perry and Collins, controlling images are the bricks and mortar that make up the walls of the room, tilted to a baffling slant for some, while providing the illusion of ninety-degree angles to everyone else. A major component of organized Black feminist thought for Collins is locating, exposing, and challenging controlling images in all their forms, thus subtly shifting the crooked walls.

Beyoncé has a long history of exposing those same bricks and reframing and remodeling the room too. She's sung about embracing imperfection in "Flaws and All," and exalted physical features not always praised by society in "Bootylicious." She's referenced accepting her body in various ways since having children, most recently unabashedly celebrating her "FUPA" in *Vogue*'s September 2018 issue. While most of her commentary has been empowering, she's also confessed the demands of the crooked room in more vulnerable ways. In *Lemonade* she says, "If it's what you truly want / I can wear her skin over mine." She concedes, "I tried to change / closed my mouth more. Tried to be softer, prettier / less awake." She's played with alter egos to express pieces of herself she felt couldn't be expressed simply as Beyoncé, or to offer critical commentary about the constraints of the world: Sasha Fierce, both King and Queen Bey, B.B. Homemaker, Yoncé, among others. Each represent a piece, but never the whole. Through her actions and performances, she constantly points back to the structural constraints of the room, bending for larger effect.

In a 2013 *GQ* interview, before going more or less media silent, Beyoncé admitted that she played the game to get to where she is today, subversively building a platform and following that she may not have been able to build had she broken more rules earlier on. She could have explicitly exposed the controlling images and constraints of the room in less subtle ways, but she likely wouldn't have attained the levels of power and access she enjoys today to make even grander statements. "I worked so hard during my childhood to meet this goal: By the time I was 30 years old, I could do what I want. I've reached that. I feel very fortunate to be in that position. But I've sacrificed a lot of things, and I've worked harder than probably anyone I know, at least in the music industry." Beyoncé's own autobiography and career history are sly, subversive testaments to the fact that she's been in on the constraints all along. And two particular performances with strong autobiographical references that bookend her self-titled album—"Pretty Hurts" and "Grown Woman"—openly expose and retell the ways in which she's built covert challenges to the crooked room and its accompanying controlling images into her own career trajectory.

Being Happy

When it comes to stereotypes around beauty, watching a pageant is a perfect way to investigate. In "Pretty Hurts," beauty is costume, and one that inflicts pain by design. Makeup, wigs, clothes, enhancements, pills, surgeries all help construct "pretty" as interchangeable artifice. Beyoncé sits introspectively judging herself in mirrors backstage at the competition for much of the video. She plays the pageant girl of her own youth as a woman in her thirties. Lyrics detail people in her life persuading her to cultivate beauty over intelligence, positing beauty for girls and women *as* knowledge par excellence defined by others. As counterpoint to other empowering anthems, "Pretty Hurts" confesses a poorly kept but deeply internalized secret: namely, that the expectation and demand to be pretty *hurts*—a soul, a body, a person—because the rules are arbitrarily determined by those with money and power, as Beyoncé noted in *Life Is But a Dream*. On the surface, the song and video follow a straightforward narrative. They provide a surefire way to start necessary conversations around beauty standards, body image, and the societal pressures and judgments that accompany them. Conversations college students, especially women, are hungry for because they face those harsh pressures and brutal judgments constantly. But "Pretty Hurts" is not without its additional layers. After providing space for the important above discussion, I also ask students to consider "Pretty Hurts" as a form of autobiographical storytelling. Pertinent given its place as lead track on *BEYONCÉ*, her first release since enacting her own public/private split following that *GQ* interview and the release of *Life Is But a Dream*.

What if "Pretty Hurts" isn't just an indictment of beauty standards generally, but a parody of pretty itself and its attendant ties to white femininity specifically? The very white feminine ideal Beyoncé is constantly accused of aspiring to. Pretty is a crooked room, one decorated with promises of privilege and freedom, but with numerous fine-print conditions that become evident over the course of the video. In an essay for her 2017 Beauty Beyond Binaries column, tackling the social privilege that accompanies being seen as pretty,

Janet Mock noted, "'Pretty' is most often synonymous with being thin, white, able-bodied, and cis, and the closer you are to those ideals, the more often you will be labeled pretty—and benefit from that prettiness." Beyoncé is widely cited as exquisitely beautiful, but, as a Black woman who does not replicate fashion's sample size, deviates from much of society's normative definition of pretty. In a crooked room, exceptions don't alter the architecture. The irony of Beyoncé competing in the pageant of "Pretty Hurts" nods to her strategy of playing by the rules only to expose them. Her overarching critique is that pretty is always a performance, and the whole world's a stage. Pageant competition is synonymous with every public space and private moment in women's daily lives.

Throughout the video, the rooms (and stages) are exposed as crooked, confining, and unequal. The white beauty ideal is unattainable performance—not just for Beyoncé as a Black woman, though that holds important weight, but for anyone. Beauty as mechanized performance becomes even more explicit during scenes where the lights come up on the contestants—Beyoncé plays Miss Third Ward, another alter ego—on stage. Smiles snap onto their faces as the light hits, along with a synchronized, robotic wave to the crowd from each woman. There's no pleasure in "Pretty Hurts," despite the lyrical claim that one can "pageant the pain away." It's not working. The room gets incrementally more crooked with additional behind-the-scenes glimpses, as more pain is exposed. The longer the pageant lasts, the more artificial it appears.

Beyoncé is being judged constantly over the course of the narrative of "Pretty Hurts," backstage, on stage, by directors and producers measuring her body, by a host, audience, judges overseeing the pageant. And though the judges appear largely in shadow, they can still be identified as mostly white men, indicating just who built the room to begin with. In other moments, women coat their teeth with Vaseline, a common pageant practice making it easier to smile without leaving lipstick stains; spray their bodies down with hairspray in order to get costumes to stick to skin, not reveal too much. These things do minimal short-term damage in the long run, but they set young girls on a course of self-harm thought to be productive and beneficial, so that when they graduate to more harmful practices, it doesn't feel like a leap at all. One contestant is shown swallowing cotton balls, trying not to gag. Beyoncé is featured excessively exercising and popping diet pills, all extreme and unhealthy practices that exist on a continuum, beginning with the seemingly innocuous Vaseline on teeth.

Given the sly focus on hair throughout—wigs are ever-present backstage, ready to be donned, in addition to shots of Beyoncé's then newly shorn locks, still dyed blond, that caused a stir on Instagram—Beyoncé ties the expectations of pretty to hair, especially for Black women. Morgan Jerkins lays out, in great and often horrific detail, the difference between "good" and "bad" hair for Black women in her book *This Will Be My Undoing: Living at the Intersection of Black, Female, and Feminist in (White) America*. Good hair equals straight, an unnatural state for Black women's hair. Relating the pain involved with getting relaxers as a child, she says, "The burning didn't just affect my scalp. My skull could feel it, too." The sodium or guanidine hydroxide most often used to relax Black women's hair "contains such a strong chemical base that it can be used to unclog drains. . . . It can cause second or third degree burns in contact with skin, blindness if eyes are exposed, and gastrointestinal damage if ingested. Now imagine this being slathered on a three-year-old's head." This is just one example of the additional bodily harm stereotypical notions of pretty cause and demand from young Black girls in order to transform themselves into "Becky with the good hair" (conversely, perms for Becky's good hair use the mildest chemical agent). And these controlling images and messages about hair are internalized by young girls and society at large.

Beyoncé continues to ratchet up hurt by depicting eating disorders too. In one scene, she appears to struggle with bulimia, contained and hidden within a bathroom stall. Even eating disorder discourse centers white women's stories in diagnosis and treatment for the most part. Stephanie Covington Armstrong's 2009 memoir *Not All Black Girls Know How to Eat: A Story of Bulimia* is one of the *only* widely available texts on eating disorders from a Black woman's perspective. Beyoncé then highlights the pernicious demand for women to seek out cosmetic surgery, mapped onto her own body, while the audience still likely recognizes her as beautiful exception. Her face is marked up with Sharpie pen, evaluated with intense scrutiny. An entire system, a diseased nation, is to blame—represented by those pageant judges—but lyrics point to a multitude of other culprits too: parents, magazines, media, perfectionism, the tendency to point out flaws at all times, diet fads, conflicting versions of beauty that can't possibly coexist in one body, individuals' souls, doctors, loneliness, a culture that sees medication as a quick fix, and maybe most pressing, internalized expectations of self that result from all of the above. The whole world is responsible and judging Miss Third Ward at every turn. She's judging herself too.

The "Pretty Hurts" video is nearly three full minutes longer than the audio track, and so those minutes stand out to the viewer even more, offering additional visual exposition that points straight to the constraints of a crooked room. As the video begins, Beyoncé is called to the stage to perform her talent. She sings the chorus of the song a cappella, initially shaky but finding strength and confidence in tone and timbre after the first refrain. A quick sonic indication that Beyoncé is attempting to stand up straight on that crooked stage. In another auxiliary scene, during the question and answer portion of the pageant, Beyoncé makes a significant statement. The words are placed at the beginning of the audio track, but gain additional meaning and focus at the video's climax. Harvey Keitel as pageant host pointedly asks: "What is your aspiration in life?" Beyoncé pauses, taken aback despite her otherwise mechanical pageant programming. The question legitimately surprises her. Why? The audience might start to get nervous, fearing some embarrassing attempt at an answer to follow. Beyoncé bides her time by asking herself the question over and over, prolonging the uncomfortable suspense.

Jump cut to a scene of Beyoncé underwater, seemingly having fallen backward into a pool or lake. She covers both ears, shakes her head while submerged, trying to drive the white noise of voices (or the noise of white voices) out of her head—the pressures of beautifully perfect conformity: how to look, how to perform, what to say, how to act, etc. She submerges herself in water to be washed clean, or perhaps end her suffering. A suicide attempt, a baptism, a rebirth, a cleansing? All possible options. The scene anticipates another moment from the beginning of *Lemonade*. In both, Beyoncé submerges herself at moments of overwhelming pressure tied to the exposure of serious flaws in the very structure of society—whether a broken promise or a crooked room—and reemerges to break shit. After "Pray You Catch Me" in *Lemonade*, she takes a swan dive from the roof of a building, hits the ground, which turns to water, and proceeds to laugh through the destruction of a city street while swinging her baseball bat; in "Pretty Hurts," the underwater scene precedes both her eventual answer to Keitel, surprising them both, and more destruction.

She, breathes, smiles, and calmly states, "My aspiration in life . . . would be . . . to be . . . happy." As Keitel and the audience digest the deceptively complex construction of her answer, the scene cuts to Beyoncé wielding a gigantic trophy with calculated rage, demolishing shelves and other smaller trophies amassed over years of trying to pageant the pain away (itself a rearticulation of bending in the crooked room). Beyoncé is smashing Collins's controlling images—the awards and rewards society bestows on those who follow the rules, who smile and look pretty because "what's in your head it doesn't matter." She reframes winning (through trophies) as insufficient, and posits destroying those indicators of success as the real position of knowledge. Meanwhile, her answer on stage lingers as subtle justification for her rage and destruction.

In a detail easy to gloss over, Beyoncé employs the subjunctive mood, rare in English, used to reference states of unreality, to answer Keitel's question. The various removes from the present in the construction of her answer are indicative of the ways bending to meet the crooked room removes a person from themselves, removes them from possibility and reality. It marks the fact that she's not even allowed to have an aspiration as a Black woman in society, and she's certainly not allowed access to happiness as it's been defined through whiteness and white womanhood in relation to beauty. The possibility is foreclosed by design. In her autobiography, *Dust Tracks on a Road*, Zora Neale Hurston noted a similar realization, her "earliest conscious hint that the world didn't tilt under [her] footfalls, nor careen over one-sided just to make [her] glad." She was referencing a trivial childhood fight with a friend about the position of the moon in the nighttime sky, but it served as metaphor for a realization that she wasn't able to set the parameters of her own happiness. That her happiness as a Black girl and woman was not guaranteed and even actively thwarted. That realization for Hurston was emblematic of the fact that the entire organization of the world was counter to things that made her glad. Counter to her own enjoyment as a Black girl and eventual woman. Hurston also realized that to seize happiness, she'd have to stand straight in a crooked room, tilt the room to *her* footfalls.

The enormity of this truth hidden within the room's walls, and the realization she's broken an implicit taboo in voicing such a truth because of the indictment it contains, is what gives Beyoncé pause while articulating her answer, not simple confusion over the question. After some internal debate, she refuses her pageant conditioning and speaks freely. She wants to be happy, if she has a choice, if society allows her a choice. But instead, society requires she perform the same tired scripts, deferred into a possible future, and smile. The answer more correctly states: "My aspiration, which I don't have because society does not allow me to have an aspiration, would be—if I was given the opportunity to express anything close to hope— to be happy at some point in the future, because I'm not currently allowed to be happy." A mouthful. The notion of happiness for women is often conflated with physical appearance and the opportunity being traditionally pretty affords. Beyoncé's pageant answer in "Pretty Hurts" further deconstructs that connection along race lines by showing her happiness, as a Black woman, is something the world works actively against. Her words connect back to the larger, overarching dynamics Hurston names too. Beyoncé doesn't win the pageant. To voice all these challenges, to name the limits of happiness and beauty and still win, would tacitly validate the crooked room all the same. Provide an easy fix by offering her another crown, appeasement. She sacrifices recognition at the pageant to illuminate her loss as proof of systemic constraint, not personal failure. Failing to win the pageant exposes a world failing her. She's beginning to stand up straight, even if uneasily.

Throughout the rest of her autobiography, Hurston proudly shares stories of defying a system that devalued her, through both struggles and uneasy successes. In an earlier 1928 essay, "How It Feels to be Colored Me," Hurston offered the tongue-in-cheek aside, "Sometimes, I feel discriminated against but it does not make me angry. It merely astonishes me. How can anyone deny themselves the pleasure of my company? It's beyond me." At the end of the pageant, Beyoncé's "Pretty Hurts" invokes that same astonishment. Played to extremes, the pageant exposes the continued erasure of Black women in a nation plagued by a perfection constructed through whiteness. And the structural constraints to Beyoncé's happiness are meant to astonish viewers, provoke conversation and action. Hurston also famously said, "I feel most colored when I am thrown against a sharp white background" in that same essay. The sharp white background is the crooked room with painted white walls. Hurston and Beyoncé both realized this through their own experiences at young ages, and turned what was meant to be accepted as a weakness into a strength. At the end of "Pretty Hurts," their astonishment lingers. Why has it taken the rest of the world so long to realize the same? It's beyond the two of them.

Ain't I a Grown Woman?

"Grown Woman" isn't explicitly about beauty in the ways "Pretty Hurts" is, but it shares the pageant theme and returns Beyoncé to the trophy room—the scene of her earlier crime, as it were—in an informal visual bookend to *BEYONCÉ* (as bonus track), building on the work she did smashing those trophies. She was breaking apart the controlling nature of beauty standards then, but "Grown Woman" calls for a revolution in the very ways the world understands Black women and the ways Black women perceive the entire world—not just attempting to stand up straight in the crooked room, but razing the damn walls. From realizing the world doesn't "tilt under [her] footfalls, nor careen over one-sided just to make [her] glad," to demanding that it does so in the future. "Grown Woman" plays with autobiography, too, through specific video footage, rewrites Beyoncé's own past to tell a story organized around Beyoncé's and Hurston's gladness. She's merging her failure to win the pageant with her extraordinary real-life success to assure audiences, like she did in that 2013 *GQ* interview, "I now know that, yes, I am powerful. I'm more powerful than my mind can even digest and understand." She even possesses the power to symbolically rewrite rules for a new generation.

Initially, "grown" and "woman" seem redundant placed next to each other. As they're repeated together throughout the song, though, they begin to remind listeners of the reality that age does not equal maturity and vice versa. Hearing Beyoncé deliver the syllables of the words "grown woman" in slightly different variations each chorus—sometimes drawn out, sometimes chopped shorter, sometimes growled, sometimes cheerfully dismissed—variously highlights equal parts empowerment, assertiveness, and an undercurrent of subtle desperation. Over the course of the song, all the versions blend and exist simultaneously. The desire to be seen as a grown woman (as an actual woman of thirty-two at the time) blends with the unapologetic assertion that she's long had to have been grown, reinvoking the childhood realization of Hurston that the world did not turn to make Black girls glad. Paradoxically, Beyoncé's every move is criticized, and she is never afforded agency as a grown woman in her art or business, at the exact same time that Black girls are always perceived as older than they are in today's racist society—already women, never girls. While Black girls are seen to be grown and responsible for too much too early, Beyoncé's independence and artistic control are ascribed to others, never her. Through repeating "grown woman," and playing with home video footage of herself as both grown woman and young child throughout the video, she is undoing that incongruity in both directions: asserting her independence and artistic maturity, while also articulating that young Black girls shouldn't be burdened with the weight of the world.

A particular piece of Alice Walker's definition of "womanism"—her own articulation of a political and theological vision deeper and more expansive than feminism generally; in her words, "Womanist is to feminist as purple is to lavender"—is ever present in the song through both words in the title. As an informal preface to her 1983 essay collection *In Search of Our Mothers' Gardens*, Walker invents a definition, etymology, and history for her conceptualization that relies heavily on the Black folk saying, "You trying to be grown." She delineates, in part:

> **Womanist** 1. From *womanish*. (Opp. of "girlish," i.e., frivolous, irresponsible, not serious.) A black feminist or feminist of color. From the black folk expression of mothers to female children, "You acting womanish," i.e., like a woman. Usually referring to outrageous, audacious, courageous or *willful* behavior. . . . Interchangeable with another black folk expression: "You trying to be grown."

Though the folk saying initially comes across as an insult or negative attribute, Walker's embrace of it also shows that it's about protection at its core—parents and other adults protect children from Hurston's realization that the world didn't "careen over one-sided to make [her] glad," since the realization itself also inflicts pain through its reification of the crooked room's walls. Walker and Hurston together expose the fact that structural racism creates a space in which some children are forced to grow up much faster, while others are allowed the luxury of a childhood because the world, the crooked room, does in fact reflect them and make them glad by design.

In other words, being able to act as a child while still physically young is a privilege largely reserved for white girls (and white boys even more so). Beyoncé's invocation of "grown woman" provides a space to talk about the ways in which a racist and sexist society both label and stereotype Black girls as older than their actual age, thus erasing their childhood, and creates the material conditions that force a young Black girl to grow up before youth is formally over or has been experienced and enjoyed. According to Monique W. Morris, that very phenomenon also detrimentally leads to Black girls' early criminalization. In *Pushout: The Criminalization of Black Girls in Schools* she says, "As children or adults, Black girls are treated as if they are supposed to 'know better' or at least 'act like they know.' The assignment of more adultlike character-istics to the expressions of young Black girls is a form of age compression." That age conflation or compres-sion then directs society to judge Black girls exponen-tially harsher than other children, funneling them into the criminal justice system unfairly. Beyoncé attempts to rewrite these limiting scripts about Black girls and women and their already predetermined racist and sexist conclusions by turning "acting grown" into a backhanded compliment, a reclamation of an insult, albeit one from a place of love and protection. She lyrically links being young, while simultaneously con-sidered grown, with being brave and having knowl-edge—with building the strategy and platform she has today. It was all part of her plan, and so "grown," in her redefinition, is celebrated and contains possibil-ity. "Grown woman" is wielded back toward the very oppressive society that shortens or erases childhood for some. Beyoncé's a grown woman and she can do whatever she wants. What she wants is to bring down the walls.

The crooked room is on full display for the major-ity of the "Grown Woman" video. Beyoncé sits slightly off-kilter in what appears to be a young girl's pageant outfit, surrounded by trophies and drinking brown liquor from a highball glass. Incongruities. She's also physically tilting her body in the chair, one leg thrown over its arm to heighten the crookedness of the scene.

An odd mix of childish antics and mature behavior. Her body stretches diagonally across the frame. A child with a curved upper lip, inexplicably chomping on gum and drunk while competing in a beauty pageant. Or a disoriented grown woman in costume, reliving a childhood memory. And despite the trophies, the money, the prestige, Beyoncé doesn't seem happy, extending the force of her answer in "Pretty Hurts." She tries to stand up straight, but still falters. The scene's framing won't allow it. Her movement seems off, lacking enthusiasm and precision at first— making it patently obvious something is wrong. Maybe it's the alcohol; maybe it's the crooked room.

Extending the incoherency of the staging, Beyoncé rewrites her own childhood in "Grown Woman" as an adult. The video features digitally altered home videos spanning her early years to create footage of a younger Beyoncé singing a song that didn't exist when the footage was originally recorded. More than once, a student has shouted out in frustration after watching the video at the beginning of class, shocked not to know "Grown Woman" was a cover song. Dismayed to have been so duped. Of course, it's not a cover song, but those less familiar with her overall catalog often sit, perplexed, watching Beyoncé lip-synching "Grown Woman" in old footage from the 1980s, 1990s, and 2000s. How? The genius of the digital manipulation lies in the way it creates a world unlike the one

Hurston encountered—a world that is particularly (re)organized around Beyoncé's gladness, that replays happy moments through time while conveying the 2013 lyrics. Another experiment with time travel. Students also laugh hard at themselves once they realize they've fallen for the trick, always acknowledging and bowing down to the powerful effect of Beyoncé's sleight of hand.

So Beyoncé reorganizes the action within the crooked room, attempts to straighten out the foundation and walls, and throw the rest of the world off-balance for once. But she still wants to demolish the entire room for effect. At the end of "Grown Woman," she confidently turns away from the camera and walks right off the set (out of the room) and into a new, previously unimaginable foreground. In pieces, the constructed set she was standing in gets pulled away, leaving her standing before a green screen on which different backdrops are then projected: a lush jungle scene, complete with wafting neon smoke and gold automobile; a plain black background with alternating falling diamonds, zebra print, psychedelic patterns, and space nebulae, among other things. The parade of seemingly random images actually makes more sense than the incongruity of the previous scenes, and eventually ends with Beyoncé, her mother, and various children on a bed floating through another galaxy. The images are so overblown and bombastic, the audience is forced to consider them limitless. Here, Beyoncé celebrates a new room of her making, a room of her choosing. Her room has no limits, the walls whisked away. An anti-room, even. The previous rooms were controlling her; in "Grown Woman," the walls finally arrange and disassemble at her will.

Significantly, at the grand unveiling of this anti-room, the audio track also shifts drastically to draw on Afrobeat percussion, complete with Guinean chanting vocals courtesy of Ismael "Bonfils" Kouyaté. The costumes contain additional African references and the choreography changes to emphasize the various forms of African movement. Beyoncé's hair is shown in more natural styles, in distinction to the iconic blond: brown, curly, and gathered atop her head in one moment; straight and black in another. Turning the short, dyed-blond cut and wigs in "Pretty Hurts" back on themselves. She features generations of women—her mother, herself, and children—all while wearing an African headdress in the style of an ankh, the ancient Egyptian symbol for life. All these things add up to define what was lacking from the previous crooked room: an affirmation of Black lives, especially Black women's lives. A theme that rushes back with striking clarity on *Lemonade*. Her new room without walls centers this affirmation, incorporating a powerful politics of gender, race, and sexuality through lyrics and visuals. And it rejects formal structure, because formal structures and systems in the United States are often rooted in the concomitant racism and sexism of the crooked room. Finally, in the last scenes of "Grown Woman," Beyoncé seems completely happy, joyful, without a care in the world. Glad.

By highlighting the room's malleability instead of its inescapable crookedness or its containment, Beyoncé suggests it may be possible to dismantle the room altogether. But it takes a lot of power, and collaborators with power willing to make immense sacrifices. Audre Lorde famously asserted, "The master's tools will never dismantle the master's house," but Beyoncé grabs the tools and makes good use of them while she has access; she snatches the master's tools to significantly damage the crooked room, if not inflict irreversible damage to its structure. Clearly, it's not a livable or even practical strategy. Beyoncé had been working in the industry over fifteen years before she amassed the influence and platform to even artistically suggest such a thing. But as an artistic statement, it does provide possibility, a moment to imagine being able to live differently. And surely Beyoncé knows that these radical changes are merely hopes and dreams in the present, as opposed to already being realities.

At the end of "Grown Woman," she sits on a bed—a place of rest, a place where dreaming happens. Sadly, an oppressive world teaches people to create only what's acceptable for them to create, to imagine only what's safe for them to imagine. To dream only what's realistic (or more accurately, approved of) for them to dream, which takes all the imagination and political capacity out of dreaming from the start. But Beyoncé gives permission to dream of more by temporarily subverting the crooked room that contained her. Even finding a little happiness along the way. As she told *Vogue* in 2018, "I'm not happy . . . if I'm not dreaming, if I'm not creating a dream and making it into something real." In other words, materializing the previously impossible. Pretty hurts, but it's possible to dream of something different, dream outside the lines and make those dreams real. "Grown Woman" is Beyoncé's actualized dream—a crooked room of one's own, remixed and redesigned to reflect and affirm the lives of Black women. And maybe when the walls come down, it becomes patently obvious that it was always already the rest of the world standing askew, not Black women. Not Beyoncé. The power of racism and sexism tricked everyone into believing in only one limited definition of right angles.

6
DON'T PARTITION ME

YOU CAN'T TALK ABOUT BEYONCÉ AND IGNORE HER shameless celebration of sexuality, for which she's been both praised and decried. Empowered sexuality and provocative innuendo were never absent from Beyoncé's music, but 2013's *BEYONCÉ* introduced an artist less encumbered by inhibition than ever before. Songs like "Blow" and "Rocket" narrate unabashed sexual pleasure, and always at Beyoncé's own direction. But it was "Partition"—a lyrical ode to sex with her husband, and a video that exposed more skin than anything previous—that elevated criticism to unforeseen heights. Conservative pundits and noted feminists alike railed against Beyoncé's now-watershed invocation of feminism alongside such sexually provocative images and lyrics, as if the two were incompatible. The debate is far from new: during the late 1970s and early 1980s, the feminist sex wars over pornography birthed a new embrace and simultaneous critique of sex-positive feminism—the idea that sexual freedom and pleasure are necessary components of women's liberation, not anathema to it. Historically, white women's bodies have been protected and venerated at all costs, virtue personified. Black women were never afforded that luxury. While white women can embrace a sex-positive feminism by simply casting off outdated, sexist assumptions, Black women's embrace of the same often provokes responses informed by the very racist stereotypes the system uses to justify their subjugation. Since Black women face particular stereotypes that are already highly sexualized, enacting a sex-positive feminism for Black women can often appear to others, on the surface, as additional tilting in the crooked room. Sex-positive feminism is a lot more complicated at the intersection of gender *and* race.

Much of the racist discourse around Black women's bodies and sexuality draws on the real-life experience of Sarah "Saartjie" Baartman, a Khoikhoi woman from what is today South Africa. Born in 1789, Baartman was exhibited under the pejorative moniker Hottentot Venus (a reference to the Khoi tribe), while both living and dead, as a human zoo attraction across nineteenth-century Europe, a kind of carnivalesque freak show. The point of the display was to highlight the ways her body differed from white women's—namely, her buttocks, breasts, and genitalia—which in turn helped fabricate a norm out of white women's bodies. Over the course of her short life, she was sold to a British doctor, managed by other various showmen, constantly exhibited, forced to stand naked at parties while ogled and touched. After her death in 1815, her body was dissected and pieces displayed at the Musée de l'Homme until 1974 in the name of science. In *Medical Apartheid: The Dark History of Medical Experimentation on Black Americans from Colonial Times to the Present*, Harriet A. Washington notes that "Baartman was not the only African woman to be exhibited as a Hottentot Venus, but she became an important exemplar of the medically exploitative display of black peoples." Word of Baartman's exhibition, along with many others, helped embed scientific racism and sexism within the foundational thought processes of Americans as justification for enslaving African people, the effects of which have still not been overcome.

Further, Baartman's buttocks, the result of a medical condition known as steatopygia, and other sexual organs—which could only be considered enlarged when citing white women's bodies as the standard—were understood as demonstrative of insatiable sexual wantonness. Immutable bodily characteristics were defined as innate desire. Promiscuity was projected onto her body by those who kept her captive, and recapitulated through her body's very exhibition. Interest in viewing her supposedly abnormal body was misconstrued as resulting from her desire to be seen, rather than the public's drive to see and consume. Being on display was tacitly understood as something Baartman wanted to do, with no attention paid to the coercion the exhibition most certainly required. Assumptions and judgments about Black women's willingness to display their bodies in ways even remotely sexual—empowered or not—are still tied back to the stereotypes Baartman's, and others', display helped create. The politics of respectability, a phrase coined by Evelyn Brooks Higginbotham in her *Righteous Discontent: The Women's Movement in the Black Baptist Church, 1880–1920*, refers, in part, to the reactionary expectation throughout history that Black women should erase any trace of sexuality or pleasure from their lives to be seen as worthy of recognition—to replicate the fictional norm associated with white women's bodies and sexuality, and distance themselves from what Baartman represented.

In fact, because Black women's bodies have been egregiously and violently displayed throughout history, and those displays have always relied on racist and sexist assumptions about sexuality, the reality is that any encounter between a Black woman's body and the public is already indisputably intimate. Sex is commonly seen as private and interpersonal, but privacy and intimacy are rarely afforded to Black women. Respectability politics create an additional impediment to claiming sex positivity for Black women: an impediment not faced by white women, nor wielded with the same historical specificity. Respectability politics also, no doubt, have a lot to do with the heavy criticism Beyoncé received upon the release of "Partition." If her only intention was a raunchy video, the lyrics to "Blow" or "Rocket" lend themselves to something even more provocative, but she chose "Partition" for a reason. It might be about a whole lot more than putting herself on display for display's sake—namely, display carefully manipulated for critical purposes.

The heightened sexuality of "Partition" doesn't exist in isolation either. It's connected to *BEYONCÉ*'s subsequent video, "Jealous." The lyrics of the two songs seem to tell different, self-contained stories (not to mention the audio track of "Partition" is first fused to "Yoncé"), but one flows directly into the other visually—the only two videos where narrative action spills from one track to another. After pointing out the track break, I ask students to consider how extending the narrative action into "Jealous" might build, complicate, or inform the performance of sexuality in "Partition," while also asking them to consider additional critical sources. Rather than sexuality alone being the focus, it becomes possible to open up much more nuanced conversations about the ways in which womanhood, for Black women, is already negatively sexualized and stereotyped. And Beyoncé's direction highlights the public's complicity in upholding racist and sexist scripts about sexuality in the present, normalized by and built off of Baartman's display—a display that created an Other in the past, used to justify the veneration of white womanhood. A display that invented an "ideology of deviant black female bodies [still] reiterated in contemporary popular culture," according to Janell Hobson in her book *Venus in the Dark: Blackness and Beauty in Popular Culture*. Beyoncé attempts to catch the audience in participation, witting or unwitting, in a system that perpetuates those same scripts.

P/art/ition

Viewing "Partition" and "Jealous" alongside consideration of a large-scale art installation by Kara Walker highlights an interactive story that counters much of the criticism "Partition" received. Walker is a visual artist widely known for creating black paper silhouettes placed over white backgrounds, literally giving Zora Neale Hurston's words about feeling "most colored when . . . thrown against a sharp white background" new life. Walker's art directly confronts taboo subjects of race, gender, sexuality, and violence in intensely uncomfortable and important ways; her art never flinches, though audiences might flinch at her honesty. In 2014 she created a massive installation (a first for her) housed in the Domino Sugar Factory in

Williamsburg, Brooklyn, and titled in full (in characteristic Kara Walker fashion):

At the behest of Creative Time
Kara E. Walker has confected:
A Subtlety
or the Marvelous Sugar Baby
an Homage to the unpaid and overworked Artisans
who have refined our Sweet tastes from the cane fields
to the Kitchens of the New World on the Occasion of
the demolition of the Domino Sugar Refining Plant.

Marked as both installation and confection, the "subtlety" of the title refers to the name of sugar sculptures placed on banquet tables during the Middle Ages in both England and France. Guests ate the sculptures after dinner was done, figuratively consuming whatever the sculptures represented. Walker's subtlety was a gigantic sugar sculpture—seventy-five feet long, thirty-five feet high—in the style of the Egyptian sphinx, but altered to include stereotypical features of a Black woman set up for public consumption. Not so subtle.

Returning to Melissa Harris-Perry's crooked room, she says that Black women are widely recognized and/or acknowledged by the public at large only when bending to re-create one of three available archetypes or characters. *A Subtlety* blended features of all three. Walker invoked the Jezebel, or the hypersexualization of Black women and their bodies à la Sarah Baartman, through the sculpture's nudity and provocative position. The sugar sphinx sat prone and exposed to the audience from all angles—no privacy. A handkerchief tied around the sculpture's head, alongside stereotypical Black facial features, immediately signified the Mammy. Tied directly to slavery and the South, the Mammy positions Black women as asexual caretakers of white families, often to the detriment and neglect of their own. And finally, Sapphire, or the angry Black woman, was projected through the sheer enormity of the subtlety—an assault on the viewing public, fierce and confrontational.

Walker was experimenting with the power of gaze and the ability to manipulate viewers' sense of scale. The installation worked to shrink spectators down in size, making them miniature in relation to the sculpture. Walker visually redirected the flow of power. By playing with scale, she attempted to confuse the space between subject and object. Despite their comparatively small size, spectators were still poised to consume a Black woman's body simply through viewing the sculpture. The audience didn't know at the time, but their gaze was also being rejected and returned by Walker herself. She later told the *Los Angeles Times*, "[H]uman behavior is so mucky and violent and messed-up and inappropriate. And I think my work draws on that. . . and it pulls it out of an audience. I've got a lot of video footage of that [behavior]. I was spying." People might have been looking, but they were also, more importantly, being watched. Walker's covert spying became the basis for a follow-up exhibit months later in New York City, a video of reactions to *A Subtlety* titled, with brevity, *An Audience*.

Walker's reversal of gaze redirected power, but audiences were willfully exposing themselves all the while too. She may have been secretly watching, but she invited the public to document interactions with and perceptions of the art from the get-go, and share those captured moments on social media using the hashtag #KaraWalkerDomino, creating a virtual version of the exhibit that would live on in perpetuity. Inappropriate selfies depicted numerous violent interactions with the Black female body, and are now preserved for posterity. The interactions weren't limited to any race, gender, sexuality, or class either—people of various backgrounds participated as an equal opportunity oppressive crowd. I visited the exhibit on two occasions and personally watched people stand in front of the sculpture with their hands up above each shoulder, fingers in pinching position. Photos snapped seemed to show that person playing with, even tweaking, the sphinx's nipples. I saw others take advantage of an obscene photo op from behind, standing with tongues or fingers strategically positioned in front of a literal ten-foot vagina, miming oral sex and other acts. Many laughed and joked while taking all kinds of pictures around the statue. Not everyone, of course. But each time I was in attendance (once at the beginning of the nine-week run and again in its final days), a fair percentage of people took part in this impolite and violent behavior. Traces of the behavior are now etched into the social fabric, thanks to Kara Walker's artistic intuition and vision.

It's just a piece of art, though, they say. *It's not like we're actually hurting anybody*, they rationalize. *We wouldn't treat a real Black woman on the street like this*, they contend. But how accurate are those words? Black women face disproportionate amounts of harassment and violence in the world and on the internet every day. How exactly are interactions under the specter of art appreciation disconnected from that reality? Beyoncé already denounced society as mere pageant stage where inequalities along race and gender lines are perpetuated, built into the walls—this is but an extension of that commentary, further indicting the rest of the public moving within the room. The parallel Walker is trying to foreground is that the way individuals respond to the Black female body when they think no one is watching is exactly the way they treat and interact with the Black female body in public. The very act of consumption, beginning with seemingly innocent actions and behaviors—like selfies from the exhibit—reinforce larger narratives. Inflict the same damage. Create the same volatile atmosphere.

Consumption is consumption, no matter the scale. Focusing on the interaction between the public and the Black female body (one of countless issues the entire exhibit tackled), and placing it next to "Partition," highlights not only the ways Beyoncé is herself a conceptual and visual artist in her music—doubled as both actor and informal director—but how the visual and lyric sexuality of "Partition" might also be about the interaction of a racist public viewing a Black woman, not merely stereotypical hypersexuality. And its counterpart, "Jealous," adds additional weight to that reading. To dismiss "Partition" as incompatible with feminism because of its sexuality is to respond to only half the story, and prove both Walker's and Beyoncé's artistic points.

The videos for "Partition" and "Jealous" begin at the same table, Beyoncé seated directly across from someone, camera looking on from behind a nondescript shoulder. Most viewers assume it's Jay-Z, due to the tendency to read the personal onto Beyoncé at all times. To be fair, Beyoncé plays with that tendency herself, just as Walker played with public reaction. Jay does appear in the video—in the back of the limo, and seated in a club while she dances. The camera shows just enough to positively identify him. However, those moments appear in stark distinction to the cryptic indecipherability featured in the table scenes. The camera's line of sight is also the viewer's own, staring directly at—or avoiding—Beyoncé from the other side of the table. The viewing public, the whole world, is positioned through the camera's gaze at the other end of that table, unwittingly ignoring, or perhaps refusing to see, Beyoncé. She's playing with the same dynamic set up between Walker's installation and viewer, and unless an individual turns off the video (which no one is wont to do), they are swept up in consumption. Drawn into and implicated in the mucky, violent, messed-up, inappropriate social and historical drama she seeks to tell, just as the audience was by simply viewing Walker's *A Subtlety*.

"Partition" opens with Beyoncé's multiple attempts to get attention from the other side of the table. She loosens her robe and runs her hand along her chest sensually—the body as go-to means for garnering attention, appearing to bend to the Jezebel stereotype. It fails. No reaction. In fact, the audience's unidentified stand-in shakes and raises his newspaper to further block Beyoncé from view. Next, Beyoncé drops her napkin in a power play, forcing the white maid to pick it up. Even after a complete reversal and rejection of the Mammy archetype, Beyoncé still gets no recognition from the other side of the table. But importantly, as the napkin drops, so does the beat. Beyoncé the artist assures she is still in control, though the character she's about to play may appear powerless on some level. Her artistic nod to the fact that she's spying, just like Walker watched from the eyes of her sculpture, as well as a nod back to the way she claimed autonomy by calling in the beat in "Déjà Vu" against Jay-Z's assertions. She's got this.

As Beyoncé carefully considers her next move, the camera jump-cuts to other scenes containing the most provocative portions of the video: various rooms in the house, backseat of a limo, the Crazy Horse stage in Paris—a legendary burlesque theatre descendent of the Folies Bergère where Josephine Baker famously performed for years. Spoiler alert: these moments aren't taking place in the narrative time of the video, unveiled at the end of the song with a cut back to the same table, back to the same exact opening scene. All the action in "Partition" can importantly be read as occurring only in Beyoncé's head. Whether fantasy or memory, its inclusion highlights Beyoncé's character contemplating doubling down on the Jezebel stereotype in order to garner the recognition she craves, bending to align with the crooked room by performing sexuality as a public demand. It's an extension of the initial come-on enacted from her seat at the table, adjusting her robe suggestively. These thoughts and choices—foreclosed options, really—are mirrored in the exasperation in Beyoncé's face at the end of "Partition." Instead of continuing to bend, she storms away from the table. But not before slyly sipping tea, which can more correctly and artfully be read as spilling tea

(Southern Black and queer slang for shrewdly exposing juicy information or deep truth).

Multiple meanings are accessible even if viewers aren't reading this larger critical narrative onto the visual progression. As stand-alone scenes, Beyoncé is still consistently empowered in her expression and performance of sexuality in the fantasy section of "Partition." Some may attack her for refusing to adhere to a modest respectability, but her performance of sexuality isn't for anyone's pleasure but her own. She's always in control and directing the action. There's physical distance between her body and others, or she's alone in rooms. The notable exception is the back of the limo, where she's in close contact only with her own husband. On a personal note, her dancing in "Partition" doubled as an anniversary gift to Jay after having spent time together at the Crazy Horse together in real life. The multiple layers and intentions end up building a political and conceptual art project commenting on the sexualization of Black women's bodies as available for public consumption, when they are never granted private autonomy to express and enjoy sex without being stereotyped—which she is also doing unapologetically, and insisting on, in the scenes divorced from the narrative progression of the two videos joined together.

There are other lyric and visual clues in the larger cinematic narrative that indicate Beyoncé isn't fully

satisfied in her sexually objectified supporting role—
or more complexly, that even if she is deriving pleasure in some ways, it's still rife with problematic racist
and heterosexist assumptions. As the striptease portion of the video begins, only pieces of Beyoncé's body
are intermittently shown, along with other disembod-
ied legs that couldn't anatomically be her own. The
Black female body is being cut apart and partitioned
itself. In fact, partition imagery and metaphors run
rampant throughout the video. Later, while dancing,
cheetah print appears on her skin, alluding to the ani-
malistic sexual wantonness stereotypically associated
with Sarah Baartman and superimposed onto Black
women—the effect achieved through a light filter (a
kind of partition) placed in front of a spotlight and
then *projected* onto Beyoncé's body as stereotype. At
the same time, Beyoncé dances slinkily amidst what
can alternately be read as stripper poles or bars of a
cage or jail cell. The double meanings here collide with
the lyrics too: "I just wanna be the girl you like / The
kind of girl you like is right here with me." Beyoncé
notes that she *is not* the girl the public likes, but rather
that the girl the public likes is a role that she's forced
to play because Black women have been split, trapped,
and caged by stereotypes, literally partitioned from
their own autonomy. She's not incorporating that girl
into her identity; she's wearing that girl as a costume.
She exposes "the kind of girl you like" as a role she's

forced into to make sense of the crooked room and appear to have a semblance of subjectivity.

In a moment you miss if you blink, the literal objectification of Black women's bodies is foregrounded too. Beyoncé turns her body into an object for effect, in choreography only meaningful in silhouette, from behind a screen or partition. As she dances, she swings her legs back and forth over a chaise lounge. For a split second, her shadow becomes indistinguishable from the chair itself. She relies on her silhouette to visually become an object while the camera is fixed squarely on her body, making it impossible to delineate where she ends and the chair begins. The audience becomes directly complicit in the objectification of the Black female body—Beyoncé's own secret spy video. Individuals might understand themselves as separate from explicitly harmful circumstances, but Beyoncé shows here that everyone is involved through her performance, whether via cheers, adoration, unwillingness to untangle the political implications of the work and thus ignore them, or simply a refusal to look away. As quick as the moment in "Partition" happens, Beyoncé pivots and tears herself away from the chair, marking a decisive turning point in the narrative and redirecting the action and story of "Partition" much more so than does the formal track break between the videos.

Partition is also both noun and verb throughout—walls, artificial separations, barriers between things that previously touched freely; dividing, severing, rending in two. Incidentally, stereotypes are also partitions. A stereotype's function is to partition and divide. Stereotypes divide people from one another and divide a person from their own humanity, both for the person who buys into or wields the stereotype and for the person who feels a stereotype's force on their body or psyche. Divisive stereotypes exist in actions, interactions, politics, minds, and are woven into the very construction of the crooked room. They force some to bend because the room wasn't built with them in mind, while others get to fade into the background standing upright. Through the framing scenes at the table while Beyoncé weighs her options, the stereotypes imposed on Black women's bodies become a massive hidden partition in the song and video that redirect the narrative. Nina Simone once sang, "You've got to learn to leave the table / When love's no longer being served," and that's exactly what Beyoncé does, after contemplating her situation, after sipping/spilling her tea. Once she gets up, finally pushing back from that table and standing up straight in the crooked room, the video for "Jealous" has already begun.

Don't Judge Me

"Jealous" sounds like a companion piece more than its own work. It eschews traditional song structure without a true verse-chorus setup, and stands out as the shortest song on *BEYONCÉ*. The sexy syncopation of "Partition" gives way to minor, haunting, eerie ethereality. The sounds of "Partition" unraveling. While the "Partition" video played with the viewer's gaze, "Jealous" is Beyoncé's unveiled returned gaze—a demand that those looking evaluate and perhaps change their actions. The true power and message of "Jealous" lie in following its subtle details and associations as a lens through which to funnel an understanding of "Partition."

Jealousy is traditionally seen as an unfavorable emotion, close cousin to anger—irrational and rarely beneficial or productive. Jealousy is also usually associated with women and femininity, which contributes to its stereotypical interpretation as negative. Jealousy only exists because society operates from an understanding of scarcity rather than one of abundance; you can't be jealous if there's enough to go around, whether material things or attention are up for grabs. It's an in-between emotion, hard to nail down. And if it's taken root, there's no easy external solution. If you're jealous in a relationship and suspect a partner is cheating, for instance, no amount of evidence will prove the contrary. Exculpatory proof often fuels even more jealousy, as if the lie is just more cleverly concealed. When I ask students what jealousy means to them—how it feels—they are *never* at a loss. Especially when it comes to following jealous hunches. I always ask what they would do if they suspected a partner was cheating, and they immediately become veritable shady private investigators. The first and most common response is to covertly go through a partner's phone, privacy be damned. It would be my go-to as well. But what if nothing shows up there? Give up and move on? Hell no. They suggest ways to dig deeper, because the story is surely not over because a phone contains no proof. After all, it could've easily been erased, right? Various off-the-cuff responses follow: I've heard "follow them," "check bank statements," or even once or twice, in jest, "kill them." The reactions create laughter and sometimes shock, but jealousy is no laughing matter. And the knee-jerk retorts are always proof that the absence of evidence only heightens suspicion.

The only real way to dismantle jealousy is to smash it within, to resolve not to give others' actions power over you (interpersonally, at least). It sounds like self-help schlock, but it's true when interrogating the nature of jealousy as a force and thinking about the phenomenology of emotion. That doesn't, however, make it any easier to practice. The directionality of jealousy seems to flow outward toward others. But it's a ruse. In reality, jealousy moves outward only to return. It can't be assuaged by an absence of proof, and so turns back to its root—which is the person feeling jealous to begin with. The true object of jealousy is individual insecurity, not anything external that is desired. As Beyoncé put it in "Pretty Hurts," "It's the soul that needs surgery." The focus on jealousy here is decidedly different from the systemic broken promises and lies interrogated in *Lemonade* and elsewhere, because those are backed up with the verifiable receipts of history. Here, coupled with "Partition," Beyoncé is exposing the deleterious effect of jealousy as yet another partition within your own head, dividing you against and from yourself and from others. The insidious work of jealousy then also mirrors the destructive work of stereotypes and fuses thematically to that last major and most brilliantly hidden partition in "Partition."

If "Jealous" encourages that jealousy be dismantled on interpersonal levels, it also demands that the partitions (stereotypes) in the world that have seeped into everyone's heads get dismantled structurally. The crookedness of the room gets internalized, and must be countered constantly. In a moment of heightened vulnerability in the song, Beyoncé demands, "Don't judge me"—don't stereotype me—which is also a call for direct action. For Beyoncé, action began the minute she ripped herself away from the chaise lounge in the silhouette scene of "Partition." The first step in her transformation was to insist on acting for herself, choosing her own agency. She transformed herself into an active subject by tearing away from objectification.

Attempting to stand straight in the crooked room also forces a necessary clash between Beyoncé's agency and the audience's gaze, creating the "oppositional space where [her] sexuality can be named and represented, where [she is a] sexual subject—no longer bound and trapped" by the constraints of history and the crooked room, as bell hooks writes in her essay "Selling Hot Pussy: Representations of Black Female Sexuality in the Cultural Marketplace." Beyoncé claims a complex, sex-positive, empowered Black feminist oppositional space by both illustrating stereotypes projected onto her, acknowledging and grappling with them, while still insisting on her own agency, as others stare on judgmentally. Her performance in "Partition" and "Jealous" calls out complicity in the perpetuation of the stereotypes she has variously embodied in the videos, from that oppositional space hooks longs for and believes is possible.

Now, hooks has been an outspoken critic of Beyoncé's feminism and her participation in all things capitalist, especially in the wake of BEYONCÉ and Lemonade. She infamously referred to Beyoncé, in part, as a "terrorist especially in terms of [her] impact on young girls" during a 2014 roundtable at the New School titled "Are You Still a Slave?: Liberating the Black Female Body." The comment was directed at Beyoncé's "100 Most Influential People" Time magazine cover, where she appeared in what could alternately be named lingerie or workout wear. Suffice it to say, the styling was not dramatically different from many performance costumes in percentage of skin visible, and wasn't necessarily overtly sexual. Beyoncé was certainly more covered than during moments of "Partition." Whatever critical problems hooks has with Beyoncé's work, I've found it even more useful to keep essays like "Selling Hot Pussy" in conversation with Beyoncé, particularly because doing so centers textual disagreement and debate for students, which is an absolutely essential aspect of critical inquiry and thinking. It opens up a space to return to hooks's earlier work and find commonalities with Beyoncé's performances, even despite hooks's more recent and vehement disagreement. Students can take a side if they desire, but are also instructed they must back it up with textual evidence as always.

It's quite possible to read Beyoncé's move from "Partition" into "Jealous" as claiming the very agency hooks wrote about but assumes Beyoncé lacked on the *Time* cover, while still acknowledging that agency isn't usually available to Black women structurally—and that even Beyoncé's agency within a capitalist system is constrained, and her participation in capitalism can be problematic. Multiple things can be true at once. In fact, the constraints placed on Beyoncé might often be major facets of what she's trying to expose in her videos and create necessary conversations around. To do that, she must first illustrate them. For what it's worth, in a 1997 *Paper* interview with Lil' Kim, hooks celebrated the same things in Lil' Kim's career that she critiques in Beyoncé's, stating, "[Kim] knows when it's fantasy and when it's real, when it's about getting paid or getting free." I contend Beyoncé makes those same distinctions clear in her own career—knows when it's about getting paid or getting free—and hopefully this reading of "Partition" connected to "Jealous" speaks to that, though I never mean to foreclose additional critical debate.

Regardless of whether Beyoncé fully accesses the oppositional space hooks names, the action of the two videos fused together reenacts Kara Walker's redirection of the audience's gaze from the sphinx's head, highlighting the fact that Beyoncé, or Black women generally, shouldn't be burdened with the stereotypes they are subjected to; it's up to the rest of society to constantly counter them. To constantly name the walls as crooked, so it becomes less necessary for others to bend. The first step is for those who have participated—which is nearly everyone, to some degree—to recognize their own complicity, whether tacit or more intentional, in upholding a "mucky and violent and messed-up and inappropriate" social dynamic. Beyoncé is foregrounding a form of accountability, just as she did in *Lemonade*'s journey. There, jealousy wasn't in play because the lies were never in question.

Here, the focus on jealousy exposes how interpersonal actions and interactions contain the power to slowly chip away at stereotypes, while still working toward necessary structural change; how incremental, small-scale change is tied to her overarching rewriting of that citizenship contract elsewhere. Doing less harm immediately, while also not assuming that small actions stand in for any systemic shift. In other words, her conflicted emotional performance in "Jealous" stands in for the fact that not all problems can be fixed by simply wiping away tears—but by wiping away Beyoncé's tears in "Jealous," owning up to their complicity in the construction of the stereotypes that immediately harm her and inflict continuous pain, the audience takes a first step toward reconciliation.

"Jealous" ends with an awkward, unsatisfying reunion. Final moments foreground various shots of people reacting to Beyoncé on the street as she presumably tries to make her way home—passersby gawk, attempt to take photos, and one oblivious white man runs directly into her shoulder, throwing her off-balance. The interactions, gradually building to physical contact, stand in for the larger critique she's been making about society's interaction with Black women's bodies and concretize her commentary. In "Partition," she wanted attention that she wasn't receiving, and couldn't receive on her own terms. In "Jealous," she's receiving attention, but not the attention she craves. It's not true recognition of her humanity. It's still funneled through stereotypes; the partitions persist. Immediately after being dismissively bumped into on the street, Beyoncé gives the camera a plaintive look and tears welled in her eyes threaten to spill over. She looks directly into the lens before swiftly turning and sprinting in the opposite direction. The distinct click of heels running on pavement is edited over sped-up, point-of-view shots from behind the wheel of a car. The two eventually merge and Beyoncé runs to the driver. Though the driver again suspiciously resembles Jay-Z, no identifying features are present. The driver is the audience, the same person who ignored Beyoncé at the beginning of "Partition." With a tentative embrace, the shot fades out on Beyoncé's face resting on that nondescript shoulder, relieved but still visibly distraught—nowhere near joyful.

Reconciliation is tempered because Beyoncé knows the entire dynamic—the stereotypes about Black women's bodies and humanity she has spent ample time challenging, fighting, subverting—will all still exist in the morning, as they've been embedded in the very ways the public interacts. Beyoncé's attempting to educate and pass along her own, and Black women's, undue burden—to share a redistributed responsibility—but knows it's a much larger project to eliminate the burden altogether. Changing just one person's mind on an individual level and having them then embrace her, give her the attention she wants and deserves as defined by herself, is an arduous, potentially never-ending process. Changing one person's mind does not change the world. But changing one person's mind is the first step to changing the world. The two videos together provide a flicker of hope. The action of "Partition" and "Jealous" will likely replay itself with the next person she attempts to educate, or might even start over again with the very same individual as they forget what they have learned by morning. Each time viewers are drawn into the uneasy reconciliation, they're also directed back to the harm caused and toward consideration of all the ways harm continues, as well as their own possible participation in it. Directed back to the stereotypes and walls of the crooked room, in the hope that additional people will pick up a sledgehammer—not leave the work to Beyoncé, and Black women, alone.

Beyoncé is subtler than Walker's *A Subtlety*, but the indictments are the same. Complicity. Partitions and stereotypes must be dismantled, both personally and structurally. There's a shared societal responsibility for seeing some as subjects and others as objects, or only ever seeing others through partitions or as partitioned—in effect, seeing the world through stereotypes. Merging "Partition" and "Jealous" together, Beyoncé can be understood as playing with the theme of history repeating itself again, but simply paring it down to day-to-day interactions. The true resolution of "Jealous"—the pained but defiant look Beyoncé fixes on the camera before turning to run—serves to capture everyone uncomfortably in a constant process, rather than offer one solution or placate individual egos. The placement of the supposed resolution also plays with formal structure, just as the pivot in "Partition" came when she tore herself away from the chaise, as opposed to the end of the song proper.

The way Beyoncé plays with gaze and audience expectation has also been noted lyrically from the beginning. The first line of "Partition"—"Driver, roll up the partition, please," an express demand for privacy—is paired with Beyoncé exposing more skin than ever before. Marked by that initial contradiction, and given Beyoncé's penchant for layering, the major statements made in each song might hold alternate meaning funneled back through one another. A feedback loop. In "Jealous," when Beyoncé says, "I wish that you were me," it's possible she's really conveying the desire "I wish that I were you." Power is always best exposed, understood, and critiqued from a marginalized position, especially one that experiences oppression in intersecting ways, by mapping Kimberlé Crenshaw's margins. Beyoncé wants access to the workings of power that she's typically not afforded as a Black woman in the US—to be the "you" who holds power—because she could unravel the ways damaging stereotypes function after having borne their force for a lifetime, wield power differently, or simply shift the margins and center as she has encouraged in her other performances. In "Partition," when Beyoncé sexily croons, "I just wanna be the girl you like"—already discussed as mere costume—she's more correctly pleading for recognition outside the crooked room: what she's really saying is, "I just want you to like the girl I am," blending newly cultivated power from the "you" in "Jealous" with the girl she is, liked or not, from "Partition." Those two things together name the kind of autonomy Beyoncé has been seeking through both videos: a simple self-determination that dictates when and where she receives attention, and when and where she can count on privacy. No more partitions. She makes the rules.

Of course, an analysis of "Partition" that follows Beyoncé's artistic commentary over and through partitions into "Jealous" and across history doesn't obliterate sexual stereotypes projected onto Black women. While some critics' reactions tried to contain Beyoncé's performance squarely within the stereotypes themselves, a closer, sustained analysis of the two videos tells a different, more complicated, story; one that directs attention back to the ways viewers and fans—as a general public—have constructed and perpetuated those very stereotypes. By placing her own body on display, even while also expressing agency and pleasure dancing for her husband in "Partition," Beyoncé highlights the additional constraints placed on Black women by history and respectability politics when trying to access a sex-positive feminism. She's laying claim to a different possibility and politics—one that re-creates empowered sexuality and sex positivity with Black women at the center, rather than being denied access or misinterpreted when desiring access. It's the constraints society has internalized, based on racist and sexist stereotypes, that prevent the public from seeing anything but the crooked room and might disguise Beyoncé's more overarching commentary. Her liberated, incisive sexual performance in "Partition," and the narrative that extends through "Jealous," fucks with the built-in stereotypes themselves, confronting viewers with all the partitions they've tried to use to box Black women in. Partitions are just more crooked walls, deceptively decorated, that need to be demolished.

7
WHAT'S SO QUEER ABOUT
SASHA FIERCE?

BEYONCÉ FORMALLY INTRODUCED THE WORLD TO Sasha Fierce in 2008 with the release of her third solo album highlighting the character, but fans were aware of her existence even earlier. Watching Beyoncé—more personally shy and introverted—fearlessly command concert stages of all sizes was to bear witness to a force of nature. It still is. But in the early days of her career, Beyoncé cited Sasha Fierce as the alter ego that made it possible to channel such unabashed confidence and attitude on stage. Though all her albums since *B'Day* have been concept driven, *I Am . . . Sasha Fierce* is a double-disc concept album of the highest order. Released on two separate discs with eight songs each, the album could have easily fit on one. The distinct separation was part of the point. Listeners had to take explicit action to move between *I Am . . .* and *. . . Sasha Fierce*. Of course, the transition might not hold the same weight now that digital music reigns supreme and physical albums have become more or less obsolete. But the original artistic intent is important to mining the album's politics.

I Am . . . Sasha Fierce tried to balance two different personas, two different characters, and Beyoncé couldn't have been clearer about that. The two characters were diametrically opposed in the packaging as opposite sides of one product. The costuming, styling, and musicality for the two exist at separate ends of a spectrum: one stark in its simplicity, featuring little to no makeup and simple fashion, styling choices, and backdrops, with slower accompaniment and more mainstream, conventional song structures; the other overexaggerated, with big hair, dramatic makeup, hybrid and almost cyborgian costuming, and up-tempo beats with loose structure showcasing some of Beyoncé's best, most unexpected, and deceptively difficult vocal work. All contained within a double-disc album concept at the precise moment the industry was embracing streaming and downloads, distancing itself from physical albums.

In the same way that partitions parallel stereotypes in Beyoncé's other work, the duality and polar opposition of *I Am . . . Sasha Fierce* can be used to explore notions of binary thinking. With any binary, one side is always slightly, even imperceptibly, prized. Power is never equally distributed. The 2008 album and Sasha Fierce herself provide the perfect opportunity to discuss and deconstruct the imbalances and limits of binaries through one of the most foundational—and most internalized—binaries: the Western gender binary, or the idea that man and woman are the two opposing poles of possibility, with man being the prized position. "If I Were a Boy" and "Single Ladies," both lead singles from *I Am . . . Sasha Fierce* that were released simultaneously, one from each side respectively, are explicitly about gender, and filmed in black-and-white. Another binary, and one that stylistically nods to the fact that binaries of race cannot be disentangled from binaries of gender in either single.

Approaching Sasha Fierce for class, I also suggest there's something decidedly queer about the character—as was already touched on in relation to "Diva"—especially when distinctly opposed to the straitlaced Beyoncé on the *I Am . . .* side of the album. While queer has been adopted as a kind of political umbrella term in reference to the LGBTQ+ movement and identity in recent years, it still carries negative associations for some. Etymologically, the word dates back to Scottish in the 1500s, when it meant "strange, peculiar, eccentric." Tracing its history further to Low German adds "oblique or off-center" associations. My use of queer (as part of the queer community that embraces the word myself) in relation to Sasha Fierce is a nod to queering the gender binary—upsetting it at its core. Sasha Fierce, then, might even be read as a kind of queer drag performance critiquing gender itself— existing outside the lines, rather than asking to be included within them. Sasha Fierce never asks for permission and she's proud to stand out.

Sasha Fierce died in 2010, or rather, Beyoncé murdered her once she had completed the I Am . . . World Tour. "Sasha Fierce is done. I killed her," she told *Allure* that February. Part outrageous marketing strategy, the incendiary statement is also further evidence that the alter ego was a critical and political experiment interrogating larger issues. Beyoncé claimed she no longer needed Sasha Fierce because the alter ego had been incorporated in equal parts into herself as a person; the binary the album and character represented was dismantled and redistributed. And technically, Sasha Fierce wasn't murdered; she can't be gone while Beyoncé still performs songs from the . . . *Sasha Fierce* side of the album live. Beyoncé may have killed her in 2010, but she lives on conceptually. She's a ghost that haunts. She even made a powerful, if largely unnoticed and unremarked upon, return on *Lemonade*, a reanimated version of her previous self. And Sasha Fierce continues to be a dangerous attack on normative thinking around race, sexuality, and gender because, as queer parody of gender, the performance character Beyoncé created epically questions and redefines what counts as real. Or, at least, what the world sees as real.

In *Redefining Realness: My Path to Womanhood, Identity, Love & So Much More*, Janet Mock insisted on redefining the concept of realness as it relates to the notion of a foundational gender binary, and her critical observations provide an instructive counterpart to Beyoncé's performances during the Sasha Fierce era. Mock critiques and challenges a normative gender binary from her own unique perspective as a Black and Hawaiian trans woman, and as someone with access to the privilege of passing as cisgender. In other words, her gender identity and expression are acknowledged as real, not Other, by society. Mock invokes the film *Paris is Burning* and one of its legendary stars, Dorian Corey, to set up the concept of realness as in ultimate need of redefinition. Realness, for Dorian, means that bodies are read through stereotypical expressions of masculinity or femininity, and line up with how an individual wants to be seen and understood—i.e., to pass undetected in a society that strictly adheres to a gender binary.

Mock further explains, "Simply, 'realness' is the ability to be seen as heteronormative, to assimilate, to not be read as other or deviate from the norm. 'Realness' means you are extraordinary in your embodiment of what society deems normative." Realness, then, marks a body's worth and value. Realness matters, especially in terms of individual safety, but it also fuels the notion that some bodies and lives are more important than others. What's more, Mock uses realness to expose an exclusive gender binary as explicit fiction, always artificially constructed. Just as Sarah Baartman's body was only abnormal when compared to white women's bodies, gender realness is not objectively fixed; it depends on its own variable starting point (which, for centuries, has been a white cis male body coupled with a white cis female body), and is always thus biased and unequal. In sharing her journey of learning to be herself in an antagonistic world, Mock takes the reader on their own journey of unlearning gender as a system of control with only two predetermined options.

Earlier in the book, Mock also observes, "Being exceptional isn't revolutionary, it's lonely. It separates you from your community." Being held to a certain standard of realness and meeting that standard isn't something worthy of praise, as it limits the options for others to thrive. Passing shouldn't have to be the goal; the goal should be exposing and redefining the entire gender binary as another crooked room. Being exceptional feeds the delusion that the ways of being are limited to begin with, that there are still rules to be followed, and realness keeps the room crooked. It's alienating and tokenizing to be granted access to realness while others are denied; it perpetuates a gender binary, just as being accepted as an exception to a rule further justifies the rule. To redefine realness exposes the fact that there are not two poles; there are infinite options. The danger in aspiring to realness "promotes the delusion that because I 'made it,' that level of success is easily accessible to all young trans women. Let's be clear: It is not," Mock notes. Just like the pageant in "Pretty Hurts," to succeed without changing the rules, or burning the whole rule book, is still failure.

When I pair Sasha Fierce performances that interrogate a gender binary with Janet Mock's writing, it's also essential to note: Beyoncé's performance of Sasha Fierce is not meant to be read as representative of trans women, nor should drag performance be conflated with trans identity. Quite the opposite, in fact. While trans women have historically found the space and freedom within drag culture to express their identities, mainstream drag and ballroom scenes, which most often assumes cisgender male bodies are performing an exaggerated femininity as parody, can be dismissive and even oppositional to any understanding of trans identity beyond binaries. In other words, drag often relies on a gender binary for its campy commentary, which sometimes results in not much subversion at all, though it can still provide great entertainment. It's a precarious balance, but one also useful to students for learning to deal with texts and sources delicately, sensitively, and respectfully. It's quite possible to locate conceptual similarities while not overstepping any boundaries or assuming anything about individual experience—something I'm constantly negotiating as a white man teaching the course regardless; students are able to practice this skill at various points as well. Mock's memoir and Beyoncé's Sasha Fierce performances converge in their queer potential for disruption, and encourage students to experiment with thinking outside of limits, rules, and realness.

I Am . . .

"If I Were a Boy" was released as the lead single for the *I Am . . .* side of *I Am . . . Sasha Fierce* on October 8, 2008. The song adheres to a fairly basic structure as Beyoncé calls out the double standards women often face in heterosexual relationships. The lyrics in and of themselves were more feminist than 99 percent of mainstream radio in 2008. Beyoncé concludes if she were a boy, she would be "a better man," because she knows what it feels like from the other side of the binary—asserting that if she had power and control, her own lived experience would lead to more empathy and careful attention in the relationship, anticipating the "I wish that you were me" and its implied inverse, "I wish that I were you," from "Jealous" years later. Essentially, Beyoncé, with societal power, would never treat her partner the ways that she has been treated, the ways countless women get treated every day, both in relationships and by society in general. Immediately, unconventional gender play comes through loud and clear. And the "If I Were a Boy" video plays with gender, too, but in intentionally tame ways that highlight the distinct limits of binary thinking, only to be explosively countered by Sasha Fierce in "Single Ladies."

Gender is flipped in "If I Were a Boy": Beyoncé and her love interest appear to be a regular heteronormative couple by society's standards, but it quickly becomes evident that she's taken on the conventional man's role, while he demurs to the conventional woman's role. She doesn't, however, invert or subvert any of the stereotypical trappings of femininity attached to her body—in fact, she heightens them. She plays a police officer, an occupation associated with masculinity and power. Though her makeup is toned down significantly, she dons an impractically tailored uniform, highlighting hypersexualized cleavage, that no cop would likely wear. She appears to be more the heterosexual pornographic fantasy of a female police officer than just a person doing her job. At every opportunity, shots show male officers checking out her ass or ogling her up and down. Simultaneously, her love interest plays the feminine role of secretary in an office. There's nothing atypical or progressive about these portrayals, as they re-create the same absurd stereotypes with different bodies. They also remain focused on the prized position and toxic, exclusive power masculinity holds in society, because Beyoncé's portrayal of a man can't fully escape the objectification she experiences as a woman. All this adds up to highlight the constraints that realness imposes on viewers' ability to make sense of the narrative. It can't be logically organized outside heteronormativity and specifically cis male-female relationships.

In her book *The Witch's Flight: The Cinematic, the Black Femme, and the Image of Common Sense*, Kara Keeling investigates the ways in which a world organized around and defined through normative conceptions of race, gender, and sexuality makes it impossible to see and understand those who exist outside the lines. The public has internalized a racist, heteronormative gender binary, whether or not it is desirable, and it's become common sense, such that it is nearly impossible to see the world outside its confines. A particular example that confounds how common sense is organized, for Keeling, is the Black femme—the Black lesbian who conforms to stereotypical femininity but does not live a life organized by the heterosexuality presumed of her. It's akin to the notion of passing or, conversely, refusing to pass and subsequently being misrecognized or misperceived. Speaking of the Black femme, Keeling says, "Because she often is invisible (but nonetheless present), when she becomes visible, her appearance stops us, offers us time in which we can work to perceive something different, or differently." Sasha Fierce's appearance might eventually be the thing that stops us, but the "If I Were a Boy" video is Beyoncé illustrating how difficult it is to think outside that notion of common sense, even when genders are swapped for cinematic effect.

A *Twilight Zone*–esque interlude at the song's climax exposes all preceding action as an attempt to crack through the viewer's common sense, but one in which the cracks necessarily seal themselves almost instantaneously, refusing Beyoncé's attempt to subvert gender expectations. The roles switch back to what viewers more easily recognize as real while the two characters argue over suspected infidelity. Beyoncé transforms back into the stereotypical woman in the relationship, while masculinity is returned to the man, complete with change in posture and adoption of a dominant swagger in mannerisms and speech. The interlude defines the role reversal as a social experiment, meant to point out the unfair treatment women face when in relationships, but one that couldn't challenge the very heteronormativity that organizes relationships. What initially felt like feminist subversion and empowerment was actually a failure, but the failure is also the video's success. It confronts the viewer with the deeply foundational nature of the heteronormative gender binary likely internalized in their own thinking. How deeply difficult it is to unlearn. Simply swapping assumptions and roles—where the two halves are treated more fairly and equally, but still attached to different expectations—does nothing to unsettle the binary itself. The impossibility of imagining the action of "If I Were a Boy" outside of binaries is also referenced in the subjunctive mood of the song's lyrics and title. Just like Beyoncé's aspiration to be happy in "Pretty Hurts," the sentiment exists in a conditional future which has not yet arrived.

Beyoncé's gender is swapped, so to speak, but hers should be the *only* gender altered when taking the lyrics at face value. "If I Were a Boy" should be, more or less, a lesbian love song, making the Black femme who haunts the lyrics visible. However, her love interest's gender is also switched in the video, as is the gender of her partner on the job (with whom she is suspected of extracurricular romantic trysts) to avoid any semblance of same-sex relationships, for which the lyrics make ample space. Beyoncé is constantly repeating that she'd "listen to *her*," would know "how it feels to love a *girl*," among other lines directed toward a female partner in a relationship. But that's not what the viewer *sees*. They *see* her mistreating a man, albeit a man stereotypically positioned as disempowered. Just like with "Partition" or Kara Walker's *A Subtlety*, viewing audiences generally aren't as progressive as they might pretend to be or think they are. Given widespread social conditioning around gender, most wouldn't know how to make sense of the storyline of the "If I Were a Boy" video if an implicit heterosexuality wasn't hovering in the background.

Everyone is constantly casually observing and delineating gender in the world in exclusionary ways, often involuntarily. Think about it. Every person you see gets quickly compartmentalized as man or woman—you're not actively thinking about it or noticing it, but it's always happening. The moment you see someone that doesn't neatly fit into either side of the binary is the moment you know you've been categorizing people all along. It causes you to pause, even if for only a split second. Society is constantly *seeing* gender and using the gender binary to make sense of the world, even while some individuals may also be invested in challenging and dismantling that boundary critically and in practice. "If I Were a Boy" serves as an acknowledgment of that fact—it's the brick wall everyone must run into to see the ways realness is internalized, another partition to demolish internally. If the video was free to follow the lyrics, who would be paired with whom? Masculinity and femininity would be loosed and free to align with all different kinds of bodies, without preconceived notions. Those associations would say nothing of the sexual interests or appetites of the bodies themselves. But first, the strict limits of what can be imagined must be starkly shown.

The rest of the songs contained on the *I Am . . .* side of the album all seem to revolve around a strict internalization of heteronormative realness too. Lyrics attempt to capture conventional gender and sexual configurations, but end up highlighting their failures—just like "If I Were a Boy." *I Am . . .* is packed with atypical material for Beyoncé that departs from the traditional empowerment anthems for which she's best known. Instead, listeners find Beyoncé not wanting to "play the broken-hearted girl," relinquishing power in and for love, claiming her "saving grace" is a man with a halo, waiting on love passively—orbiting romantic partners like satellites, never meeting. A far cry from the Beyoncé of Destiny's Child, celebrating "Independent Women" and choosing to be "Through with Love" over being controlled, or the *B'Day* Beyoncé asserting that no man is ever "Irreplaceable." Seen against her other work, the more submissive themes of the songs on *I Am . . .* heighten dramatic effect. It's Beyoncé reinforcing the limits of binaries, and even a commonsense compulsory heterosexuality, along with the dissatisfaction and pain both often create, in contradiction to the endless possibility she unleashes as Sasha Fierce.

. . . Sasha Fierce

Beyoncé plays with queerness and stereotypical rules of gender—the spaces between and outside the poles of the binary—as Sasha Fierce on the opposite side of her 2008 album. In "Single Ladies," Sasha Fierce is "brave enough to fuck with the grays," like Joan Morgan demands of hip hop feminism in her 1999 manifesto *When Chickenheads Come Home to Roost: A Hip-Hop Feminist Breaks It Down*. The video returns to the black-and-white conceit of "If I Were a Boy," but with starker lighting and drastic flares, while throwing into question the normative categories of gender and sexuality easily recognized by mainstream American society. Focusing on the interstitial spaces. Over the course of the eight songs on the . . . *Sasha Fierce* side of the album, lyrics describe happiness, fulfillment, and pleasure outside traditional norms and binaries of gender and sexuality, and experiment with alternate possibilities: "Single Ladies" embraces independence; sexual attachments to technology and not people abound in "Radio" and "Video Phone"; Sasha Fierce rails against the concept of "lonely," terrified of the ways society forces relationships on women, not actually afraid of being alone, in "Scared of Lonely"—an aspect especially highlighted in 2009 pared-down, intimate live performances of the song. In the videos and album art, it's also Sasha Fierce's eccentricity, performance of overblown confidence, and dramatic makeup choices that align Beyoncé's alter ego with drag performance, or at least the possibility of Sasha Fierce as a drag queen.

Drag is often understood as campy impersonation.

And much of drag does rely on heteronormative, commonsense gender assumptions by featuring artists identifying with one pole of the binary performing as the other. But, at the same time, it's more complicated. In her autobiography *Hiding My Candy: The Autobiography of the Grand Empress of Savannah*, The Lady Chablis, a famous transgender Savannah drag staple, notes, "There was a safety and security in this area of employment: drag offered me a legitimate way to earn a living not as an *impersonator* like some mighta called it, but as a woman." Though some traditional theorizations of drag highlight the impersonation aspect, Chablis shows how gender has always operated more fluidly in drag, even while positioning herself on the binary as a woman. So we cannot read Beyoncé-as-Sasha-Fierce as simply female, either stereotypically or through impersonation. Merging all the associations of drag together, Sasha Fierce becomes a complex alter ego that confounds our expectations— Sasha Fierce parodies the parody, as it were. A strictly cross-gender version of drag only holds when an intact gender binary is its driving force or backdrop anyway.

Later in her memoir, Janet Mock writes, "Femininity in general is seen as frivolous. People often say feminine people are doing 'the most,' meaning that to don a dress, heels, lipstick, and big hair is artifice, fake, and a distraction." This very association comes out of a binary that privileges masculinity over femininity, men over women. But femininity is also a means of survival for many, a means of expressing oneself, embracing possibility not always normatively aligned with said body in society's eyes. Beyoncé is already seen as feminine, of course, but she draws out various meanings of femininity from the distance drag allows, insulating her own body from being seen as spectacle personally. Beyoncé is doing the absolute most performing as Sasha Fierce and close cousin of Keeling's Black femme, creating pause to ask: What exactly do male and female, or masculine and feminine, even mean? The confusion created by an inability to understand gender outside of normative, binary terms creates the very space where Sasha Fierce *can* confound an audience. Sasha Fierce doesn't just deconstruct gender, she explodes limited notions of gender, parodying the entire concept—not just one of the poles.

In stark contrast to the ballad "If I Were a Boy," the almost manically up-tempo "Single Ladies" introduces Sasha Fierce through simplistic excess. Lights come up on Sasha Fierce and two dancers, Ashley Everett and Ebony Williams. All three wear variations of a basic black leotard and heels, nothing more (save Sasha Fierce's robotic metal glove). "Single Ladies" is deceptively edited to look as if it was shot in one take, a feat in and of itself—the camera revolves around the dancers at all times and gives the illusion of an open, free space, despite the fact that it's shot on a run-of-the-mill soundstage. Viewers can't even differentiate the walls from the floor due to the glaring lights, don't know which way is up or down. More manipulation of the crooked room. There's one key moment toward the end of the video where all three dancers inexplicably run up the wall, further driving home the point that the video doesn't exist in a room society has built, like the anti-room of "Grown Woman." This room doesn't follow the rules, it's surreal. Sasha Fierce is standing straight and bending the room to her will—viewers are the ones with a sense of crookedness, a political vertigo.

The electronically cosmic soundtrack adds to the surreality. Apart from handclaps and a back-beat, much of the music of "Single Ladies" sounds like 1950s intergalactic camp. Sasha Fierce's robotic glove emits computerized sounds to provide additional otherworldly, even posthuman vibes. Beyoncé's real-life wedding ring sits on top of the glove in the video's final moments, shimmering under the lights. She flashes it repeatedly to viewers while catching her breath once the choreography ends, breaking through the frame to announce to the world for the first time that Beyoncé privately was a newly married woman. More than a simple wedding announcement, Beyon-cé's wedding ring does two key things for an analysis of "Single Ladies." First, it functions to slyly negate one of the two words that make up the song title. The song unapologetically celebrates being single while simultaneously announcing Beyoncé as just married. The ring also directs attention to the contract of marriage generally—its history and politics. Just as *B'Day* and "Déjà Vu" respond to their immediate history of Hurricane Katrina, "Single Ladies" was released at a particularly contentious moment in the US battle to legalize same-sex marriage, worthy of revisiting with students alongside the video to uncover other political connections.

In late 2008 the nation was embroiled in vitriolic debates over Proposition 8, an amendment to the California state constitution defining marriage as between one man and one woman. The proposition, if passed, would also invalidate same-sex marriages that had taken place in the previous few months in the state, during which they had been deemed legal and celebrated. Prop 8 initially passed in the 2008 election and marked the first time the public *took away* previously granted rights, but the finding was eventually overturned by the Supreme Court in 2013. The debates and vote in 2008, however, stand as a landmark moment in the longer history of debates over who is deemed worthy to enter the state-sanctioned institution of marriage in America, from slavery—when Black people were barred from marriage or any recognition of meaningful partnerships outside of their own ceremonies—to fights over interracial marriage, which were only legally sanctioned in 1967 via the Supreme Court decision in *Loving v. Virginia*. Further, throughout history, marriage itself was initially seen and understood as a necessary property relationship, not as the romantic milestone it's marketed as and imagined to be today.

Though the issue is by no means settled, and marriage is not the most radically queer issue by a long shot, the weight of this fraught historical baggage is attached to the release of "Single Ladies" through Beyoncé's clever wedding ring maneuver. And she pulls this sleight of hand as a Black woman in America performing a critical drag. Contradictions abound. What if the single ladies aren't single? That question necessarily slides into other, deeper questions, given all this context. What does it mean that only certain groups of people are allowed to be interpolated by the state as no longer single? How does the very nature of marriage as an institution reinforce racial hierarchies and a gender binary, given that the validity of a marriage rests squarely, or has rested, historically, on the race and gender of the participants? In what ways has marriage in the US always been a tool of white supremacy and heteronormativity? How does all this history relate to how marriage is conceptualized today? And while the incongruity of the wedding ring and the "single" ladies opens up many avenues of inquiry, it also points back to the other word in the title. Negating one necessarily calls the other into question by association.

If the wedding ring symbolically empties "single" of its meaning, what about "ladies"?

Lady is a specific linguistic choice. Sure, it fits the meter of the song, but nothing Beyoncé does is careless. She has invoked "girls" and "women" and even "females" elsewhere, but "lady" carries a sense of propriety with it, invokes respectability politics, decorum, even nobility. Etymologically, "lady" comes from Old English for "mistress of a household," and was also associated with "woman of superior position in society" as far back as the 1200s. Today, "ladies" can be pejorative and dismissive colloquially, or refer to formal royal titles in some European countries in contrast to "commoners." In America, Black women have never been embraced or celebrated as "ladies." Femininity itself was defined in US society specifically as white women's domain, set up against the stereotypes projected onto Black women's bodies. And so what does it mean, now, that the single ladies who may or may not be single are also Black? Sasha Fierce is reclaiming and redefining the raced, classed, and gendered notion of "lady," and also emptying previous formal associations of meaning.

Following each textual clue, it becomes increasingly clear that Beyoncé as Sasha Fierce is carefully challenging who counts in the eyes of the state, through a slow unraveling of both "single" and "ladies." And not just linguistically, either. As soon as the video was released, controversy erupted online over the gender identity of the dancers, directed specifically at Ebony Williams. Ignorant and bigoted comments demanded to know whether Williams was a woman or man (as if those were the only two choices). Devout Beyoncé fans that were active online during the time often bring up the heated debates when discussing the video together in the classroom. It's not important how any particular person in the video identifies or expresses gender (though Williams is a cisgender woman), but it's quite interesting to see how invested the public was in *questioning* and *knowing*. That piece is worth investigating. What cues or features of Beyoncé's dancers' bodies did viewers immediately associate with masculinity, in attempts to pin them down on the binary? Because it must be their bodies themselves, as nothing else is shown in the video. When asked, students name muscular legs—the most exposed and featured parts of these women's bodies—as masculine. They note the women's jawlines, hardened and intensified by light and shadow, as seemingly less feminine. They cite shoulders set broadly and highlighted through the simple leotards as distinctly gendered.

This is precisely where Sasha Fierce in drag in "Single Ladies" becomes a more decidedly intentional queer performance. Watching the video carefully, drawing distinctions between it and Beyoncé's other videos (even other Sasha Fierce videos), viewers see that Beyoncé is slyly cultivating a kind of stereotypical masculinity in all the ways mentioned—performed by her two dancers, but also clearly mirrored and played up in her own styling as Sasha Fierce—to create gender confusion. Makeup choices, harsh light and shadow, and severe camera angles aid in that confusion by conjuring and exacerbating features stereotypically associated with masculinity. And this gender confusion is ultimately more impactful and meaningful than the simple and incomplete gender swapping in "If I Were a Boy." Because viewers stare directly at these three bodies for the entirety of the video, with no distractions. The gaze is intentionally filtered so that assumptions get thrown back and defied. The desperate public need to pin the "single ladies" down on the binary also exposes how the same single ladies are pushing against commonsense gendered assumptions of masculinity and femininity.

The choreography throughout "Single Ladies" additionally fuses and confuses stereotypical masculine and feminine movement via a mix of Bob Fosse–inspired steps with a style called J-Setting. J-Setting is an energetic dance form from Jackson, Mississippi, influenced by marching band and cheerleading; an exaggerated majorette routine, without batons, where one dancer models the steps and others quickly fall in formation. A popular female dance team called the Prancing J-Settes created the style at Jackson State

University in the 1970s. J-Setting also quickly became a queer staple, a hit among gay Black men who took the movement to bars and parties, spread it to additional cities, and blended it into other dance styles across gender and sexuality. The queer embrace of J-Setting invokes the same histories of realness, resistance, and subversion noted by Dorian Corey in *Paris Is Burning* and quoted by Janet Mock. Punctuated and fluid steps blend, causing the audience to question what even counts as masculine or feminine in the end, performed by all kinds of bodies across differences. Sasha Fierce's queer(er) drag performance reaches beyond the simple reversal of men's and women's roles that began in "If I Were a Boy." And the performance becomes an expression of visible survival outside the confines of the binary, meant to confound common sense and connects back to Mock's words about rethinking exceptions as revolutionary. It won't be until an exception is no longer necessary, because the binary cannot hold, that everyone will be truly able to thrive.

Sorry Not Sorry

Even though Beyoncé proudly killed Sasha Fierce in 2010, Fierce refused to go down without a fight. She gets unexpectedly but powerfully resurrected on 2016's *Lemonade* as one of the visual album's many ghosts. In what was already an intensely complicated and complex drag performance, Beyoncé adds even more layers by casting Serena Williams as Sasha Fierce during "Sorry" while she plays Williams in another role swap, hell-bent on further undoing assumptions rooted squarely within a racist gender binary. "Sorry" is the only solely black-and-white portion of *Lemonade*, and I've suggested that the black-and-white motif signals time travel. Not only does the section travel back historically, it returns to the heyday of Sasha Fierce in Beyoncé's own career.

As "Sorry" opens, Serena Williams descends the staircase of a New Orleans plantation house in almost slow motion. Beyoncé lounges, splayed across an ornate throne. The shot re-creates exactly the December 21, 2015, *Sports Illustrated* cover Williams posed for after being named "Sportsperson of the Year." As with anything Williams does, the cover drew brutal personal criticism of her physical appearance, the very strength of her body—not unlike the racist and sexist criticism Ebony Williams received after the "Single Ladies" video. Serena Williams's femininity has often been called into question by the media and players on the tennis court too. Beyoncé re-creating that infamous cover signals something critical immediately, especially as Williams circles and dances around where Beyoncé sits. She moves with typical Beyoncé-on-stage swagger, both seductive and empowered (a.k.a. Sasha Fierce). They've effectively swapped roles, mirroring binary opposition again, but one in which both sides are represented by Black women. In September 2017 Williams opened up about the body shaming she'd faced her entire life, reflecting on her hope that her own daughter won't go through the same, in a note posted to her Reddit profile. Speaking of her daughter, she wrote, "She has . . . my exact same strong, muscular, powerful, sensational arms and body. I don't know how I would react if she has to go through what I've gone through since I was a 15 year old and even to this day. I've been called man because I appeared outwardly strong."

The implication that strength is incongruous with a woman's body, and further stereotypically constructs and differentiates a Black woman's body as something other than feminine, is highlighted in "Sorry" in order to be symbolically undone. Beyoncé as Williams rewrites the criticism Williams regularly receives by deploying her own stereotypical femininity back at Williams's critics from that same throne, essentially standing in for Williams. In turn, Beyoncé also directs attention away from Williams's body and back to the very system that created the expectations and assumptions then hurled at Williams as racist and sexist attacks. Because the gender cues those attacks rely on were arbitrarily fixed, never real, to begin with. Meanwhile, as Sasha Fierce, Williams also shamelessly and fiercely rejects all the criticism she's faced and will likely continue to face; she turns the critique on its head, denouncing it while wearing Sasha Fierce's extraordinary, unshakeable confidence. Williams flaunts her strength and beauty and shouts back, "I ain't sorry," noting that she can't be contained by normative scripts or binaries, just like Beyoncé's "I'm just too much for you" immediately prior in "Don't Hurt Yourself." The dual performance opens up possibility for self-determination in the very space of the racist plantation house in which the action takes place. Rewriting racist and sexist history at once in the very place where a gender binary was used to justify and define white women's virtue, while simultaneously violently excluding Black women from femininity—all to bolster and tacitly support slavery. Neither Beyoncé nor Williams is sorry for calling it all out. They're sorry they're *not* sorry. There's no excuse for such a sorry fucking system.

Beyoncé also plays with gendered assumptions of bodies in the lyrics when she demands the system "suck on my balls." As she did by sexually anthropomorphizing her "Ego" as Sasha Fierce in 2008 ("It's too big / It's too wide / It won't fit"), she's upsetting which body parts are expected to attach to specific gendered or sexed bodies, undoing even binary assumptions of biological sex as real (anatomy previously understood to be male becomes part of her own cisgender female body through the lyrics)—a move she returns to on

The Carters' "Apeshit" with the instruction, "Get off my dick." The social construction of gender tends to neglect biology and anatomy, even though society's very understandings of biology and anatomy are also funneled through the way gender has been understood socially in any given historical moment and often fused to scientific racism. Biological sex is no more real than social gender cues; it, too, is made up of endless variations and described through the social norms of the time.

The appearance of Sasha Fierce always signals deviation and unrestricted possibility. So "Sorry" introduces the prospect of gender, along with gender's attendant racist suppositions, breaking free from its past inscriptions and ascriptions to bodies and spaces. Binaries fall apart. Assumptions crumble. Beyoncé resurrects Sasha Fierce by way of Serena Williams to accentuate a queerly redefined realness once again. Or no realness at all, because the concept would cease to exist under the critical interrogation Mock demands and Sasha Fierce performs. In a world that devalues and perpetuates violence against bodies in greater numbers when they don't fit neatly within predetermined gender categories, Sasha Fierce becomes a kind of revolutionary figure, not for representing an exception but for exposing the messier truth. Beyoncé exposes binary oppositions as fiction—in gender and all things, including the construction of her own *I Am . . . Sasha*

Fierce. Typically, the "I" functions as the central identifier in Western culture, but with that 2008 album, Beyoncé broke down the barrier that partitioned the two sides, ultimately showing that Sasha Fierce was part of her all along, and more true to life than the side claiming "I am." The division never existed. The limit was what was artificial, never real. Real is whatever you want it to be. Through Sasha Fierce, real gets redefined, or maybe, more correctly, real finally becomes undefined and undone.

8
THE WHOLE DAMN SYSTEM
IS GUILTY AS HELL

BLACK FEMINIST CRITIQUE DEMANDS POWER BE CON-
fronted at intersections and dismantled at the root,
or else it reemerges transformed, more resilient than
before. The crooked room that relies on beauty standards, binaries, and intersecting stereotypes of race,
gender, and sexuality to demand that some inhabitants
bend, while others are free to stand tall, is itself built on
the firm foundation of capitalism. Obviously, Beyoncé
works within a capitalist industry and system; she
maintains a brand, and her music itself is a product,
but that doesn't mean she hasn't also included layers
in the music that critique the same system that makes
her massive success possible. They could, of course, be
stronger or more explicit, but they're there. Notably,
on "Ghost," she asks why everyone on the planet has
to keep working "nine to five just to stay alive"—one of
her more direct indictments of capitalism (by way of
the music industry). Overt critique or not, her music

can be used to create conversations about the toxicity inherent to capitalism and its insidious organization of society. To approach the various crooked rooms and individual stereotypes piecemeal is to pluck the weeds at the stem, rather than grasp them at their root.

bell hooks has centered capitalism in the web of all other oppressions, inseparable from racism, sexism, homophobia, etc., by insisting on using the overarching descriptor "white supremacist capitalist patriarchy." Challenging capitalism is nothing new in Black women's work or theorizing, either. Claudia Jones tied the exploitation of Black women directly to capitalism, and was eventually deported in 1955 for voicing communist principles. Both Angela Davis and Assata Shakur were targeted and jailed by the US government in the 1970s because of their work and affiliation with revolutionary movements opposed to capitalism. Davis was eventually acquitted; Shakur was convicted of the murder of a New Jersey police officer (even though forensic evidence proved it impossible for her to have been the shooter) after being profiled, targeted, and acquitted on other charges (some of them dismissed), but was broken out of jail by the Black Liberation Army and ultimately fled to Cuba, where she still resides. She remains on the FBI's Most Wanted list. Both Davis and Shakur wrote indispensible autobiographies detailing their experiences.

The Combahee River Collective also forcefully denounced capitalism's overarching domination, especially for those experiencing multiple, interlocking oppressions—which spawned the theorization of identity politics—in their famous 1977 Black Feminist Statement. The statement itself, authored for the collective by Barbara Smith, Beverly Smith, and Demita Frazier, was a response to both the whiteness of the feminist movement and the maleness of civil rights and the Black Power movements, not a wholesale denunciation of either. Composed by a strategic coalition positioned at the intersections, the statement formed a cornerstone of what came to be known formally as Black feminism. The CRC insisted that it was "difficult to separate race from class from sex oppression because in our lives they are most often experienced simultaneously." From this position, they posited that "the liberation of all oppressed peoples necessitates the destruction of the political-economic systems of capitalism and imperialism as well as patriarchy." While some of these radical, paradigm-shifting assertions are more commonplace today, bringing the CRC's statement into the classroom, alongside some of Beyoncé's allusions and references to capitalism, helps students trace various inequalities already discussed even further back to their origins in a capitalist system. By zeroing in on individual weeds in previous chapters and lessons, it's then easier to hone in on the root.

Throughout her catalog, Beyoncé has seemed to mark commentary about capitalism through fire. In "Diva," which was discussed earlier, Beyoncé redefines work, while expectations and assumptions around race, gender, and sexuality stemming from capitalism are blown up in a fiery explosion before she calmly sashays away. "Ring the Alarm," a song about retaining material possessions—and in the context of Hurricane Katrina, Black women exerting ownership over things can be situated as a critique of capitalism rather than its simple unfettered embrace—warns, "You ain't never seen a fire like the one I'm-a cause." When it comes to looking for other unlikely critique of and commentary on capitalism in Beyoncé's work, I ask students to keep following the flames.

Burn, Baby, Burn

"Mine" from *BEYONCÉ* begins and ends in fire, with additional explosions between. The title appears in two bookended scenes, the only track on the album where it appears visually more than once. Fade in, fade out. But what exactly is Beyoncé torching? Lyrically, "Mine" is about the work involved in a relationship, but the word "mine" itself denotes ownership, property—the devious, driving force of capitalism. In contrast to owning *things* bought with money, the ownership in "Mine" refers to ways ownership is implied or outright claimed interpersonally. The dynamics between two people, and the ways they relate to one another, have typically also exhibited a core element of ownership or possession. It's the same element of unequal power that builds stereotypes, binaries, crooked rooms, but injected into all the other seemingly more innocuous relationship dynamics between people and internalized: *my* boyfriend, *my* girlfriend. *Your* father, *your* sister. Though ownership of other people has been and remains an actual reality in some places, more diffuse echoes of ownership underwrite almost all relationships. All language and thinking is tied back to toxic impulses expressed elsewhere.

In "Mine," Beyoncé challenges all the ways people interact transactionally with one another, the covert ways the system has been internalized to varying degrees. The song opens with a vulnerable, extended stream-of-consciousness verse. It's visually accompanied by whorls of silk, seamless movement, and a re-creation of Michelangelo's *Pieta* with Beyoncé as Mary. Lyrics during that intro conjure internal struggle; Beyoncé confesses shameful thoughts and doubts that women, mothers, and romantic partners aren't supposed to voice openly because they upset the so-called natural order. At the same time, she tentatively holds an alabaster ceramic mask to one side. The juxtaposition of hard and soft as the song begins to transition—angelic melody fading into explosive musicality—represents a split or partition capitalism has constructed, keeping her from her own humanity as a Black woman, private person, and highly visible celebrity/artist all at once. Speaking and expressing doubt as a new mother, she's revealing herself in ways she isn't supposed to, and those revealing moments question the very ways the system expects or even demands that people interact with one another.

Beyoncé also marks the transition in "Mine" by placing that mask on her face, signaling a move out of the personal and individual realm. She sings, "We're taking this a little too far," over and over, invoking a collective "we" as all of society, and indicating that society has been overpowered by the system itself. Read politically, what's being taken too far is not just personal feelings in a relationship, but the very cultural assumptions and expectations around race, gender, sexuality, even motherhood, that stem from capitalism to obscure its root. Things are spiraling out of control. Beyoncé uses the mother-child relationship as a foundational or universal bond to ground her critique and then work outward. The parent-child relationship isn't devoid of capitalist traces, as children have been historically used as free labor even outside of institutionalized slavery. Beyoncé's critique extends to the dynamics of *every* relationship, the ways people interact on a larger scale, as evidenced through the other actors in the video who are paired off in couples. To unsettle viewers for this substantial critique, she pulls the rug out from underneath them completely, upending herself as well. In the frame, she falls backward into darkness, desperately reaching out as her hand slips from another unidentified hand—positioned as the audience's own. She's falling away from the viewer as the viewer falls further away from her, because the bonds between individuals are being called into question as capitalist fabrications. The bonds are unraveling. As she slips further back, the video takes an abrasive turn—explosions, percussive choreography, and masked dancers litter the shots.

The next section of "Mine" performs additional ownership. The chorus finds Beyoncé reiterating, "You're mine, you're mine." Less obvious, though, is the fact that another line divides the chorus and is in opposition to that claim: "All I'm really asking for is you." The repeated claim of ownership, however, overrides the plea that another person give of themselves willingly. It outnumbers the more benevolent request: six claims of "You're mine" to a single alternative. Beyoncé's marking an intrinsic competitive grasp for power at the heart of many relationships through the construction of the chorus. What's more, despite all the uncontested claims of ownership, it's not enough. It's never enough. She wants more. Everyone is constantly conditioned to want more. As the chorus repeats, the earlier plea is swapped out for the more forceful, "As long as you know who you belong to." No room for debate. She's dictating conditions already in place, whether or not the "you" recognizes the claim of ownership—and, in the process, demonstrating how power gets exerted over others, even unwittingly.

Every dancer in the video is shown with heads covered by hoods inscribed with either YOURS or MINE. It becomes evident, given heteronormative gender cues, that everyone labeled YOURS is a man and those labeled MINE are women. They dance and perform as heterosexual couples too. Though the labels can be stereotypically seen as completing one whole equally, there's a significant power differential in the words, expressed in the video along gender lines. Think of the two statements: You're mine; I'm yours. One is claiming; the other acquiescing. They can be uttered by the same person, but they don't exist with equal power. Another deceptive binary. The first claims; the latter gives away. And despite the inequality, the very means by which "yours" and "mine" are applied in the video further exposes that both sides subtly lose through an internalized ownership model. The hoods depersonalize everyone across the board—blind them, suffocate them, even possibly torture them when dancers appear underwater. One person can utter both "You are mine" and "I am yours" to another without contradiction, but the kernel of ownership isn't being subverted, just reconfigured, and the power differential passed back and forth. This goes for platonic, familial, and romantic relationships—*all* relationships.

The video begs a number of questions that arise

in class, some from students and some from myself: Is there a way to have a relationship without implying ownership? Is ownership at the heart of the way people fundamentally function, and will it always be? What does engaging with others in the most human, least harmful ways look like? Am I challenging concepts of ownership as they appear in my daily life? Is there a way of speaking about those closest to me without claiming them as my own? Who would they be to me without the label "mine"? Conversely, who would I be? These are nearly impossible questions to grapple with. It's easiest to think about possible solutions through the concept of friendship, but neither students nor myself have ever come up with any surefire solution. Attempting to shift something so foundational and internalized is painstakingly difficult. At the same time, students always approach the questions and contemplation with hope and enthusiasm. I think even opening up the questions feels like a win, because doing so points to at least the potential of moving beyond the constraints of the system—begins to identify cracks through which roots become visible and within reach. The questions further open up Audre Lorde's directive, "The master's tools will never dismantle the master's house," too, because often the master's tools are all that can be identified; other tools seem impossible to imagine, making the search even more imperative.

I always want my classroom to be a space to weigh options, no matter how far-fetched and seemingly impossible or implausible; a place where different scenarios get played through to their logical conclusions without judgments. A place to simply practice thinking. Sure, there are alternatives to heteronormative coupling, but different romantic and/or sexual configurations like polyamory or nonmonogamy—whether queer, heterosexual, or something else entirely—can fall into similar ownership traps. There are also examples of thinking and/or alternative social and political organization that don't understand or have any use for the concepts of private property or ownership, but early US ideology labeled them as primitive in order to devalue and discredit them. This is what capitalism has wrought, and it's obscured the ability to see anything else from within, just like the hoods in "Mine."

Part of the problem also returns to an economy of scarcity rather than one of abundance, and the notion of jealousy that Beyoncé used to investigate stereotypes earlier. Here, jealousy is tied up in the competition of capitalism and an American sense of rugged individualism. Always wanting more, desiring the things someone else has. But if the "I" in any situation is decentered, and possession not prized, society might be able to leave behind the "I" at the heart of ownership and scarcity in exchange for an "us"—always keeping in mind that the "us" must also be formed at the intersection of multiple issues and identities. Socialism as a de facto alternative to capitalism isn't adequate without qualification. As the Combahee River Collective warned, "We are not convinced . . . that a socialist revolution that is not also a feminist and anti-racist revolution will guarantee our liberation." The CRC echoed some of the same sentiments as Claudia Jones nearly thirty years prior and for which she was deported, additionally stating, "Although we are in essential agreement with Marx's theory as it applied to the very specific economic relationships he analyzed, we know that his analysis must be extended further in order for us to understand our specific economic situation as Black women." Understanding that situation is the key to answering the above questions and creating alternative possibilities that don't default to toxic, internalized capitalist impulses.

Beyoncé's not wearing a hood on her head, but she is still labeled MINE in the video just like every other woman. Her label is painted directly on the center of her bare back. At various times she appears to be trying to wipe it off, but it's just out of reach. As a Black woman facing multiple interlocking oppressions, her mark is more shrewdly unreachable and hidden, more difficult to identify at first glance or from certain angles. Her mark is harder to redress; she can't simply uncover her face. The letters of MINE on her back never fade, but they do smear while counterintuitively remaining distinct and pronounced. Like poison spreading through the bloodstream. In a poem from her 1993 collection *The Book of Light*, Lucille Clifton wrote, "come celebrate / with me that everyday / something has tried to kill me / and has failed." The paint on Beyoncé's back represents those murder attempts— from capitalism and all its subsequent systems of control, a toxic, overarching institution—even while she may collude with the same system in order to survive, and even though some individual Black women make the system work for them. Like Clifton, she invites celebration for each time something has tried to kill her and failed, but also alludes to the fact that true, lasting celebration won't be possible until the mark finally comes off, evidenced through her continued attempts to wipe her back clean.

Beyoncé's back in "Mine" also connects back to the opening moments of *B'Day* and the feminist anthology *This Bridge Called My Back*. There, she was exposing the work Black women are expected to do in order to bridge differences; here, capitalism possesses Beyoncé, her back effectively branded with MINE. The placement forcefully speaks to capitalism as built on the backs of women of color and particularly contingent on subjugating Black women, as noted by the Combahee River Collective. Some of the earlier questions "Mine" poses also find the beginnings of answers in a popular essay from the *Bridge* anthology by prominent Black lesbian feminist poet and scholar Cheryl Clarke. In "Lesbianism: An Act of Resistance," Clarke suggests looking to the intersections of race, gender, and sexuality and a kind of ideological lesbian feminism to mine relationship dynamics (both romantic and platonic) that have the potential to exist outside of capitalist impulses. She says this reorganization in thinking "purports an anti-racist, anti-classist, anti-woman-hating vision of bonding as mutual, reciprocal, as infinitely negotiable, as freedom from antiquated gender prescriptions and proscriptions." Because of this, Clarke asserts, "all people struggling to transform the character of relationships in this culture have something to learn from lesbians." Beyoncé obviously isn't portraying identity-based lesbianism in "Mine," and Clarke's "lesbian resistance," too, moves beyond strict identity in its full praxis. June Jordan metaphorically uses the notion of "bisexuality" similarly in her essay, "A New Politics of Sexuality"— political praxis that begins as an identity but opens wider through investigation of the ways that particular identity is positioned to challenge, or escape, toxic power dynamics. Aligning with those politics and ideologies doesn't necessarily require claiming the identity itself, just learning from it.

In Clarke's formulation, mutuality, reciprocity, open dialogue, and negotiation take the place of ownership and possession. Those ideals are theoretically rendered visible through her focus on lesbian relationships as they potentially resist or rewrite patriarchal norms, particularly interracial lesbian relationships that are also working to deconstruct power along racial lines. Not by their existence alone, of course—there is still much necessary work involved. And the work begins by first naming the ways capitalism has infiltrated even the most intimate relationships in order to push back against those dynamics. As all of this analysis swirls over "Mine," explosions erupt across the landscape and the hooded dancers themselves perform convulsive, violent choreography—a battleground shown in long shot. The explosion from the final scene of "Diva" returned and reenacted many times over. The last moment mirrors the beginning: the word "mine" engulfed in flames. It's being burned down, destroyed, fire lapping the edges of the frame, before the scene ultimately fades out, with no discernible attempt to extinguish the blaze. It's been necessarily burning the entire length of the video, given the opening shot, and will continue to do so. Suggesting, perhaps, that society would do well to let the motherfucker burn.

Emptiness

And that's exactly what happens in "6 Inch" on *Lemonade*, the next place where flames blaze in Beyoncé's catalog. A focus on money and work, more immediately referential of capitalism than "Mine," returns as well. In "6 Inch," Beyoncé's no longer celebrating all the times the system has tried to kill her and failed, she's punching back. Kill or be killed, and fire functions as fulcrum. It redirects the narrative in *Lemonade* from description to prescription, explanation to solution, as Beyoncé writes that new social contract. In "6 Inch," more than anywhere else in *Lemonade*, viewers see the gears turning, the mechanisms of capitalism rotating, to keep Beyoncé entangled so deeply in work—stacking money, grinding to achieve power, to find some elusive self-determination through the American dream—that, though it's a nonsensical contradiction, she's "already made enough but she'll never leave." An addiction to capitalism. Even though money is power and Beyoncé has achieved it all, "6 Inch" is *Lemonade*'s nadir, fused to emptiness. Not a moment to be celebrated. Because capitalism ultimately empties everyone.

Red light illuminates all the action. The stylistic choice invokes the illicit economy of red-light districts and women's bodies as commodities. Of course, sex work need not necessarily be exploitative, but Beyoncé uses the metaphor to reference capitalism's dehumanization of workers in all ways here, as well as her character's own internalization of that impulse. She appears intermittently on a stage at points throughout

"6 Inch," a smaller stage than those featured at any other time in *Lemonade*. One that completely contains her physically. She's trapped behind a glass wall, on display specifically and expressly for the pleasure of others—another possible allusion to Sarah Baartman—in a first-floor corner of the larger plantation house. At times, she references, "She don't gotta give it up 'cause she professional," which speaks to the differentiation of work, and differential judgments about or flat-out erasure of some kinds of work deemed less worthwhile, necessary for the few to continue profiting off the many. The line also speaks to the heightened divide between exploited and exploiter, though it's definitely possible to occupy both positions simultaneously.

A red light also signals the withdrawal of consent, a refusal to participate any longer or at least the realization that she needs to extricate herself from capitalist clutches. Red references a simple no. She played with similar themes earlier in *B'Day*'s "Green Light"—referencing "green means go" in the lyrics, all the while cloaking strategic areas of her body in the color red in the video, creating conversations around consent and sexual stereotypes. The lyrics of "6 Inch" are largely in third person, but the juxtaposition of visuals and lyrics indicate Beyoncé is playing both characters. She's both the one giving it up *and* the professional. She's been divided within herself again, kept from true self determination by American capitalism. Alongside red's associations with refusal, Beyoncé drops additional hints for the audience to insinuate that something more subversive has been going on. She's been working, grinding, yet all the while "too smart to crave material things." For what reason is Beyoncé stacking paper, if not to fulfill a craving of material things? Remember the analysis of money and power she began in *Life Is But a Dream*—perhaps she's about to use that money and power against the system that has tried to kill her and failed. Aim her own kill shot.

References to material things, money, and wealth appear throughout Beyoncé's catalog, and often appear to run counter to any claims of her work as critical of capitalism. From the purple labels she stresses as necessary to improve her partner in "Upgrade U," to the chinchilla coats and VVS stones she claims ownership of in "Ring the Alarm." From the "Black Bill Gates in the making" named in "Formation," to the countless references to the Carters' lavish lifestyle sprinkled throughout the tracks of *Everything Is Love*. Even renting out the Louvre to film the "Apeshit" video, flaunting power and wealth throughout, seems to rub viewers' noses in the enormous kind of wealth disparity between Beyoncé and the vast majority of her audience that only a complete embrace of capitalism can provide. And it's true. But the very flaunting creates conversations around that money and wealth. Alternately, it could be read as making a mockery of the fact that capitalism creates such disparity. Bill Gates might be disgustingly wealthy, but he's also known as a philanthropist, and that gives the "Formation" line additional meaning too. Beyoncé herself gives back generously, much more than is even shared with the public. So discussing and analyzing her music in relation to capitalism is always a balancing act: one in which critique of the system becomes just one layer—still a productive one to focus on—in the overall narrative of the course.

Tension ratchets up continuously in "6 Inch," to the point where Beyoncé is pushed to commit and witness murder simultaneously—the only way to move the action of *Lemonade* forward. Beyoncé, referencing herself doubly, sings, "She murdered everybody and I was her witness." She turns her murderous rage against an internalized capitalism, the very pieces of herself that crave money and material things and tie her to a toxic system despite her own protestations and acknowledgments. The performance also indicates that the system is internalized in most everyone, not just in interpersonal relationships like in "Mine," but internalized at the very core of one's being. To live is to compete and work oneself to the bone, and often, that's still not enough when compounded by race, gender, sexuality, etc. Beyoncé couldn't wipe that paint off her back in "Mine" because it had spread through the bloodstream, but in "6 Inch," she's ready to stop her own heart from pumping poisoned blood, no matter what it takes. Over the course of the song, she slows and stops the heart of capitalism, even as it kills a part of her. Capitalism takes root and sucks the life out of a person from the shadows. Beyoncé's left no choice but to travel deeper into the emptiness "6 Inch" represents in order to commit her own restorative act of violence.

The song begins and ends with a syncopated, modulated bass drum, reverberating in and out, slowly but regularly. A pulse. An apathetic heartbeat on the verge of flatlining, but still pumping just enough. It's both Beyoncé's own heartbeat *and* that of the system she's challenging, because they've merged. She has to kill that thing inside herself that makes her crave the validation of the system. That thing that convinces her "she loves the grind," every day and night with no respite. She must sever her own heartbeat from that of the system, in an act of destruction that doubles as one of creation. "She gon' slay," and slay she does. She takes the fire of "Mine" to the walls of the plantation house in *Lemonade* and slowly, casually walks down the hallway and out the door, as she walked away from the exploding car in "Diva," and as Sojourner Truth walked away from slavery. Then she stands outside, flanked by others, not to put out the fire or ease the destruction but to ensure it burns. A hoarse cry of "Come back" in Beyoncé's possessed voice repeats into nothingness as the pulse flatlines at the end of "6 Inch," the system begging to be spared though Beyoncé's own mouth. The line gets raspier and less alive with each repetition. She resists and stares into the camera as the crackle of burning wood fades into the background.

In a symbolic transubstantiation, Beyoncé turns the stiletto heel of "6 Inch" into another metaphor for capitalism: one that foregrounds its vulnerabilities with all its attendant byproducts—racism, sexism, homophobia, etc.—balanced precariously on top like a body's weight. The heel is constantly in danger of snapping. But whether heel or root, Beyoncé scorches the earth, feet planted in the dirt, to make sure it all burns to ash. Fire isn't simply destructive, it also signifies rebirth and cleansing. Controlled or prescribed burning is often used in farming and forestry to prevent or contain anticipated forest fires, or to better prepare soil for coming crops. Destruction tied specifically to growth or preservation. Octavia E. Butler wrote of the necessity of fire for transformation in *Parable of the Talents*: "In order to rise / From its own ashes / A phoenix / First / Must / Burn." Burn the motherfucker down, indeed. Then, from the ashes, build something new. From the ashes, coax a phoenix.

FUTURE

9
OUT OF THE RUINS

ON "UPGRADE U" BEYONCÉ SINGS, "I CAN DO FOR YOU what Martin did for the people / Ran by the men, but the women keep the tempo." Once again, she's stressing that building a better world takes centering Black women, while also never forgetting the ways Black women especially have received less recognition for participating in and creating revolutionary movements over time. From Sojourner Truth to Ida B. Wells, who brought national attention to the epidemic of lynching as a journalist and activist from the 1890s through the first decades of the 1900s. From Ella Baker, a community organizer who worked tirelessly behind the scenes for Martin Luther King Jr. touting a radical vision of what democracy could be, to Patrisse Cullors, Opal Tometi, and Alicia Garza, three queer-identified Black women who founded Black Lives Matter as a decentralized movement-building network in response to the racist murder of Trayvon Martin. Students consider all these women, in addition to so many more, over the semester. They've all kept the world moving in various ways. Though charismatic men often get more public attention, Black women have indeed kept the tempo. Without a steady tempo, a song devolves into noise.

At this point in the course, after chasing ghosts through the past and discussing attitudes and systems that continue to haunt the present, it's time to pivot more explicitly toward the future. What might Beyoncé's new world, built out of the ashes, look like? How does Beyoncé imagine the future? The videos for "Run the World (Girls)" from 4 and "Superpower" from *BEYONCÉ* take viewers directly into those futures—postapocalyptic landscapes, worlds where everything has burned but resilient groups of people are still navigating the changes. Dystopias not without their own problems, they serve as Beyoncé's blueprints for better, more equitable worlds. Octavia E. Butler guided students back and forth through the past and present while they looked at *Lemonade* and some of Beyoncé's other work, and they return to Octavia E. Butler to approach the future.

Butler's *Parable of the Sower* transports the reader into its own near-future dystopia, eerily reminiscent of the current United States. The book is constructed as journal entries by Lauren Olamina, a young Black girl in Southern California, as society crumbles in real time and she's thrust into more and more chaos and violence. The gated community where she lives burns to the ground, her family is killed or unaccounted for, and she's forced to strike out on her own. She begins a journey north, trying to escape a newly elected fascist US government (set in the 2020s, though published in 1993, and literally including a president who utilizes the slogan "Make America Great Again"), but also in an attempt to build community around a new religion she has created called Earthseed. She's looking for a tribe of people with common beliefs to construct a new nation. The central tenet of Earthseed is not a god to worship, but the philosophical concept of Change itself. Every action and interaction creates and facilitates change, so submission to and adaptation in the face of change become the ultimate goals for survival. Everyone is shaped by change and, in turn, by listening to and honoring change, can be part of a generative spiral.

One of the central problems for Olamina is that her religion eschews the notion of leaders and hierarchy, yet as its founder, trying to proselytize and amass followers, she must, at least initially, take on something of a leadership role to spread her gospel. The entire process mirrors Beyoncé's own leaderless formations that require her to first teach viewers the steps. It also mirrors the decentralized nature of Ella Baker's community organizing and the Black Lives Matter movement. Olamina's other major hurdle is her hyperempathy disorder: an invention by Butler that afflicts certain members of society, where an individual who witnesses another's pain physically, viscerally shares it as if it were their own. She also shares pleasure, but pain is in near-constant circulation in Butler's future. Interestingly, an exaggerated empathy doesn't make Lauren more compassionate and understanding. It toughens her and sharpens her edges for her own protection, and the protection of others afflicted by the same syndrome that might be in proximity to her pain. A sacrifice in service to a less harmful time.

Lauren Olamina is trying to make sense of a future that the US today is hurtling toward with lightning speed. Her blueprint for a better world is Earthseed, but *Parable of the Sower* itself, as Olamina's journal crafted by Butler, is a kind of blueprint for the reader too. Butler published a sequel, *Parable of the Talents*, in 1999, which features the later years of Olamina's life, but her early days in *Sower* speak most powerfully to Beyoncé's visual world building, especially in connection with "Superpower." Students put Lauren Olamina into conversation with Beyoncé as both navigate their own dystopian landscapes, and they funnel connections and discrepancies all back through other real-life visions and movement building by Black women over time. A continuum. A trajectory. Through the analysis, they're encouraged to hold critical conversations about their own dreams and hopes for what that future will look like too—while Beyoncé keeps the tempo.

One Nation under Beyoncé

"Run the World (Girls)" opens with people filing in and out of the frame, militaristic, rapid-fire, over a soundtrack of chanting voices. A call to arms. Beyoncé rides up on a rearing dark horse—the symbol of the underdog in any fight. Viewers are immediately transported to battle in the middle of a desert. Fire, concrete, debris, a crumbling highway overpass, all mark a dystopian future; a different version of the world with alternative possibilities. Beyoncé received criticism for lyrics detached from reality when the song was initially released. Some said the song lied to young girls, implied that girls could run the world without any recognition of the obstacles that sexism and inequality legitimately pose. But that's exactly the point—the song is a vision of the future, not an exposition on the present. It's a reconstruction of a world after fire where men might no longer have a monopoly on power. A fact the video makes clear. In my experience, students always cite the song and video as hopeful, not over-reaching or disingenuous. Beyoncé also signaled the nature of the song as command, not description, in an epic Billboard Music Awards performance. Before the music kicked in, she shouted, "Men have been given the chance to the rule the world, but ladies, our revolution has begun. Let's build a nation. Women everywhere—run the world!" and immediately snapped into formation with a stage full of female dancers.

Building on the prior work she's done to deconstruct gender categories and binaries, "girls," in the lyrics and in the title, marks a political identity tied to an understanding and willingness to dismantle power, not a strict gender delineation, similar to Cheryl Clarke's ideological conceptualization of "lesbianism." Beyoncé is laying the groundwork for identifications across differences (but not *erasing* those differences) that are organized around a common politics of affiliation. In the 1997 article "Punks, Bulldaggers, and Welfare Queens: The Radical Potential of Queer Politics?", political scientist Cathy Cohen imagines "a politics where one's relation to power, and not some homogenized identity, is privileged in determining one's political comrades." Placed in conversation with Beyoncé, Cohen creates space for "girls" to be decidedly queer as well. Sasha Fierce may be "dead" by 2011, but her politics live on in "girls." Cohen's demand to organize around "the *nonnormative* and *marginal* position of punks, bulldaggers, and welfare queens, for example, [as] the basis for progressive transformative coalition work" is similar to the outcasts from society that organize in political coalition with Beyoncé and her "girls" in the video.

There are not *just* those who identify as or are stereotypically perceived to be women with Beyoncé's group. The camera shows two young men who also dance with her, border crossers flanking Beyoncé on either side but never in the center of the frame. They're actually the entire basis of the choreography for the whole song too, highlighted in *Life Is But a Dream* in scenes that showed the rehearsal process for "Run the World" and told pieces of the young men's story. Beyoncé first saw Mario Abel Buce (known as Kwela) and Xavier Manuel Campione (known as Xavitto), collectively known as the Tofo Tofo Dance Group, on YouTube, and fell in love with their movement. Her team searched for them for five months, because neither she nor any of her choreographers could recreate the steps. They flew Kwela and Xavitto in to teach the dancers and be featured in the video. *Tofo* means "body shaking" in a local Maputo dialect, the area of Mozambique from which the men hail. The dance style itself is called *pantsula*, set to Kwaito music (similar to house music); it originated in South Africa, where it was popularized as a means of resistance to apartheid in the 1980s—comparable to voguing and ballroom culture for queer folks of color, or hip hop and break dancing for Black and Latinx communities in the United States during the same period.

The Tofo Tofo Dance Group challenges any strict gender definitions, not only through their presence, but through the ways their movement has been incorporated as ammunition, locked and loaded throughout, by Beyoncé's entire army. They aren't the only border crossers, either. In a portrait-like shot, a male lion sprawls alongside Beyoncé's group. She uses hyenas, leashed by heavy chains to her grip, in another scene, to further deconstruct traditional gender roles and power. Hyena packs are led by females, who typically distract prey as the rest of the pack circles and traps. And hyenas are vital in most African ecosystems, although they are often devalued and seen as useless. Some species of hyena even feign death when attacked by predators, so as to be left alone, rather than advance on opponents. A blurred mix of passivity and action, stereotypically feminine and masculine traits, led by women. Hyenas are also commonly thought to be scavengers, recyclers of leftover carcasses. Despite the fact that they do hunt and kill much of their prey, the scavenging myth persists because they regularly chase much bigger lions and lionesses away from their own kills. Hyenas are fearless, scrappy, cunning, and in many ways feminist. They represent much of what Beyoncé is incorporating into this new political world.

Undone gender lines and upset power, then, are also politics that queerly unite Beyoncé's tribe. Add to that a critique of whiteness. While the two armies assemble in the opening shots, the camera briefly jump-cuts to a white woman tied to a cross. As religious symbols, crosses represent sacrifice of the highest order. Here, the sacrifice is not literal or individual, as the white woman appears later in the video and in subsequent videos, but symbolic and collective, in order to define the new nation under construction. It doesn't mean that white women—or white people in general, since girls isn't strictly gendered anymore—are not welcome; it means white participation and coalition is dependent on decentering whiteness as a politics by interrogating the construct of whiteness's connection to power. While Beyoncé invokes feminist principles and empowerment, the sacrifice also denounces white feminism—a mainstream version of single-issue feminism that sees the plight of women as monolithic, and usually prizes white women's experiences as universal, at the expense of interrogating intersecting oppressions. The very opposite of Kimberlé Crenshaw's intersectionality and of Black and other women of color feminisms.

Geography also becomes important, and tied to the political work of the white woman on the cross. There are some African elements referenced, and many read the setting as just a general placeholder for a postapocalyptic world, but one single road sign, shown for only a split second, names the actual location: just outside Tbilisi, the capital city of Georgia. Modern-day Georgia exists in the direct vicinity of the Caucasus Mountains—from which the category Caucasian takes its name—and is the very location out of which the history of whiteness as a racial category was born. In *The History of White People*, Nell Irvin Painter traces how whiteness emerged as a racial classification: never quite nailed down, always shifting and malleable, for the purposes of exerting power over others. Though many white people believe the category has existed as static throughout history, Painter exposes it as a fiction with no concrete referent—a category that has shifted drastically over time. The first so-called Caucasians weren't even white as society understands the label today. Historically, geography was used as the primary way to classify people—not the color of their skin or any modern "scientific" notions of race and racial difference. Racial classification systems have always only been implemented in ways that were already biased, anyway, and not to be objectively trusted. There is visible racial diversity among Beyoncé's "girls," but her new nation rejects the premise of the divisions and differences racial classification systems have wrought. She uses geography to mark whiteness writ large as a necessary sacrifice.

Beyoncé is also building her new nation out of the ashes of capitalism, or, at the very least, trying to imagine something more equitable. But she continues to reference money, just like in "Diva" and "6 Inch," to highlight its heretofore unequal distribution. Questioning money's role is another central tenet of her constitution. Socialist systems use money, of course, but they value work differently, leading to a reorganization and ideally more collective distribution of wealth. In the middle of each verse, before declaring that her persuasion (not just in the sense of influence, but her *kind* of people, politically) can build a nation, Beyoncé playfully jokes with the occupying army, using stereotypically feminine sexual wiles to seduce them. But her seduction is about proximity, infiltrating enemy territory to deliver the real message: "F— you, pay me!" While the recorded version opts for the sanitized "eff" over the full obscenity, the demand for payment comes through loud and clear. As she voices that demand for the first time in the video, the camera zooms in rapidly to a tight shot of her contorted face and raised middle finger—a visual fuck you to accompany the more polite lyric. In Beyoncé's world, money doesn't work the same way, and "pay me" might also be considered reparations, as opposed to capitalist greed. What is she going to do with money in the middle of the desert, anyway? (Though, of course, it's also trenchant critique of wage inequality in the United States' present.)

So, fuck you and pay what you owe. Immediately, the scene cuts to Beyoncé punching her fist to the sky, which signals a giant explosion of an abandoned car behind her. Like in "Diva," she's blowing up the constraints and inequalities named variously through "girls" and her expansion of the category, whiteness, and money. The entirety of Beyoncé's tribe also unifies through that same fist in the air, shared choreography. The gesture is commonly recognized as a Black Power salute. Used prominently during the 1960s and 1970s and associated with the Black Power movement, it's often read as confrontational. It's *meant* to defy and challenge inequality. A famous moment at the 1968 Olympics, when African American athletes Tommie Smith and John Carlos saluted the American flag with this gesture from the medal podium, was recorded for history. Their protest ultimately resulted in their expulsion from the Games. It was decried as inappropriate and even vulgar by some. Beyoncé's group offers this same salute together over the closing lines of the song, fusing the already queer political category of "girls," a denunciation of whiteness, and a recalibration of money and capitalism with an affirmation of Black protest. It all becomes part of this new nation's origin story and foundation, rather than functioning simply as reactionary responses to a previous (current) system.

Even the music of "Run the World" itself rises from ashes, repurposed and subverted. Beyoncé uses a sample of Major Lazer's "Pon de Floor" as the backbone of her entire song, a sonic scavenging by the hyenas featured earlier. The first explicit indication that it's not, in fact, Major Lazer playing is the word "girls" echoing over the top of the beat. Major Lazer's original song and video can easily be read as misogynistic objectification of women set to a catchy, appropriated dancehall beat. Listeners or viewers familiar with that original can't help but note the juxtaposition of diametrically opposed subject matter over identical sounds. "Run the World" rises from the ashes of "Pon de Floor" as an altogether different kind of phoenix, replaying Beyoncé's entire political strategy: a new nation figuratively and sonically reconstructed from the ruins of an unacceptable system. She's hoping her version will highlight and avoid the mistakes of the past. More foreshadowing of the kintsugi bowl from *Lemonade*. Like Tina Turner's Aunty Entity from *Mad Max Beyond Thunderdome*—who viewers are hard-pressed not to see referenced and reflected in Beyoncé's "Run the World" desert dystopia—sings, "Out of the ruins / Out from the wreckage / Can't make the same mistakes this time."

The video closes on Beyoncé's group uniformly advancing on the line of demarcation created by men in riot gear. Inches from one man's face, Beyoncé reaches out and snatches a badge from his pocket. Literally snatches his power. Once she does, her side of the fight immediately freezes in a new formation. Many of them mid salute, a traditional military salute this time rather than the Black Power salute already performed. It's possible to read that ending as Beyoncé ultimately deferring to the traditional stereotypes and power that she just spent the entire song challenging. But don't forget that Beyoncé has already subverted and reworked the power dynamics—this is her world, not that of this alleged military. They're a vestige of the past. Students consistently categorize the gesture as confrontational when asked, and I have to agree. Her salute is much more likely a sign of disrespect, given it mocks rules she doesn't subscribe to. Another middle finger. Another fuck you. Endless power devoured and redistributed among the girls. That final shot subsequently ties "Run the World" to another dystopian setting from her next album that ends in an almost identical scene.

Tough Love

Fast forward to Beyoncé's next postapocalyptic experiment. "Superpower" begins in an underground, more metropolitan setting than that featured in "Run the World"—cement walls, dumpsters, more debris. The ruins of one of the most recognizable paeans to captialism and consumerism. The action ultimately moves from a parking garage through a deserted and destroyed shopping mall. Surveillance camera footage names the time and location: Los Angeles, California, 7:33, though Beyoncé's future takes place in no specific year. She appears at the far end of the shot, and heels striking cement echo with each step as she approaches the camera. Her clothing looks torn, battle worn. Conspicuously, she sports a balaclava with only her eyes, nose, and mouth showing. Before the song begins, she adjusts the balaclava to further hide her face, covering her mouth. As she's not visibly performing the lyrics, attention is directed back to the visuals and action. In "Run the World," a collective fell into formation against an occupying army—a hyena pack fighting together. In "Superpower," Beyoncé enters alone and gradually builds her misfit tribe, many of whom, noticeably, are the same dancers from "Run the World."

Styling, particularly the balaclavas and facial coverings mixed with an overall punk aesthetic, invokes what has come to be known as antifa (originally *Antifaschistische Aktion* in Germany), a loosely decentralized and informal network of groups sharing a militant politics opposed to fascism in all its forms. Antifa is sometimes defined by members' willingness to engage in more violent forms of protest, and a tendency to mask and anonymize themselves so as not to be recognized by the state. Not as prominent at the time of the video's release in 2013, antifa notoriety has surged since the intense right-wing backlash of the 2016 election. In the United States, anti-fascist action dates back to the 1920s, but today's antifa stems directly from Anti-Racist Action networks that came out of punk movements of the 1980s. The aesthetic of "Superpower" both anticipates and validates this kind of radical politics, which also shares similarities with Cathy Cohen's shift from strictly identity-based coalitions to strategy-based ones.

The way Beyoncé calls in additional members and slowly builds her following directly links the action of "Superpower" back to Octavia E. Butler's *Parable of the Sower* and Lauren Olamina's own congregation. The slow procession through the abandoned structure could easily be a scene directly from the novel. Where Beyoncé may have been channeling Tina Turner's Aunty Entity in "Run the World," she's Lauren Olamina in "Superpower" for sure. And Olamina's hyperempathy is part of the narrative too. Hyperempathy doesn't easily translate into simply *more* empathy, more compassion, more love as a solution. It causes her to be more critical of simple emotional connection. In "Superpower," Beyoncé et al. rally around love as a possible corrective to a problem. It's featured prominently in the lyrics and scrawled on makeshift flags and banners, graffitied throughout. But it's not simply love for love's sake. It's inflected with a critical hyperempathy. Love doesn't erase all oppression overnight. It might offer a slight salve interpersonally, but it's not an end in and of itself. "Superpower" is fundamentally a love song, illuminating how people are stronger together than apart, but the caveat is that the individuals who are stronger together must first be strong on their own, and continue to be. Love can amplify strength that already exists, perhaps exponentially, but it doesn't automatically do so. It has to be critically sharpened and charged into something else: tough love.

Tough love isn't the absence of conflict or pain. Or even the absence of violence. Beyoncé's ethics of tough love actually creates space for violent outbursts too, as shown throughout the video and through an antifa parallel. The two ideas have never been mutually exclusive, despite the attempts by those in power to pit one against the other. During the civil rights movement Martin Luther King Jr. and groups like the Southern Christian Leadership Conference advocated a kind of nonviolent protest, while Malcolm X and the Black Panthers encouraged Black folks to arm themselves for protection. But they weren't in direct opposition—that's a divisive misconception still propagated today, often by white people. They shared more in common than American history wants highlighted. Ijeoma Oluo speaks to this fallacy, and white America's investement in controlling the narrative through disingenuously ascribing value and credence to nonviolence above all else, in *So You Want to Talk About Race*. "What Martin Luther King Jr. and Malcolm X fought for was the same: freedom from oppression. At times they used different words and different tactics, but it was their goal that was the threat," she states. Both King and X were assassinated, and those assassinations took place just as each of them began highlighting the similarities in their positions, joining forces, focusing on their common goal.

Ella Baker, still keeping the tempo, also merged the two positions in her own work, even while closely aligned with King and nonviolent protest organizationally. Historian Barbara Ransby's account of Baker's life, *Ella Baker and the Black Freedom Movement: A Radical Democratic Vision*, details how Baker celebrated and supported the importance of nonviolent protest wholeheartedly, but also stressed her personal decision to not preclude violent re-action as part of her own overall survival strategy. Ransby states, "For her, nonviolence and self-defense were tactical choices, not matters of principle," and as such required context and more careful, critical deliberation on multiple levels. In short, Baker was a realist. And that's the heart of Beyoncé's "tough love"—merging seemingly contradictory positions for both strategy and survival, while not conceding either side. Holding reality and ideals in tension. Nina Simone, upon meeting King, whose tactics she greatly admired, also famously and shamelessly announced, "I am *not* nonviolent," to which he's said to have warmly taken her hand. In "Superpower," Beyoncé is blending complex histories and sometimes contradictory views under the umbrella of tough love as critical force, one that pushes her to carefully advocate for and create better worlds. Honoring emotion as affliction, gift, and tool at once; a lesson taken from from Olamina's hyperempathy. Years before it was even released, Beyoncé extended the Carters' 2018 album title as a postapocalytic pledge: everything is tough love.

This interrogation of tough love takes place in a video with eerie, uncanny similarities to present racial unrest in cities across America. Though it predates protests in Baltimore and Ferguson, Missouri, it clearly doesn't predate racial unrest generally. Which is even scarier. Because Beyoncé, like Octavia E. Butler, is able to conjure such realistic visions under the guise of dystopian fictions that they come to fruition in a few short years. Less than a year, in Beyoncé's case. Images in "Superpower" sadly evoke the very same scenes witnessed in August 2014 following Michael Brown's murder in Ferguson, which reinvigorated Black Lives Matter protests by beaming the literal aftermath of his murder into homes around the world on multiple news networks—something that hadn't happened directly following Trayvon Martin's murder, for which the hashtag had first been used. Michael Brown's body lay in the street for over four hours after he was killed. At one point in "Superpower," Beyoncé bends over a body lying prone on the ground amidst chaos—not dead, but at first seeming to be—in an anticipation of that exact scene. She puts her head to the man's chest and lifts him up, embraces him with his head to her chest in a reciprocal gesture. Viewed post-2014, Beyoncé might even be seen here as breathing life back into premature deaths that haven't happened yet, but that she knows will come, given US history—a move she highlights more explicitly in *Lemonade*. She resurrected ghosts in "Formation"; she anticipates ghosts in "Superpower."

Not only does the video invoke contemporary racial unrest in America, it joins historical rebellions and uprisings across time. The surveillance footage places the action of the video in Los Angeles, California—the site of a momentous racial uprising in 1992 after Rodney King was brutally beaten by LAPD officers the year before; though the incident was caught on film, the officers were acquitted of all charges. That acquittal sent the city of Los Angeles, especially its Black residents, into a justified rage. Considered warranted civil disobedience from one perspective and unruly riots from the perspective of the powerful, the uprising lasted over six days, as citizens grappled with how the verdict could have been possible after such a brutal, unprovoked attack had been recorded. It's the same question many ask today when police murder Black people, are caught on tape, and rarely, if ever, face consequences. Eric Garner and Philando Castile stand as prime examples. Other cities where these murders occur and go unpunished are fused to the action through the greater Los Angeles reference. And it's not the only specific city directly layered into the song either.

"Superpower" is built on vocal arpeggios, sung by Frank Ocean (cowriter of the song, though he doesn't appear in the video) as bass line, over which the melody is sung. They exist as classic throwback to doo-wop and Motown styles funneled through Ocean's own contemporary vibe. Motown, Berry Gordy's record label and an entire genre of music, was created in Detroit, Michigan—also the location of large-scale revolts around race, both in 1943 and again in 1967. In 1943 a three-day riot found white folks actively attacking Black people as the culmination of extreme racist tension in the area (tension that continues to this day). Black residents were rightfully angry about explicit discrimination, a shortage of affordable housing, police brutality, and a host of other issues. Speaking out about their anger drew white ire and ultimately violence. The 1967 uprising involved the police raid of an unlicensed bar in one of the poorest Black neighborhoods in Detroit. Though many white people participated in the 1967 uprising as well, and it wasn't as specifically polarized as the LA riots, the revolt itself initially erupted in response to more unjustified police brutality against Black people.

Mapping references to all this violence further into

the margins, it's not just Black and Brown bodies brutalized by police regularly. Historically and contemporaneously, LGBTQ+ folks have been squarely in law enforcement's crosshairs—especially queer and trans people of color who face oppression on multiple fronts and garner the least attention. Marsha P. Johnson, Sylvia Rivera, Miss Major Griffin-Gracy, and other trans women of color initiated and led the uprising at the Stonewall Inn, a New York City gay bar, in 1969, after one too many police raids, probably *the* most famous revolt against anti-queer police brutality. Three years earlier, the Compton's Cafeteria riot in the Tenderloin district of San Francisco found many trans women of color fighting back against years of police brutality they had endured. Today, homeless LGBTQ+ kids, a disproportionate number of whom are also people of color, are at direct risk of being targeted by police in major urban areas. Even when police aren't actively targeting LGBTQ+ people, they are rarely investigating violence against them. In 2017 alone, at least twenty-nine transgender people were murdered (actual numbers are most certainly higher, as murders go unreported, or trans people are misgendered in death, skewing statistics), making it the deadliest year for trans people on record—an ongoing trend that Laverne Cox has called a "state of emergency." All these references to violence and brutality against queer bodies also bleed into the song through

Frank Ocean's writing and vocals. He publicly came out as not strictly heterosexual in 2012 in a Tumblr post, and in lyrics on his album *channel ORANGE*; he eschews labels overall, but has had relationships with both men and women.

Beyoncé is using a veracious and voracious tough love to name and expose all these various threads of violence against bodies that don't fit US norms throughout "Superpower." And she's noting that history repeats, that change never comes fast enough. The music of "Superpower" moves painstakingly slowly. Even students that love the song admit that it drags, even more so in the video. They get frustrated with the pacing. It clocks in at nearly five and a half minutes. Watching "Superpower" feels like slogging through eternity when compared to a typical upbeat barely three-minute pop song. But it's replicating history and the entire US political process: s . . . l . . . o . . . w. The system moves at a snail's pace by design, a built-in protective measure and failsafe for power. The system itself prevents progress, allowing the status quo to continue unchecked as long as possible. The desire for a tempo increase mirrors a demand for more from the system. And we know Beyoncé is running the tempo, so the lag is clearly intentional. The video is filmed in slow motion too. It incorporates sonic dissonance as artistic misdirection—viewers see violent explosions, but hear only the soothing but *slow* melody—reflecting how some are able to ignore political realities to remain comfortable. The video catches the audience in a dissonant lag that replicates the political position of privilege, comfort, and inaction. Beyoncé is creating frustration to incite action.

She runs the tempo in "Superpower" to highlight an overall failure of the US political process. The song culminates with the closing refrain of "Yes we can," over and over again. A simple hopeful phrase, but one now universally associated with the campaign of Barack Obama when he historically won the presidency in 2008, the first Black man to do so. Obama didn't fix America by any stretch of the imagination. He enacted and furthered harmful neoliberal policies and engaged in violent imperialist actions, like every other US president. Just because one is not the worst doesn't make them the best. Yes, America can and did elect the nation's first Black president, a watershed moment for representation, but ultimately, what changed? His election, through no fault of his own, even fomented conservative and white supremacist rage exponentially over his eight-year tenure. It exposed the true racist underbelly of the United States that usually stays hidden, and emboldened racists to create a reactionary movement to retake the country they thought was theirs, culminating in the 2016 election and its aftermath, literally bringing to life the fascist government elected in Butler's *Parable of the Sower*.

Earthseed states, "The only lasting truth is Change," and the results of the 2016 election were certainly an abrasive change for those hoping to build a kinder, more equitable world. But Earthseed also says one must submit to change in order to shape it, redirect it into a future. Simple submission to post-2016 American reality is unwise, but perhaps placing the seismic shift of the election in context, and understanding the ways that moment is connected to longer histories, will better allow people to wield tough love in order to shape the next chapter. It's no silver lining, but maybe a tiny consolation: The enemy was more clearly exposed and lines more clearly drawn, just like the two sides that clearly assemble at the end of both "Run the World" and "Superpower." Beyoncé's "Yes we can" is surely a nod to the historic election of Obama, but it doesn't have to exist solely as an endorsement of the system that elected him or all his choices in office. It's an illustration and reminder of the system's failure too. Especially given what came next; what will now forever shamefully mark the next phase of American history. But, yes, keep going. Yes, do things differently.

The final moments of "Superpower" return to police in an almost exact reenactment of the final scene in "Run the World." Equally confrontational, but comprised of one key difference. In "Run the World,"

Beyoncé's girls were advanced upon; in "Superpower," they advance. After amassing a collective army over the slow minutes of the video, they encounter a police barricade, but stop a few yards away to create their own alternative barrier. They pause as a collective . . . and then they charge. Still in slow motion, but a moment that breaks the monotony and pace of everything before. There's no salute this time, just aggression. The slow motion highlights the determination, defiance, and anger contorted on the faces of Beyoncé's group: Mouths are open, lips snarled, eyes boiling over with fury. Just as they reach that line of demarcation, the entire advancing army, running at full speed, stops dead in their tracks, inches from the visors of the riot police. They pause. And the audience, no doubt, takes a deeper breath.

Beyoncé stands next to an unidentified man. He's now wearing the balaclava she cast aside over the course of the video. Maybe he's disguised to be another unidentifiable stand-in for the viewer, like in "Partition" and "Jealous." But here, he's quickly roped into impending collective action. Beyoncé exchanges a meaningful glance with him—plotting next moves, devising strategy. The shot then zooms in on Beyoncé's hand reaching toward his. Fingers interlace. They join together, charging superpower in real time while preparing to charge forward. Gazes revert directly back at police and the video abruptly ends. When the last arpeggio hits its lowest note, the camera cuts to black and the bottom falls out of the song. But Beyoncé's eyes, the eyes of everyone assembled alongside her, leave little room for doubt. Conceding to this military power is not an option, damn the consequences. The charge will, *must*, continue. Earlier lyrics referenced even gravity and physics being unable to quell Beyoncé's charge; "The laws of the world never stopped us none." So, full speed ahead. Carrying tough love as a critical strategy, carrying visions of the future ahead with the charge. Submitting to and shaping change on the fly. And the seething fire in Beyoncé's eyes in that very last moment—not just angry, but resigned to rage—also points critically forward to the slow burn of resentment as its own potential superpower.

10
POLITICS OF RESENTMENT

IN AN ESSAY CALLED "KILLING RAGE: MILITANT RESIS-tance," bell hooks confesses the longing to kill an anonymous white man sitting next to her on an airplane. "I felt a 'killing rage,'" she says. "I wanted to stab him softly, to shoot him with the gun I wished I had in my purse." hooks was traveling with a friend, another Black woman, who was denied her correct seat next to hooks in first class because the airline printed the wrong boarding pass. The friend was called out over the loudspeaker and humiliated, though she had made no mistake—the error was theirs. A white man took the seat next to hooks while her friend was forced to sit in coach. The rage that bubbles up and explodes in hooks as she sits and writes on the plane is not just tied to that one incident, though; it's the culmination of a lifetime of experiencing and viewing microaggressions against Black women, seemingly minor everyday occurrences that reinforce a racist and sexist system in which white men constantly reap privileges for no other reason than that they were born white men. She doesn't literally want to kill the man. Her rage is directed at the system that created the situation and reinforces the white man's actions as normal and acceptable time and again.

"By demanding that black people repress and annihilate our rage to assimilate, to reap the benefits of material privilege in white supremacist capitalist patriarchal culture, white folks urge us to remain complicit with their efforts to colonize, oppress, and exploit," hooks explains. With no viable outlet to express her rage and frustration, she ends up weeping. Asking students to meditate on hooks's essay holds up rage as another critical force, and allows them to connect hooks's ordinary experience on that plane with other examples from the news and their lives every day. It forces students to reflect on individual reactions to the rage hooks expresses, and any possible complicity with what the white man in "Killing Rage" represents. To see the ways that all interactions carry histories with them, even when individual people's everyday interactions may seem immediately removed from those histories. hooks's rage isn't trivial or irrational—it's illuminating. It draws attention to the small choices everyone makes daily that hold power to exacerbate or alleviate rage and subsequent despair for hooks and others.

Though Black women's rage is often stereotyped as

superfluous in order to hide its sociopolitical import, Carol Anderson explores how the exact opposite is true for white people, particularly white men. In her book *White Rage: The Unspoken Truth of Our Racial Divide*, she succinctly explains how white rage and resentment have been the constitutive discriminatory forces in United States politics, legislation, and imagination. Despite the appearance of progress over time—more legal protections, antidiscrimination statutes, some technical equality under the law—the underlying racism and interlocking oppressions of the nation weren't eradicated, just more cleverly disguised. They still bubble up regularly, as hooks's experience on the plane makes clear. "With so much attention focused on the flames, everyone had ignored the logs, the kindling," Anderson says. As a few large overarching race issues—the biggest flames—appeared to get extinguished (even if in name only) throughout history, white resentment and rage at Black people, and at the perceived loss of a fabricated privileged status, continued to seethe under the surface, find new expression even from within seemingly progressive reform. The 2016 election found that white rage undeniably come home to roost. Beyoncé is attuned to her own rage as well. And she may also be especially attuned to the kindling, which is why fires are never fully extinguished in her videos.

Beyoncé invokes rage and anger sparingly in her

catalog, but they are there. The unmitigated rage of "Ring the Alarm" is an anchor to *B'Day*. Anger permeates much of the first half of *Lemonade*: the gleeful destruction she perpetrates along the street with a baseball bat in "Hold Up," and her impassioned delivery of "Don't Hurt Yourself." Audre Lorde, like hooks, addresses the indispensability of anger in speaking back to power in her own essay, "The Uses of Anger." Rather than questioning anger, she questions its absence: Why *wouldn't* a Black woman be angry at the system? And following Lorde, why aren't more people angry at the system's treatment of Black women? Lorde says, "It is not the anger of other women that will destroy us, but our refusals to stand still, to listen to its rhythms, to learn within it, to move beyond the manner of presentation to the substance, to tap that anger as an important source of empowerment," and thus, an important way to critique power. Beyoncé has occasionally tapped that anger as a productive force, and as a position from which to swing a fist back at the oppressive systems and privileges that allow white people's harmful actions to continue unchecked.

hooks's rage, seen by society as irrational stereotype, devolves into tears for lack of modes to express that rage and be *heard*. White rage, on the other hand, is translated into discriminatory policies and strategies. Fighting fire with fire only goes so far, because rage is only seen as productive when wielded by certain people. Because rage from the oppressed becomes all-consuming, hooks ultimately argues, "[i]t must be tempered by an engagement with a full range of emotional responses to black struggle for self-determination"; that rage must be felt, harnessed as connective force, but also can't exist in isolation. What does a tempered but still simmering rage look like? How can rage, wielded critically, counter oppression, create new possibility, and highlight various complicities all at once? Anderson's writing shows how white rage created a resentment that has maintained the racist status quo for centuries. Beyoncé, too, highlights resentment as a basis that can guide politics to challenge that status quo, resentment from an alternative direction that gets truly heard and understood. Anger and rage explode, and explosions are often necessary. But resentment smolders.

Why Don't You Love Bey?

Beyoncé first posed her infamous question, "Why don't you love me?," in 2008. The song was never officially released as a US single, but appeared on various deluxe versions of *I Am . . . Sasha Fierce* and a bonus tracks EP, not quite conceptually attached to either side of the album proper. The video, released in 2010, finds Beyoncé playing a new character altogether, B.B. Homemaker, introduced by name during 1950s-styled opening credits. Beyoncé has also translated the song into an impactful interactive live performance, notably part of both the Mrs. Carter Show World Tour during 2013 and 2014 and the On the Run Tour in the summer of 2014. Both video and performance highlight aspects of what a strategic resentment might look and feel like.

The question itself seems almost comical: After all, who *doesn't* love Beyoncé? Sure, she has critics and naysayers like any artist, but even those same critics can't completely discount Beyoncé's work ethic, talent, and cultural impact. While playfully ironic on its surface, Beyoncé's performance of the question reveals an anger, rage, and critique lurking underneath. Put another way, in a moment when Black lives are explicitly and uniformly devalued, especially in America—when Black women are de facto seen and devalued as angry simply for existing within a racist and sexist system—what does it mean for Beyoncé to ask, *as a Black woman*, hey, why don't you love me? Perhaps she's even alluding to the absurdity of the question by not including a question mark in the formal song title. The question isn't about Beyoncé at all, but should be seen as political commentary uttered by a Black woman, like hooks's "killing rage." Besides, it's not even Beyoncé asking; B.B. Homemaker is, which brings with it another host of associations. The question to which she repeatedly demands a satisfactory answer, is really: Why doesn't the United States love Black women? It serves as a tweaked predecessor to the question actress Amandla Stenberg poses in her YouTube video, "Don't Cash Crop My Cornrows": "What would America be like if we loved Black people as much as we love Black culture?" The question is modified and posed again in *Lemonade*—in which Stenberg conspicuously appears—by Beyoncé as, "Why can't you see me? Everyone else can."

The video for "Why Don't You Love Me" opens with the kind of bouncy, happy-go-lucky instrumental music associated with sitcoms from the 1950s, and all the regressive, stereotypical messages contained in them. A male radio announcer's voice speaks the title of the song and introduces B.B. Homemaker, cementing this performance as more character-driven commentary. Her own forceful spoken intro follows. She speaks to her (presumably male) partner on the other side of a telephone she haphazardly swings to-and-fro, warning him that she's about to leave if he doesn't make some drastic changes in behavior. He must have bumped his head, but B.B.'s there to talk some sense back into him. He hasn't been treating her right and there's no excuse for it—even all his friends recognize her worth. She'd hate for him to return to an empty house. A slightly passive-aggressive threat, followed by the demand that drives the entire song: "All I need to know is why . . ." and she begins singing, "Why don't you love me?" She relates all this matter-of-factly, but with martini in hand and smoky eye shadow streaming down her face. Despite the setting and various allusions, B.B. Homemaker is certainly no stereotypical 1950s housewife.

The song is a point-by-point presentation, down to poster board and easel touting the titular question, refuting reasons one might give not to love her. Beyoncé as B.B. Homemaker is not only demanding an answer to the question, but demanding that audiences sit in the rhythms of "Why Don't You Love Me," to learn within it, and ultimately move from Beyoncé's presentation of the question to contemplating the substance of her claim. A demand following Audre Lorde. Although at times she appears cheerful and happy over the course of the video, it's anger that drives the ferocious force of the song forward. The vocal delivery is full of angst; Beyoncé works through a full arsenal of guttural emphasis, with high-powered, punctuated attacks on consonants in each word, searing highs and lows. And the soundtrack is up-tempo and unrelenting, never offering a moment to breathe—the rhythm repeats in a swift, cyclonic four-count and sweeps the listener away. It's like a hurricane with a heavy kick drum. Like storm winds, the video also offers a brief eye, only to quickly thrust the audience back into its raging gusts and an interrogation of a system that creates the title question in the first place.

Before the eye of the storm, though, cultural references cycle through the video's whirlwind. Though the styling places the action in the 1950s, viewers are immediately whisked back even further in time via the red kerchief Beyoncé dons in early shots while working on a car. Not only is the kerchief reminiscent of Mammy stereotypes Black women have constantly faced and challenged, it also invokes Rosie the Riveter: that now-iconic feminist image originally painted by Norman Rockwell, thought to be based off real-life Rose Will Monroe and popularized on posters in the early 1940s. Beyoncé explicitly revisited and remade that image in her own likeness in a separate photoshoot posted to Instagram on July 22, 2014. And Beyoncé-as-Rosie does some significant political work. Rosie the Riveter is a white woman, and her image was initially used much like the Uncle Sam poster was—to entice support of the war effort through various forms of service. Rosie posters were emblazoned with the slogan "We can do it!" in order to get women to take on the factory jobs men were leaving during World War II. Women could help the nation in wartime by getting to work. Trouble was, many Black women and women of color were already working outside their homes. The previous luxury of not having to work was largely reserved for privileged white women.

B.B. Homemaker, styled as Rosie, exposes those contradictions and further subverts the imperialist underpinnings too, by exposing "at home" as their own form of imperialism, still reminiscent of slavery. Rosie empowered women to join a workforce specifically in service to the state. Black women and other women of color, however, were already working in domestic jobs, usually in the households of white women. The ability of white women writ large to join the workforce, which in turn supported the war effort, was often already contingent upon Black women's labor. And it's been historically revised as a major (white) feminist victory. Black women were still expected to do the multiple forms of work necessary to create the possibility of white women's demand for work. Beyoncé's shown doing not only the traditionally feminine work around the house of dusting, cooking dinner, and washing the clothes, but also the traditionally masculine work of landscaping and fixing an overheating car. And she's tired. And rightfully angry. Beyoncé's saying no. She doesn't perform any of these domestic tasks satisfactorily. All while styled quite provocatively—another taboo for sitcoms of the fifties. She burns dinner. She's terrified of a garden snake. She can't figure out how to fix the car, rejecting the expectation of her already doubled workload through her parodied, overwrought failures. They expose the expectations as unfair and unequal while Beyoncé's makeup runs, smears down her face and she spills martinis all over the carpet and bedspread. She never attempts to clean up the mess.

She chain-smokes throughout the video, steam coming from her nose and mouth in unseemly, unfeminine ways—more refused expectations blown back into the winds of the song.

It's also easy to see Bettie Page—known as *the* iconic pinup girl from the 1950s—in the video's aesthetic. The sitcom nature of the video and the Page-like costuming put sexuality and housewife duties in tension—multiple demands, not disparate things. This blending shows Beyoncé playing a character who was largely unavailable to Black women during the time in which the video is set. Page was a white woman, and Beyoncé's invocation exists as another subversion by pointing out the lack of ways Black women were able to embrace sexuality in the mainstream, though Eartha Kitt, who would come to be known as an iconic sex kitten, was beginning to make waves in cabaret and stage productions during Page's heyday. Another parallel to the Page-esque centerfold was Josephine Baker, already a strong influence on Beyoncé from the *B'Day* era forward. Baker fled the US for Europe decades earlier, to escape the blatant racism she regularly experienced in her youth. She had cultivated a distinguished career abroad, and was still well-known in the 1950s. Baker seamlessly blended erotics, sexuality, motherhood, and politics. She became a civil rights activist and even did a stint as a spy for the French government during World War

II, while Rosie was emblazoned on those US posters. Baker absolutely eschewed all preconceived notions or rules about what a Black woman could be, and Beyoncé as a Black woman invoking Bettie Page is also certainly an invocation of Baker as celebratory (and predated) counterpoint to mark the limits of the US imagination.

It wasn't until 1968 that a Black woman was given a main role as the protagonist of a major television sitcom. Diahann Carroll starred in *Julia* as the title character on NBC for three seasons. Julia was a single mother, working as a nurse and supporting her son. The show marked an important pop culture first in terms of representation of Black women on TV, but also stands as evidence of how long it took and how little progress has been made since. Beyoncé, merely through her presence in this video and the time period invoked, is challenging the whiteness of pop culture in general, and carrying that challenge forward in time. Aside from a few popular shows—a majority of them produced by Shonda Rhimes's Shondaland production company or Oprah Winfrey's OWN—mainstream television remains largely whitewashed, and diversity gets embraced only in niche markets, or written and cast only as stereotypes. Parts for which race is not expressly named continue to be seen as white by default, reinforcing the unspoken universality of whiteness.

In her historic 2015 win as the first Black woman to take home an Emmy for Lead Actress in a Drama Series, Viola Davis quoted Harriet Tubman to reinforce this exact point. "In my mind, I see a line. And over that line, I see green fields and lovely white flowers and beautiful white women with their arms stretched out to me, over that line. But I can't seem to get there no how. I can't seem to get over that line." Beyoncé positioning herself as a Black woman in roles that were never meant to belong to Black women—by channeling the outsider energy of Eartha Kitt and Josephine Baker while subverting Bettie Page and Rosie the Riveter iconography—calls out the same line Tubman and Davis invoked, reframing it all as "Why don't you love me?" Beyoncé's got everything anyone needs, as the lyrics attest: beauty, class, style, ass, a full bank account, knowledge, smarts, sexual prowess, empowered pleasures and desires, success. But she still runs up against the line. Davis mentioned the only thing that separated those white women over the line and the Black women who couldn't get across wasn't any innate quality like talent, which Black women have in excess—it was opportunity. Beyoncé forces the viewer to see and grapple with the racist, arbitrary nature of that line. And she demands an explanation.

The eye of the storm mentioned earlier takes place during the video, not the audio track. The rhythm of the song throughout has been fast, persistent, relentless.

But the video breaks where a traditional song's bridge might appear. The exuberantly hokey sitcom music returns while B.B. Homemaker relaxes, away from her expected chores. The one chore she does perform during the brief respite is dusting off a line of Grammys on the mantelpiece—some of the sixteen Beyoncé had won at the time. The scene interrupts the repeated "Why don't you love me?" by showing that Beyoncé is actually loved and respected as a performer, though the Grammys themselves have a long history of pushing Beyoncé's work in particular, and Black women's work in general, to the margins of niche categories, just like Black women's representation in pop culture overall. She's the second most awarded and single most nominated female artist at the Grammys (twenty-three awards and sixty-six nominations at the end of 2018), but has been egregiously snubbed for the Recording Academy's most prestigious Album of the Year award three times (an award only three Black women have ever won)—2017's *Lemonade* snub being the most heinous. Significantly, the "Why Don't You Love Me" video was released directly following the first of her three Album of the Year snubs for *I Am . . . Sasha Fierce*. Just because Beyoncé is one Black woman loved by many, it doesn't mean all Black women are loved or celebrated by society. It doesn't even mean she's given the full respect she deserves from those in power. It shows that she's still an exception that proves the unfortunate rule, just like in "Pretty Hurts."

There's no husband or romantic partner shown in "Why Don't You Love Me." There's no children or dog, both of which she threatens to take with her when she leaves. Only Beyoncé as B.B. Homemaker singing—sometimes shouting—into a phone. The "you" is, in large part, America, the system, just like in *Lemonade* and much of Beyoncé's other music. Rosie the Riveter and a featured red, white, and blue motif throughout the video speak back to America as well. This is Beyoncé as a Black Rosie the Riveter, calling Uncle Sam on the telephone to ask why he doesn't, hasn't, and might not ever love her. All she really wants to know is "Why?" Though the video uses the conceit of a 1950s sitcom to undercut some of the severity, Beyoncé's performance actually seethes with anger and resentment, the rhythms of which demand to be taken seriously.

She re-creates this critical, political force when performing "Why Don't You Love Me" live too, at the same moment the eye of the storm appears in the video. While singing the song, she abruptly stops the music and threatens to walk off stage. She demands those in attendance cheer for her. Loud. And audiences always do, of course. But Beyoncé builds her dissatisfaction into the performance. She begins to dramatically repeat the title question with increasingly impressive runs and riffs, pausing after each refrain to elicit even bigger reactions. She mimes leaving, walks away and turns her back to insinuate the audience hasn't given her exactly the reaction she wants. She won't leave, though, will she? For a moment, sitting there in arenas or stadiums, or watching the performances back at home, people might get scared, because she draws out the pause to uncomfortably long lengths. During her feigned retreat, twin dancers Laurent and Larry Nicolas Bourgeois (collectively known as Les Twins) perform as hype men, begging the audience to scream and applaud louder so she'll return. So audiences scream their lungs out. She's asking, "Why don't you love me?" and they're trying to prove she is loved above all else.

The entire performance is kitsch to make a larger political point. Beyoncé, a Black woman, is refusing to continue performing until she receives *exactly* what she wants. She holds all the cards. She's trying to illuminate the disconnect between loving Beyoncé but not loving Black women generally—trying to erase Davis's and Tubman's line, not toe it. She's pointing out the inconsistency in the public's unyielding adoration and love of her and the treatment of Black women in society on a daily basis. Her brief refusal to perform stands in for a much larger objection and refusal, thrown back at America. Only when she deems the reaction by the crowd *enough* does she drop her hand, signaling the band's return to finish the song. She then increases the already blistering tempo, further spinning the winds of the hurricane as she repeats the chorus. The eye in the storm during her live performances is reconfigured, because she's the only one experiencing the calm. For the audience, it's a mad, exasperated frenzy to prove they love her and can be trusted to behave accordingly. During the video, viewers could enjoy the respite with her, but on stage, she's the only one standing still. Everyone else is jumping and spinning in the stands. The shoe is on the other foot in a reversal of traditional power dynamics. A boss move fueled by her resentment, not of her audience, but of a system. The move forces everyone watching to ask: Am I doing everything I can to counter the very system that perpetuates the need for Beyoncé to angrily ask, "Why don't you love me?" to begin with?

The song ends conspicuously. After countless attempts to prove herself worthy, deserving, exceptional, Beyoncé plainly states, "There's nothing not to love about me / I'm lovely . . . Maybe you're just not the one / Or maybe you're just plain . . ." and trails off. She refuses to finish the lyric in line with the beat of the song, while the drums continue to roll. "Why Don't You Love Me" displays the tempering of rage into resentment in real time. There's no answer to the question she's asking that doesn't admit at least a modicum of complicity with the system that forces her to ask it. She's orchestrating her anger, fine-tuning her resentment while pointing back with condemnation. The only explanation for why she isn't loved lies with the "you" in the song, not with her. She's lovely. It's America's problem. She finally finishes the last lyric unexpectedly on an odd, as opposed to even, count of the measure, after a prolonged musical outro. "Maybe you're just not the one / Or maybe you're just plain . . . dumb." It ends midmeasure with an indictment thrown back at the listener. A slap across the face. It's the metaphorical, imaginary soft stabbing bell hooks wanted to perform on that airplane. And the word echoes into the silence, leaving viewers and listeners reeling. Maybe Beyoncé's right. If some individuals can't see their own complicity in all of this, maybe they *are* just ignorant.

You Lied

Beyoncé's "Resentment" first appeared as the last official track on *B'Day*—what listeners were left with as the music faded and the album closed. The final taste of *B'Day* proper. Rather than wrapping the record up with a bow, it provoked more questions through what Daphne Brooks noted was an especially unusual and dissonant "uncomfortable crescendo, a jagged little pill for fans to swallow." It's not just a song about a cheating partner and the difficulty of repairing a breach in trust, loyalty, and fidelity. It foregrounds a lie and prefigures the main thrust of the narrative of *Lemonade*. "Resentment" painstakingly lingers on that lie, never lets it go. Moreover, the song was a centerpiece of both iterations of the On the Run Tour, and cited as evidence for personal relationship and marriage turmoil at different moments in Beyoncé's career. Once again, though, the "you" Beyoncé is singing to is a romantic partner on one register, but the "you" is also the liar more generally, the one who doesn't love her—society, the system, America. Because America has lied, broken promises it never intended to fulfill. Repeatedly, and to Black women especially.

There's no music video for "Resentment," which caused it to stand out more against the *B'Day* video anthology. It's the only song from *B'Day* without one. The first time Beyoncé performed the song live was in 2009 during a set of small concerts in Las Vegas, later released on DVD as *I Am . . . Yours*. Before starting the song, she asked the audience, "How many of you have ever been lied to? I'm sure everyone has; we all have. This song is about a relationship after you've been lied to, and you're trying your best to forgive. It's really difficult 'cause you never forget." Her extended introduction returned to the lie more than once, while not taking a stand on what repair might look like. Rather, she keeps the lie alive by holding forgetting and forgiving in impossible tension. More than just introducing a ballad about a lying partner, she was mapping resentment as politics. She left the circumstances vague, though cheating becomes obvious in the song's lyrics, choosing to highlight the lie itself and not its substance. Building on everything else Beyoncé interrogates about race, gender, sexuality, and class in America, the lie becomes the entire premise and promise of America itself. The lie of equal opportunity. The lie/line Harriet Tubman exposed that imposes separation. The lie of freedom broken down in *Lemonade*.

Beyoncé drew the audience into the lie to open the song, asking everyone witnessing the performance to read their own experiences onto the dynamics of a broken promise. She created an intimate atmosphere—even through her choice to sit on the steps leading to the stage as she sang the song to an already intimate, smaller audience—in order to make a powerful statement: You can't forget; the lie will always exist whether it's forgiven or not. She asked how many knew what it felt like to be lied to, but she also drew some members of the audience close to accuse them of being the liar. The urgency and intimacy of the message was paired with some of her most soulful, roof-shattering, sidesplittingly emotive live vocals and meticulous runs. She transmutes the hurt and pain of the lyrics into an impassioned political plea to expose the underlying lie and her own refusal to let it go, despite multiple attempts. She's simply "much too full of resentment," indicating that some hurt remains regardless of societal or even personal pressure to forgive and/or forget. Some lies or actions are simply too egregious, and individual forgiveness can slide uneasily into the erasure of systemic complicity. "Resentment" keeps the hurt and anger alive, refuses to let the system off the hook. Another palimpsest, impossible to erase. In more words of Brittney Cooper, "However important forgiveness may be as a personal act, it does not make for sound and effective politics." So Beyoncé won't forgive or forget. She'll continue to give liars a hard time, even. She's still giving them a hard time a decade later on *Lemonade* and beyond.

Resentment says, structurally, that lies shouldn't be forgotten or forgiven, though individuals may personally choose to practice one or both. As a politics, lies should be resented—acknowledged and remembered, constantly keeping accountability alive as a process—never forgotten. Remember the example of the cracks and fissures of the kintsugi bowl. Imagine what resenting America looks and feels like, using Beyoncé's experience as a Black woman in the United States as an example. To imagine that resentment is to also practice using intersectionality as an analytic lens. At the same time, imagine being resented and trying to determine how to remedy that resentment. Because everyone can be a liar and lied to variously, often simultaneously, on a sliding scale. Everyone plays different or multiple roles in this metaphoric relationship. Acknowledging harm doesn't erase good. One should expect the most from any relationships or system that they are part of, in which they participate daily. Constructive critique should correctly be seen as *more* beneficial than ignoring a problem, as it leads to more critical conversations around healing and repairing lies, mending broken promises. And it all begins with resentment, fermenting anger and rage, attending to them with a dash of tough love and critical dialogue.

In addition to the Las Vegas performance, "Resentment" was featured in its entirety as part of the narrative of *Life Is But a Dream*. The performances (and subsequent On the Run versions) incorporate a significant lyric change from the recorded version on *B'Day*, a quick change Beyoncé might even intentionally muffle so as to allow multiple interpretations. Especially given her precise enunciation and diction elsewhere. While refuting any potential justifications for the infidelity in the song, Beyoncé originally recorded, "Like I couldn't do it for you / Like your mistress could." However, in live versions the lyrics are aggressively altered, infusing even more anger and rage into the thrust of the song. I always say a misheard lyric can create just as much meaning in its reception as the correct lyrics, and though Beyoncé changes "your mistress" to "that wack bitch," students always and without prompting express shock at Beyoncé unleashing fury against "that white bitch" after viewing both the 2009 concert and *Life Is But a Dream* performances of "Resentment" together. I misheard it many times myself before discerning other possibilities. Either way, that initial mishearing sticks with me as meaningful, especially as students continue to hear it.

"Wack bitch" is certainly less polite than "mistress," but "white bitch" goes further to name the political root of all the system's lies. It nods to Carol Anderson's study of how white rage, unleashed and unchecked, has produced such inequality today. Who knows? Maybe Beyoncé wants audiences to hear multiple phrases simultaneously. Squeeze the words together yourself, coupled with dramatic delivery, and it's easy to disguise one phrase for the other. What would it mean for a Black woman to pour out her heart and simultaneously express distress and resentment over the "white bitch" that isn't even half of her, yet gets celebrated on every magazine cover, TV show, fashion runway? The possible use of "white bitch" here calls out the entire system of white supremacy and white feminism once again, and is not out of line with Beyoncé's other artistic commentary. The "white bitch" in "Resentment" is the predecessor of "Becky with the good hair" in "Sorry." And Beyoncé can't forgive. She can't forget. Or more correctly, she *won't* forgive, *won't* forget. During the final leg of the On the Run II tour, Beyoncé validated the above reading, altering the lyrics even further to denounce that "desperate, mediocre, *white* bitch" explicitly, leaving much less room for speculation. Despite her naked candor in early versions of "Resentment," most still failed to hear the political complaint she was voicing years before *Lemonade* and On the Run II; it mainly got subsumed into gossip over her personal marital issues. It often still does.

Beyoncé still can't believe at the end of "Resentment." She wishes she could, but all the excuses used to justify the central lie "really don't apply." Just like any answer to the question "Why don't you love me?" pointed straight back at the system. She rejects the simple solution—forgive or forget—and she chooses to trust herself. She won't reconcile with the white bitch of a system. And so, the resolution of "Resentment" is much like the resolution of "Why Don't You Love Me": nonexistent. Because there's no real satisfactory, quick-fix resolution when it comes to racism and sexism in the United States, so audiences are necessarily thrown directly back into the thick of it. But with a redistribution of power, Beyoncé no longer has to justify her resentment; others have to explain what created that resentment in the first place. By insisting on fostering resentment, not getting over it, Beyoncé is taking the white rage and resentment Anderson named and turning it back against those who wield it. She's exploring alternative outlets for hooks's killing rage so that it doesn't dissipate in tears for lack of options. In tempering rage, Beyoncé cultivates resentment and fully embraces the double entendre of hooks's title: that a killing rage is justified, and also that the killing of rage births new meaningful possibilities. Beyoncé's resentment keeps lies of the past alive, unflinchingly holds them to the light and shines the spotlight even brighter. In so doing, she suggests it's the only way to heal.

11

FRESHER THAN YOU

MOST OF BEYONCÉ'S MUSIC IS KNOWN FOR BEING FUN; some of it is even *about* fun. It's fun to listen to, hopefully fun to analyze and study. It also investigates healing in a number of important ways—Beyoncé as both the one being healed and the one doing the healing at different times; both healing for those at the margins and healing for the larger audience. I like to end each semester with a consideration of the healing present in Beyoncé's catalog as a way to carry the entire course forward into the world. And so I always assign a selection of chapters from Toni Cade Bambara's *The Salt Eaters* to highlight healing, too, as complicated work, not the absence of trouble. Which doesn't mean it can't also be fun. As Beyoncé says as *Lemonade* pushes forward to its climax, "If we're gonna heal, let it be glorious."

Bambara's 1980 novel opens with, "Are you sure, sweetheart, that you want to be well?"—a question posed by healer Minnie Ransom to the novel's main character Velma Henry, a community activist, before she undergoes a healing ceremony that lasts the novel's entire length. Minnie wants to be sure Velma is warned. "I like to caution folks, that's all. . . . A lot of weight when you're well," she states. Perhaps the weight in Minnie's caution is the very weight of Beyoncé's resentment, a continuous, tempered negotiation that eschews easy solutions. Getting and staying well does not mean letting go of resentment; it means incorporating it, balancing its weight against the toxic systems that create it, while also carving out small moments to enjoy oneself. Beyoncé creates these same moments with her music, for herself and, once she's brought the entire audience into alignment, for them too. Bambara's novel explores health and wellness as a presence, not an absence of weight. Getting well means resisting forgiving, resenting forgetting, remembering. It's the new social contract Beyoncé sought to forge in *Lemonade* that places Black women's experiences at the center. Seen this way, Beyoncé's performances of "Resentment" might be their own healing ceremonies. By extension, resentment might also get refigured as a powerful form of self-care.

Caring for oneself often still gets read as selfish—even more so when the world is in complete disarray and everything seems dire. Taking a moment to breathe, unplug from technology or social media, or do something kind for yourself often feels shameful or weak, like you're ignoring more important issues. Levels of privilege can also affect who is able to regularly indulge in a practice of self-care. Though today it is being increasingly embraced, many still burn out by neglecting those breaks necessary to refuel and recharge. The world has worn Velma down. That's why she seeks healing to begin with in *The Salt Eaters*, and her need for healing sheds specific light on how the health of Black women, whether community activists or not, is severely impacted by America's lies and broken promises, present everywhere if you're looking. Audre Lorde popularized the notion that self-care is absolutely vital in her epilogue to "A Burst of Light: Living with Cancer." She recounted, "Caring for myself is not self-indulgence, it is self-preservation, and that is an act of political warfare," especially as the world and cancer tried to annihilate her. Beyoncé has waged political warfare throughout her catalog always while taking important care of herself by insisting on boundaries between her personal and public life. To do anything but—to be more polite, demure, or conciliatory—would have been Beyoncé not being fair to herself, as noted in *Life Is But a Dream*. Her political warfare/self-care is often blended with a call to see through the lens of intersectionality and a demand of her audience to get information, to actively unlearn. A demand that they see the world differently to join Beyoncé in coalition and solidarity, amplify the warfare being waged.

Beyoncé's music as insurgent healing ceremony works on multiple levels. She heals as she tells her story and creates her art. She narrates the healing through highs and lows, joy and sometimes pain. She fuses celebration and indictment as essential aspects to healing, nodding toward the weight of being well. She heals by dancing, performing, and shedding light on crucial issues; couches her political warfare within the healing beats and rhythms of the music. She also heals her audience by empowering listeners of various marginalized groups, by entertaining and educating. She inspires people to dance, have a good time, stabilize the weight of the world for a moment, however brief. Listening to Beyoncé or seeing a live show becomes its own form of self-care for an audience, a break from a depressing and violent racist, sexist, homophobic, imperialist society and any current personal troubles. But even when individuals take a self-care break through Beyoncé's music, she's still foregrounding political warfare and building that better world.

She creates a scenario in which fully and critically engaging with her work is to critique the world that has kept Black women down, historically and currently. Using her music in the classroom has shown students how essential intersectionality is as a lens through which to see the world, for everyone to use while respectfully honoring the work and voices of Black women. All of Beyoncé's songs and videos become their own healing ceremonies in different ways, and work across different registers on the listener depending on their own identities, encouraging everyone to proportionately share the weight it requires to make the whole world well. Assuring everyone that better things are possible. As Tina Lawson said in a 2014 speech sampled in Beyoncé's "Ring Off," "If you're going through it, just know it's called going *through* it. You're not gonna get stuck there. You're not gonna die. You're gonna survive." I like to end each semester with what I believe are two of Beyoncé's more forthright healing ceremonies as reminders. As an added bonus, the two songs also encourage everyone to have fun, be defiant, be flawless.

Three Stars

Some consider "***Flawless" a place to begin, a watershed feminist pronouncement that might serve as a cornerstone to a Beyoncé course and inspire subsequent analysis and discussion. But I like to position the song as a place to rest and celebrate after other hard work gets done. Beyoncé structures the multipart song as a progressive lesson in learning, listening, and finally enjoying oneself that mirrors her own journey to formally embrace feminism. As such, it works perfectly as a culmination. Besides, at this point in the semester, it's impossible to deny Beyoncé's (Black) feminist politics whether she used the word pre-2013 or not, which makes building to "***Flawless" even more useful. The alleged, elusive, and possibly mythical "white bitch" from "Resentment" resurfaces on the song, alongside Beyoncé's unapologetic demand for said white bitch to bow down. For many, name-calling from the queen of pop female empowerment came as a shock, especially featured in a song espousing feminism for a whole new generation. But it's also a political rallying cry funneled through all the rest of Beyoncé's catalog and commentary.

The original demand emerged earlier and was criticized as part of a stand-alone track, "Bow Down/I Been On," released on SoundCloud and then revised and extended to create "***Flawless." "Bow Down" is the first of three distinct sections, imported in full from its earlier iteration despite criticism received. Beyoncé even acknowledged the critique by slyly backing off the word "bitches" in the video, not mouthing it to the camera, though it clearly and powerfully rings out in the vocal line while she feigns shock and partially covers her mouth. People have debated intensely the utility of reclaiming pejoratives previously wielded as insults or slurs. These words—names used by white people against people of color, words used by men against women, or words describing LGBTQ+ identity wielded from a heteronormative perspective—have no easy equivalent to direct back at the more privileged or powerful position. There are no words to wield in that direction because slurs are about power being exerted over the marginalized. So Beyoncé is both reclaiming a word used to belittle women and subverting power by throwing it back simultaneously. "Bow down, bitches," merges with the "white bitch" from earlier to target those in privileged positions and demand they check their privilege while also indicting the whole system. "Check your privilege" can even be said in the same cadence, number of syllables, and near exact internal rhyme as "Bow down, bitches," but the more incendiary obviously makes a better cathartic hook for a song. Besides, as Brittney Cooper succinctly offered in defense of Beyoncé's feminism and 2013 album, "Sometimes bitches do need to bow down." Especially when confronted with such an undeniable power amassed by a Black woman with the odds of American history staunchly against her.

The video opens with more of Beyoncé's time travel to drive her provocative point home—footage from *Star Search* in 1993 featuring the "hip-hop, rapping group Girls Tyme" (the first iteration of what eventually became Destiny's Child). The video cuts between Ed McMahon introducing Girls Tyme and the actual "***Flawless" video of 2013, positioned so that the 2013 footage takes the temporal place of Girls Tyme's

'93 performance in the narrative. After the song ends, the video abruptly cuts back to the *Star Search* stage to watch Girls Tyme lose to returning champion Skeleton Crew—three stars to their perfect four. It's clear to viewers today that that loss is being resituated as an undeniable win. After all, Beyoncé now runs the world, and how many people know the name of even one member of the now-defunct Skeleton Crew? Replaying this memory also unleashes resentment and critique of that past judgment.

Asked to ponder the video's setup, students often ask: Why is a group of grown white men set up in opposition to these young Black girls to begin with? It wasn't entirely uncharacteristic of *Star Search* to pit vastly different contestants against one another, but through Beyoncé's clever recapitulation, it's meant to rub modern viewers the wrong way. The dreams of young Black girls get dashed while older white men smile and cheer into the camera. It feels eerily similar to US history. And Beyoncé is insinuating that not much has changed by reviving it, despite the colossal evolution of her career. Moreover, the editing of the video shows Beyoncé's current song losing to Skeleton Crew, not her past performance. She's illustrating that no matter how successful and powerful the Black woman, there is still a hierarchy in play that favors cis white men above all else. Explaining her use of "bitch" in "***Flawless" to iTunes radio, she said,

"Imagine the person that hates you. Imagine a person that doesn't believe in you." Though it can be interpersonal, it's also powerfully systemic and structural for Black women. This is the "white bitch" she resents, the expression of systemic white supremacy. And she's also rewriting, correcting the past. She's taken the three stars Girls Tyme received for their performance and placed them at the beginning of the song title as asterisks.

As typographic symbols, asterisks have two main functions, and Beyoncé plays with both. One use of an asterisk is to indicate a footnote, to direct attention to extraneous information not quite relevant to the main text, but still useful. The redirection points back to the often disguised, unfair white supremacist system represented symbolically in the *Star Search* footage, judging white men more favorably than Black women or girls by default. Through clever redeployment of her autobiography for political reasons, as she's wont to do, Beyoncé directs viewers back to white supremacist power at the core of the current system. Second, an asterisk placed on either or both sides of a word or phrase is commonly used to rectify a previous misspelling or mistake in online communication. The three stars stand alone as a reclaiming and mistake to be rectified (because they should have been four), but also exist *as the correction*. One asterisk on either side of the middle asterisk marks that middle symbol as an additional corrective star to augment the former three. Three plus an extra one equals four, tying Girls Tyme's score with that of Skeleton Crew. Leveling the playing field through a shout of goddamn three times (once for each star of the lower score) right before Ed McMahon reads the results; redefining an imperfect score—three out of four stars—as "flawless."

Where the previous "Bow Down/I Been On" segued into a slow, modulated, chopped and screwed verse of "I Been On," the new second section of "***Flawless" is a remixed sample of a 2012 TEDx talk by Nigerian author Chimamanda Ngozi Adichie titled "We Should All Be Feminists." An unusual and unlikely addition—one meant to jar and teach the listener. The transition occurs directly after Beyoncé commands bitches to bow down, to check their privilege, to listen, to sit in the rhythm of her anger. She organizes pieces of Adichie's speech out of original order, making them her own while still honoring Adichie's original intent. A political speech enters a popular song out of nowhere *as the lyric*. After repeated listens, most fans singing along also begin repeating Adichie's words, having memorized them verbatim over time. It's an educational moment, one that listeners internalize. The speech centers young girls and the ways they are taught differently than boys, especially when it comes to marriage. Beyoncé's already assured everyone she's no one's little wife earlier in the song, so the speech is also aligned with her own experiences and education. It speaks back to feminist criticism over her use of the word "bitches," but continues to double down and nod to the fact that, in her formulation, bitches means something more. Remaining lines of the speech stress hypocritical, gendered expectations girls unfairly face in the world, more major themes of much of Beyoncé's work.

This section builds finally to Adichie reciting the claim heard 'round the world, which is just a bare-bones dictionary definition of the word "feminist." The line rings out at the very end of the second section, providing a link to the third and final piece of the song. "Feminist: a person who believes in the social, political, and economic equality of the sexes." The definition comes last because Beyoncé has already built a case using information it's impossible to disagree with throughout her career and catalog. She's simply attaching it to the description of what constitutes a feminist now. Where Adichie's title for her speech is "We Should All Be Feminists," Beyoncé's midsong remix of the speech flips her suggestion to an imperative. We *must* all be feminists, and Beyoncé's larger body of work, both before and since, complicates and inflects that simple dictionary definition with a more nuanced understanding of power and interlocking, intersecting oppressions—a Black feminist analysis.

Beyoncé could have easily used her own voice to relay that feminist definition, but she instead enacts another feminist principle of coalition by highlighting Adichie's voice alongside her own, honoring and building on the past.

bell hooks stresses the importance of *advocating* feminism as a political commitment to transformative change, which often stands in distinction to merely identifying as a feminist, in her essay, "Feminism: A Movement to End Sexist Oppression." Sometimes a focus on identity even masks a lack of substantive action. Advocating feminism is about actions to end harmful systems over words, and working together over centering oneself—a key difference in orientation. Note that the lyrics never explicitly claim feminist as an identity either—they focus on the politics. Beyoncé appears as part of a group of young Black girls, and she appears as one of many people in the video, downplaying her individual self for the sake of advocating a movement. And the movement, from one section of her song to the next, rests on the transformative potential of Black feminism. Beyoncé stands next to Adichie to embrace a politics over an identity; and the move also shows that Black feminism overall, like intersectionality, can be wielded as an analytic tool and perspective in addition to being an identity. Because much of Adichie's work deals specifically with Nigeria, her feminism also opens up Beyoncé's analysis and coalition globally, more so than Beyoncé standing alone, speaking for others or centering herself.

The song performs the process of cultivating a Black feminist consciousness as a restorative, healing journey for Beyoncé herself: from an indictment of the system demanding that bitches bow down to identifying specifically Black feminist politics, and ultimately moving into a critical embrace and redefinition of waking up flawless as its own political stance. It also exists as a suggestion to the listener to heal the world through changing perspectives, if this perspective is not the one already held. "We Should All Be Feminists" slides even further into "We must all advocate a Black feminist politics and analysis." Many derided Beyoncé's invocation of feminism in 2013 as a marketing tool. There's validity to the critique as Beyoncé is still selling a product, but alongside her other critiques of capitalism, her insider/outsider dynamic, the surprise release of *BEYONCÉ* with no marketing or promotion, and a closer look into the layers in this video, other readings are possible. Alternately, her invocation of feminism and advocacy of Black feminist politics grounds "***Flawless" in a risk she's willing to take, *despite* trying to sell a product. Beyoncé actually made it popular for other celebrities to subsequently "come out" as feminists without impacting their careers (including many who had previously denounced the label), rather than just riding an already in-motion feminist marketing wave. When the album dropped in 2013, feminism wasn't a mainstay in mainstream pop culture. Beyoncé initiated the wave and though it paid off, it could easily have gone another way.

Feminism is not the only political influence associated with risk, resistance, and defiance in "***Flawless." The fashion throughout nods to punk rock: shaved heads, combat boots, torn jeans, flannel shirts. The action of the video also revolves around a punk-rock mosh pit. Punk is a direct rejection of establishment norms that fits in perfectly. Although punk is often seen as a predominantly white and masculine space (despite its origins in reggae, ska, and Blackness), and its fashion is sometimes mirrored in a neo-Nazi aesthetic, Beyoncé challenges those perceived dominances here through her inclusion of a diverse crowd all moving to the music together. In her opening line, Chimamanda Ngozi Adichie states, "We teach girls to shrink themselves" (again, "girls" by now is a more diverse political identity in Beyoncé's work), while Beyoncé and the mass of people she's assembled do the opposite. They collectively make themselves bigger, stretch out in slow motion, expand their bodies in defiance of society's demand to shrink. Taking up space they were never meant to inhabit. Growing, healing. Although mosh pits have also been sites of misogynist violence, the scene in "***Flawless" prizes a mosh pit's capacity for collective action, collective growth, over time. Even a mosh pit can be a form of self-care, though it might not appear relaxing to most.

The other dominant musical influence in "***Flawless" is hip hop, foregrounded even more explicitly in the song's remix featuring Nicki Minaj though it's abundantly present in the original. Hip hop is another subculture born out of rebellion and rejection of the status quo. Poor Black and Latinx communities pioneered rap (alongside the other three major hip hop pillars: DJing, breakdancing, and graffiti) as a way to speak back to power about the issues they faced in everyday life and as a way to have fun, to celebrate survival, to take care of themselves. Mainstream hip hop may be more commercial than it used to be, but its original politics still inform the form. The mixture of punk, hip hop, and feminism in the song not only demands bitches bow down, but implicitly echoes the additional demands of punk and hip hop respectively: "damn the man" and "fuck the police." Punk and hip hop blend in another act of solidarity, reenacting more of the song's feminist politics.

Just as Adichie finishes giving the definition of feminist, Beyoncé reenters the song with another rallying cry, "I woke up like this." "This" being "flawless"— which becomes the driving force of the song's final section. Beyoncé is turning her new, redefined sense of flawlessness into an everyday state of being which she invites audiences into through the lines immediately prior, highlighting a larger "you," not just an "I." She woke up this way, but so did you. Visually, the collective you is displayed through the video's outcast congregation—a group eerily similar to the misfit tribes in "Run the World" and "Superpower." Flawlessness is no longer the sense of perfection or winning it used to be, because that sense relied on the unspoken rule that whiteness, maleness, cisgender identity, heterosexuality, etc., perpetually held invisible advantages. Beyoncé rewrites that previous rule. Being flawless is messy. Being flawless can be contradictory. And now, being flawless is also part of that other big f-word: feminism. It refuses easy categorization or definition, exposing and exploring the contradictions contained within feminism too. Inconsistencies Roxane Gay named and broke down in her tongue-in-cheek embrace of the moniker "bad feminist," which is also the name of her 2014 collection of essays exploring the topic. She says, "If I am indeed a feminist, I am a rather bad one. I am a mess of contradictions. There are many ways in which I am doing feminism wrong, at least according to the way my perceptions of feminism have been warped by being a woman." Like Beyoncé's three stars redefined as perfection, rolling out of bed flawless regardless, Gay's bad feminism shows it's okay to fail at some things as long as you remain "deeply committed to the issues important to the feminist movement," and acknowledge the ways race, gender, class, and sexuality inform those issues from various intersections.

Beyoncé's performance of "***Flawless" at the 2014 MTV Video Music Awards included the powerful image of her posed in front of the word "feminist" on a conveyer belt (again, not a verbal identification)—a moment iconic for the ways it captured Black women's previous erasure from mainstream feminist movements through Beyoncé's mere presence, pointed straight back to white feminism's historical failures and contradictions. She complicates feminist discussions by positioning her own Black body as essential to the dialogue in "***Flawless," alongside Adichie, and adds Nicki Minaj through the remix of the song too. Minaj brings a grittiness and more explicit brand of feminism outside traditional respectability to the table, one that Beyoncé's image doesn't quite allow her to access, though her own challenges to respectability continue to amass. In fact, each of the women and the feminisms they invoke do something the others can't. Chimamanda Ngozi Adichie's feminism is intellectual, not without its shortcomings, and expands potential for application outside the United States; it deploys a simple dictionary definition only to prove it insufficient with its own limits and blind spots. Beyoncé's feminism is empowering, claims motherhood and sexuality, and perhaps casts the widest net. It also reinvokes

Black feminism's foundational intersection of race and gender by incorporating her "daddy," "mama," "sister," and "man" all taught her in the opening of the third section of the song. Nicki Minaj's feminism is explicit, raunchy, and makes absolutely no concessions or apologies for its ostentatious excess. Each connects to and reinforces the others, like the three sections of "***Flawless" themselves. None exist in isolation. They work across their own differences and highlight those differences as strengths, not weaknesses.

They embrace one another, contradictions and all, as facets of a larger Black feminism and, alongside Roxane Gay's own bad feminism, can't be neatly organized. In modeling all this for the audience, Beyoncé imparts knowledge and reenacts her own progressive Black feminist education over time, part of her own healing. In an important scene toward the end of Velma Henry's healing ceremony in *The Salt Eaters*, Velma begins to dance in her mind. Another character cautions Minnie Ransom, the healer, "Let her go, Min. Dancing is her way to learn now. Let her go." Beyoncé and her collective group expand themselves, releasing years—perhaps centuries—of pent-up frustration before snapping back into tight choreography in "***Flawless." Learning and dancing, just like Velma Henry. The beat makes it nearly impossible not to let go too, throw caution to the wind and begin dancing along with Beyoncé.

Fresher Than You

The perfect opportunity to do just that arrived with Beyoncé's next chronological release in late 2014. "7/11" presented an explosive, fun-filled epilogue to the *BEYONCÉ* era, dropped again by surprise and later included on the *Platinum Edition* of that self-titled album. Appearing at first to be complete nonsense, "7/11" slowly reveals itself as more of Beyoncé's trenchant, layered political commentary and encouragement to heal. When initially asked what "7/11" might be about, students usually say, "It's just fun," "It's got a great beat," or "It makes me wanna dance." They regularly do dance in their seats watching the video in class but are often hard-pressed to mine any deep meaning. It's a fun song and a song *about* fun. The lyrics do sound like repetitive gibberish made up on the spot, but they're deceptively complex. They're also directives for audiences to perform the movements and fun alongside Beyoncé and her friends, similar to the "You wake up . . ." line that begins the third section of "***Flawless." All in all, "7/11" proves quite the high note on which to finally end a semester.

It's also immediately apparent that this video exists as antithesis to Beyoncé's meticulous narrative videos that comprised the 2013 visual album. "7/11" appears to be filmed by Beyoncé herself—she's shown putting the camera in place, then moving into the shot to dance and sing. It gives the illusion of home-movie footage and is purposefully deceptive. There's actually a constant interplay of "high" and "low" forms of culture working back and forth through one another. These juxtapositions explode the very stereotypical notions that give one form of culture value while draining value from others. All while Beyoncé, and everyone watching, has a damn good time. "7/11" is meant to heal while forcing everyone to confront possibly silly assumptions, but ones that inform and sustain broader inequality on a continuum. And to start, she demands coordination in performing the movements she calls out.

Alice Walker emphasized the benefits of dance as self-care, a critical means of maintaining balance and distribution of weight throughout the body, particularly for Black people, in her poetry collection *Hard Times Require Furious Dancing*. In "7/11," Beyoncé dances furiously and wildly, but not in her typical, tightly choreographed way. She's goofy, drinking, and appearing to have a shit ton of fun—in private spaces alone, sometimes with friends. It appears she's creating the movement in the moment, improvising what is necessary and most useful and simply shouting it out. She's reacting to an oppressive world by rejecting its demands. Walker writes about how the restorative utility of dancing is connected to African American history and politics too. "[T]he marvelous moves African

Americans are famous for . . . came about because the dancers . . . were contorting away various knots of stress. Some of the lower-back movements . . . were no doubt created after a day's work bending over a plow or hoe on a slave driver's plantation," she writes.

African American dance traditions actually seek to circumvent the violence and oppression done to Black bodies historically and contemporaneously while healing the body. Walker goes on to say that to "still hold the line of beauty, form and beat" is "no small accomplishment in a world as challenging as this one." As a 2015 internet meme and hashtag prove, Beyoncé is nothing if not *always* on beat. Moreover, she has continuously incorporated resistant dance practices into her choreography—from the Alvin Ailey–inspired African Jazz of "Déjà Vu" to the pantsula of "Run the World (Girls)" to the J-Setting, vogue, and drag ball creations incorporated into her various Sasha Fierce performances and "Formation," and more. In "7/11," she's embracing improvisation as a way to balance the weight of living, including unreserved, unrehearsed, fun movement—simple bodily response, shaping change as it comes—as part of that resistant practice that draws on African American history as well as experiences of queer communities of color. And demanding that others get in formation.

The instructions of "7/11" require no formal dance training, unlike some of Beyoncé's other choreography.

The movement is simple and energetic, precision be damned. Squaring shoulders, smacking, clapping, spinning, throwing hands up, moving legs from side to side. And Beyoncé models it all as she calls it out. It's silly, but she's enjoying herself without apology, turning fun into a weapon. Fun, as a form of self-care, can be political warfare too, as Lorde suggested; and, conversely, political warfare can, and perhaps should, be fun. The same might also be necessarily applied to education in general, as Beyoncé showed more explicitly in "***Flawless." Expanding minds, challenging assumptions, shouldn't be a chore, it should be enjoyable, though complete with its own necessarily uncomfortable and difficult transgressive moments—the discomfort bell hooks noted as central to education as the practice of freedom, and that Beyoncé drew out of conservative audiences in some of her post-2016 performances. Learning, or unlearning, can also be deceptively simple, like in "7/11." Education can (and, I would argue, *should*) impart complex ideas in plain, seemingly simple ways—proving Beyoncé, once again, a master teacher.

There's deeper meaning hiding underneath the deceptive simplicity of other silly elements of the video—the costuming, structure, and some of the nonsense lyrics. The video begins with Beyoncé in a sweatshirt emblazoned with the word KALE across her chest. While maybe originally a joke sweatshirt, the intentional presence of it in a Beyoncé video opens a kind of Pandora's box of political layers. The word is printed in collegiate typography, specifically mimicking Yale's. Yale is immediately recognizable as an elite (and elitist) private Ivy League institution. Reference to the school invokes privilege, power, and prestige usually accessed through whiteness and judged against supposedly lesser public institutions. Yale was founded on unequal opportunity and tied to the spoils of slavery, like other Ivy League schools (and many other universities). While it's true anyone can be accepted into an Ivy League institution today, it doesn't mean that actually attending is attainable, for a host of reasons. Featuring KALE in place of YALE on a facsimile college sweatshirt poses questions about the validity of the education received at the satirized school. In reality, Yale is just a name used to open doors for some, the education received not quantitatively or qualitatively better or worse than anywhere else. Beyoncé, with no formal postsecondary education, is once again "schoolin' life" and challenging perceptions held of the Ivy League and ivory tower, even when viewers might not be immediately aware they hold those perceptions.

Kale often elicits unexpected passionate reactions in the classroom too—a bitter leafy green students either love or hate. There's never an in-between. It's fairly well-known as trendy and hip, to some people's delight and others' dismay. Kale is a simple leafy green, but its associations are distinctly high-class. How many New York City or Los Angeles eateries can be found *without* a kale salad on the menu? Plus, the kale salad usually clocks in at a higher price point for the elite, Whole Foods–devoted, gentrification-inclined eater. Which is all to say, kale is often associated with white people—perhaps the same elite, powerful, privileged, prestigious, moneyed white people holding on desperately to their association with places like Yale. Kale contains a lot of implicit messaging for such a simple vegetable.

A close cousin of kale, collard greens, don't hold nearly the same privileged, elitist messages and associations. Quite the opposite, actually. Collard greens are a similar bitter leafy green but typically differ in preparation, usually served as a side dish to kale's main event. Collard greens themselves hold just as much nutritional value, but are often perceived as unhealthy. Why have two closely related dark leafy greens been so greatly separated and differently valued? Collard greens are a staple of traditional Southern African American cooking, and since Blackness is heavily devalued in the United States, food associated with African American culture is also devalued. But the difference doesn't exist inherently in the vegetable, just as differences don't lie de facto in Yale's education but rather the school's funding, endowments, and history as a bastion of elite connections. Difference is expressed through stereotypes and perceptions of the two things, and the object associated more closely and heavily with whiteness is prized and celebrated, while the object associated with Black cooking and culture is devalued. Associations regarding elite education and elite foods and vegetables aren't dissimilar. Part of healing and unlearning is recognizing these associative differences and the ways they've been used against different groups of people, used to proliferate unearned privilege and stereotypes.

What about the title of the song itself? 7-Eleven is a well-known franchise of relatively cheap convenience stores, but that's not what Beyoncé is referencing. The lyrics point to a dice game, craps; they actually serve as instructions for winning the game—rolling a seven or eleven repeatedly. Additional players place bets on the shooter's roll. Rolling a two, three, or twelve is considered "craps." Odds can vary based on the particular version of the game being played, but given the number of possible dice combinations, odds don't typically favor the shooter. Just as the odds are not usually stacked in any given Black woman's favor in America. Beyoncé is the shooter in "7/11," but the results of her roll are never shown. She's saying she wins regardless. She's flawless, remember. The outcome is irrelevant, just like those three stars from *Star Search*. The dice she rolls are winners, either because she's impeccably skilled or because she's rewritten the rules, but, to invert a Nina Simone song title, in the game featured in "7/11," either way, Beyoncé wins.

What's more, she rolls the dice on the bare back of a white woman lying prostrate on the ground, replaying and extending that sacrifice on the cross from "Run the World." Beyoncé has used imagery of her own bare Black back to illustrate undue burden forced onto Black women and other women of color as bridges, in "Déjà Vu" and "Mine" specifically. Here, Beyoncé explicitly refuses and redistributes the work of being the bridge by turning the back of the white woman into that bridge. She's instead imposing the work of the bridge back on whiteness through her craps shoot. To be clear, the white woman is superfluous. Beyoncé could easily roll the dice on the ground. But the white woman's back critiques the foundational nature whiteness and white feminism hold as norms. Also significantly, the dice roll *off* the white woman's back. In craps, when the dice fall off the table, they must be formally inspected before allowed back in play. Beyoncé's intentional overshot is meant to force a closer examination of the system itself—the very master's tools, the dice. Beyoncé asserts major power with a careful sleight of hand that again appears as loss symbolically reframed as victory. She places her own bet and the bet of the audience back on herself.

The overall structure of "7/11" subverts formula and form too by conjuring almost every single line as a chorus through repetition. A traditional chorus contains the hook or main theme of the song, repeated regularly throughout. Beyoncé's repetition of near every line confuses the listener as to what the true chorus is. There isn't one . . . until the end. And it's counterintuitive. A final significant stanza stands on its own, holding the actual meaning a chorus traditionally would by contrast. One that contains a multitude of clear cultural references and point of view absent in all the earlier lines. Though the main thrust of the song has been encouraging listeners to throw caution to the wind, forget any immediate cares, and have fun, Beyoncé intermittently shouts backs, "I know you care!" signaling she's still aware of the political work of the song—the blend of Audre Lorde's self-care as political warfare and fuck-it-all fun she's creating. She shifts tone dramatically in the final stanza and relays strong references invoking Black culture, firmly tied to Black women's style and hair: dashikis, Nefertiti, kinky edges, sweating out blowouts and presses.

Beyoncé ends the stanza and resolves the entire song through presentation of a beef between her and another "trick about to go off," mad because Beyoncé's "so fresh." How fresh? "Fresher than you. . .," which gets repeated once, shouted back, and lingers, driving home the point that the preceding lines stood alone. The "trick about to go off," the trick Beyoncé's challenging and defying here once again, is the entire system—the white bitch of "***Flawless" and "Resentment," Becky with the good hair. And the word "trick" functions triply: as a pejorative identifier for those critiquing her; as the magic trick performed by the system in rendering the structural violence and inequality of racism, sexism, and homophobia invisible to the naked eye; and, finally, as Beyoncé's own sly misdirection tossing the dice off the makeshift table and exposing what the system seeks to always keep invisible.

The most meaningful, freshest lines in "7/11" are brave enough to stand alone, while the repetition of everything else empties out meaning, turning the rest of the song into nonsense. Beyoncé constructs the last stanza as a political outlier. Beyoncé herself is an outcast in the song as well. She's standing alone against a system, doing something truly different—subverting song structure and even her own meticulously curated image from earlier videos (and after another contentious Album of the Year snub from the Grammys for *BEYONCÉ*). Alice Walker also celebrates the power of outcasts and outliers in her 1976 poetry collection *Revolutionary Petunias*. The poem "Be Nobody's Darling" encourages individuality; Walker insists on the importance of standing out from the crowd, even when—especially when—it's uncomfortable, because contradictions and discomfort are the only places true learning and change happen. In the final stanza of the poem, she resolutely advises, "[B]e nobody's darling / Be an outcast. / Qualified to live / Among your dead."

In "7/11," Beyoncé performatively blends Walker's words on dancing and outcasts across time. She embraces her outcast identity, refusing to be anyone's darling but her own. It's all mirrored in the outcasts she's gathered to build new nations, to challenge normative power structures. She's shown her qualifications and camped out in haunted cemeteries among the dead—consistently mapped the margins with ghosts unattended to by history, given them new life. Her lyrical assertion that she knows others care extends an invitation for everyone to formally join her. To become one of the "girls," to exhibit coordination by following her movements, by getting information and falling into formation. Who doesn't want to be "fresher than you" like Beyoncé? And she's laid out a roadmap to her new nation that centers being or embracing outcasts from the current order, qualified to live among America's neglected dead.

Beyoncé is now the healer, enticing her audience to dance, making it damn near impossible *not* to dance. And then, like Minnie Ransom does with Velma Henry, she lets her audience go. Until the next lesson. And everyone must answer the implicit questions for themselves: Do you want to be well? Can you bear the critical weight wellness requires? Do you want others to be well? Can you work to redistribute and share the weight, unfairly borne by marginalized groups throughout history, to make the entire world well? Can you acknowledge your various privileges, sacrifice them when necessary, and direct your energies and experiences toward challenging the status quo? Are you ready to fight? Can you heal and make it glorious? Only time will tell . . .

We Were Here

And so we're dancing, if we accept what Beyoncé is teaching. Together. We're awake. We woke up like this. We're fresher than you, having followed and respected Beyoncé's lead. She invites us all to see through Black feminist lenses regardless of our identity, but always knowing our place. Her work is ultimately so powerful and resonant to various marginalized groups and individuals because she expresses a simple truth: you have always mattered, despite a system that told you otherwise. Whether you identify as a Black woman, as LGBTQ+, or as any number of innumerable combinations of identities at the intersections, Beyoncé creates hope. She uses the particularities of her own experience, frames intersectionality as an analytic lens, and extends all she has learned as a set of empowering political tools. We locate the tools by studying the associations, layers, politics—the very information—she packs into her art. By celebrating imperfection and redeploying it as a perfect win, she enacts healing for those that need it most, including herself. By accepting and highlighting occasional failure, but always having fun, we actually become flawless. In learning what it costs to lose, we know exactly how to win. We're poised to take good care of ourselves and others. We redefine the margins as a new center, upset the meaning of margin and center across the board. Throw the dice way off the table and force critical examination of an unfair system alongside Beyoncé.

She sings, "I wanna leave my footprints on the sands of time / Know there was something that meant something that I left behind" in the opening of "I Was Here" from 4. We all want to matter. To someone. Somewhere. We hope our existence changes something or someone for the better. I'm no different. I'm a teacher and writer hoping to encourage students to look deeper into Beyoncé's music, deeper into history, deeper into the words, work, and ideas of Black women, because I believe Black feminism holds the answers to heal the world. And though my experience is drastically different from Beyoncé's, I'm also just a person that has felt marginalized for being queer. I've struggled through days hoping I'll eventually have something to leave behind because I don't want to be forgotten either. I want to leave a mark or a footprint. But sands shift and there are no guarantees. I continue to advocate a Beyoncé-inflected Black feminist politics because I believe that means advocating freedom for everyone, demanding a better world. Working with young people in classrooms over semesters, or just for individual hours, has shown me exactly how important that message can be. Though Beyoncé has access to enormous amounts of class privilege, money, and fame, she is still a Black woman navigating the streets of America. And her defiance to a system that would rather she suffer in silence—that all marginalized people suffer in silence and disappear—is nothing short of inspirational.

As Beyoncé repeatedly sings "I was here," she transports herself and us as listeners into a future where we have mattered. With each repetition, she reinforces the possibility that we have left a mark on history. The construction of the lyric is multitemporal, past-present-future all merged, giving those beaten down by society in any number of ways power over time. In her essay "The Personal," Wendy S. Walters notes that a "speaker's demeanor during the telling alters the past," and thus creates a new future unbound by the restrictions of that past. The simple speech act, "I was here," marks a present, projects it into the future by invoking past tense, and rewrites the past that might otherwise have erased us. Beyoncé's seemingly simple "I was here" is a final, radically hopeful healing we can feel in our bones. She sings it to us over and over and over. And we sing it back even if no one is listening. We sing it back to Beyoncé, and to ourselves.

With all this background (over twelve years of Beyoncé's career and more than two hundred years of history, referenced in these pages), critically attending to Beyoncé's work serves as a fuck you to the entire system. And a celebration of saying fuck you to the entire system. And a healing ceremony. And the first steps in building a better world. We were here. Together. We are here, but we refuse to play by the system's rules because we have better worlds to build. To roll out of bed chanting, "I was here" and "I woke up like this" and "We flawless" are emancipatory statements. Other campaigns have notably reached out to marginalized youth to tell them, "It gets better." But that's a false, albeit well-intentioned, assurance: it doesn't get better for everyone or in all places. Sometimes it gets worse before it gets better. And, sadly, sometimes it just gets worse. But to wake up just as you are, and to liberate yourself through the reminder that you are here, is to survive. It's a celebration often borne from resentment. And you *are* here. You were here. We are here.

Say it loud. Scream it loud. It's a battle cry. Raise a fist in the air. In "The Transformation of Silence into Language and Action," Audre Lorde said, "What are the words you do not yet have? What do you need to say? What are the tyrannies you swallow day by day and attempt to make your own, until you will sicken and die of them, still in your silence?" Don't be silent. Beyoncé teaches us not to be silent, to break our various silences alongside her and Lorde and to carry that message forward. Because we woke up like this. *We woke up*, and that's an accomplishment. We're awake. We gave our all and did our best, just like she sings in the bridge of "I Was Here." And we will build a better world because we are here. Or we'll die trying. We're part of her new nation. Some already knew some or all of Beyoncé's political commentary because they've lived it, or various versions of it. Others may be learning for the first time through Beyoncé, attempting to deconstruct privileges and make connections across differences. Together, we're all dancing to the beat while she provides the tempo. We're organized around a common politics. Beyoncé not only stopped the world in 2013, she's changed it over the course of her career, made it better. And she's encouraged all of us, no matter who we are, to get information and get in formation—to have been here, there, and already shaping whatever is to come. She's empowered us to see differently, stand on new ground, and insist others do the same. We're going to be okay.

World stop . . .

. . . Carry on.

***

EPILOGUE
LET'S START OVER

ENDINGS ARE BITTERSWEET. I DREAD THE END OF
"Politicizing Beyoncé" each semester. I never want the
analysis and clever, engaged conversations to end. I
don't want to lose the energy produced in the classroom that I so look forward to each week—count on
to raise my own spirits, even. But at the same time,
the end of each semester is one of my favorite parts of
the course—not because it's over and I'll get a break
from grading, but because it's a chance to start again.
Endings are also always beginnings. Just as I often
don't want a Beyoncé song, video, album, or concert to ever end, I know they technically must. One
thing I've learned from teaching and studying Beyoncé's work is that there are always endless possibilities,
additional layers to uncover in the work you think
you already know. Chances to start over. Endings are
never endings.

Though the semester formally ends with healing
and dancing in "7/11," my personal mental soundtrack

to the end of a semester is always "Start Over" from 4. An inauspicious song in the middle of the album, it foregrounds the idea that just when something appears to be over, it's useful—imperative—to return to the beginning and reevaluate. See what can be saved and what must be burned. On the surface, it's about a relationship in crisis, but if you trade the personal register for a political one, as is the explicit demand of "Politicizing Beyoncé" overall, it recapitulates the skillful demand of her music since 2006: a radical transformation of society that's not as harmful or discriminatory as the previous version. Level the foundation, wipe the slate clean, but never forget the mistakes of the past. Highlight them. Start over from a position of greater knowledge, from a different center. On a pedagogical level, the same is true.

For me, that means forgetting what I thought I knew and starting fresh, not weighed down by preconceived notions or attachments to my own favorite songs or videos. Taking note of what worked especially well over the course of any individual semester, and what produced too many pregnant pauses. Staying open. Remembering that there are infinite possibilities, so any particular low point can just be refigured as an opportunity for the future. I reevaluate readings and the stories the songs tell each semester in hopes of creating the best, most exciting conversations next time. Try to reorganize the syllabus into the most impactful narrative possible. Often that means carrying through the most productive pairings—ones where time ran out and no one wanted to leave—and swapping out readings or songs that dragged or failed to create much useful analysis. Moving a reading to a different song after having noticed, during conversation, it made more sense connected to another video. Sometimes shuffling and reordering the flow. No semester has ever used the exact same syllabus as the one before. Plus, there's no telling what Beyoncé will do next, or when. She doesn't play by industry rules anymore; she writes them. A new album or single could further rearrange everything at any moment, and the potential for a Beyoncé surprise looms literally around *every* corner.

Chances are high that Beyoncé has released new material by the time you hold this book in your hands. I had a finished manuscript before *Lemonade* was released, but that monumental piece of work necessitated a near-complete overhaul. Just days after turning in *this* "final" version, Beyoncé and Jay-Z, as The Carters, released their long-rumored joint album and a video for the song "Apeshit" live from the stage during their On the Run II London show. *Everything Is Love* is an undeniably fun, carefree collection of songs that serves as brief coda to the *Lemonade* era—a bit of closure on the healing, redemption, and reunification named as possible at the end of that album. Luckily,

I've been able to add some references throughout before publication, but the album deserves much more consideration and analysis, on its own and alongside everything else Beyoncé has released. She continues to reinvent herself and push the boundaries of music, visuals, and business. There will, no doubt, be even more coming—probably, with my luck, dropped with no warning just weeks before this book's June 2019 release, giving me no time to integrate any of it. I don't know where her next major artistic statements will fit in with the story of the previous pages, but that's also part of the fun. I hope this book has offered tools necessary for readers and thinkers to incorporate whatever comes next into their own version of a curriculum to take out into the world. In addition to Beyoncé's constant surprises, there's also always new, exciting Black feminist work being written and created that can draw additional layers out and speak to students in important ways. And older work still being uncovered, discovered, republished. The possibilities for new or reworked pairings are endless, but I'll never know what resonates most in conversation until I experiment in the classroom.

My main hope in building a syllabus around Beyoncé's work is to inspire students to look deeper, more critically, at Beyoncé, at pop culture, at themselves, and at the world around them. To reframe the margins and the center, starting with the words of Black women, not looking to them as an afterthought or supplement. To practice wielding a Black feminist lens to deconstruct and dismantle the ways power works. To encourage them to get politically involved and join in creating the world they want to see. It's complicated to talk about these things from a largely privileged position, but my goal has always been to listen to my students, facilitate conversation, and never prescribe analysis. To just share what I find in my own explorations and ask questions. To guide. Today's ally scripts are often about those with various privileges checking themselves, speaking less and listening more. That is certainly crucial, but it can also become a liability or easily turn into an excuse for those of us with privilege to do nothing in the long run. Personally, I don't believe in allyship—"ally" is an unnecessary and usually self-appointed identity that takes the place of proactively advocating a certain politics and distracts from simply doing the necessary work. I continue to find utility in talking and teaching, while always researching and learning the best, most responsible ways for me to use my voice, position, and privilege. I don't and won't consistently get it right, but I'll always try to be part of the change I want to see, and use any skills at my disposal to work tirelessly toward that change.

I believe that white people need to talk *more* about race. I believe that cis men need to talk *more* about gender and feminism. Not in ways that speak over others whose experiences give them specific knowledge, but respectfully and carefully and always *with* others, in community and coalition. Solidarity. Yes, that often means deferring and simply listening. But privilege can additionally be used to create important opportunities for change through speaking when it's prudent and including others whenever possible. I want to model an example of what that can look like through my teaching, writing, and speaking. The classroom is a unique space where diverse groups of people come together to interact and learn. And we all have so much to learn from Black feminism—Black women have been telling us that for centuries, and continue to do so. I always want my classroom to foreground their voices. There has to be something useful in those with access to certain privileges being visible and willing to speak against those same systems and privileges, to advocate other options, too. I hope there is, at least. I believe there is. And I hope it might remove a tiny bit of the weight others feel to describe and defend their own experiences if they wish, though I know it's a hair's-breadth margin between offering something useful and causing additional damage. I'll keep trying.

We need to start over, recenter Kimberlé Crenshaw's original theorization of intersectionality as about exposing, challenging, and dismantling intersecting systems of power and oppression, not simply about representation or collaboration. Black women laid the foundation, but everyone has a responsibility and stake in creating a more just world. Activist and lawyer Flo Kennedy believed these connections across our own differences were the unique, transformative ability and goal of Black feminism. She also believed that protest and education should always be fun—a directive I've long taken to heart, clearly. Kennedy's biographer Sherie M. Randolph states, "Kennedy saw black feminism as a praxis created and led by black women but available to everyone. She provided activists of all stripes with a theory and practice that centered on challenges to racism and sexism but expanded widely to include challenges to all forms of oppression." It's this belief of Kennedy's that I hope to carry forward and pass on to students through Beyoncé and all the other work on the syllabus. "Kennedy's main objective was to build pragmatic coalitions of the 'outs in society,' an 'alliance of the alienated,'" Randolph continues. These are the alliances I hope to create in the classroom as well—the very outcast alliances that Beyoncé highlights on "7/11," drawing on Alice Walker's poetry—by using analysis of Beyoncé's music as a foundation for negotiating everyone's individual positions, investments, and commitments across whatever differences might at first seem to separate us. Some may be personally alienated by society in any number of ways, while others may just be learning to alter their perspectives and offer support through acknowledgment, recognition, and subversion of their own privilege, but together, pragmatic coalitions materialize.

I'm including two appendices to this book: a kind of master syllabus with a formal course description and list of pairings from various iterations of "Politicizing Beyoncé" over the years (many more than are included in the preceding chapters), and a formal bibliography where all the assigned articles and chapters, along with additional sources mentioned throughout the book, can be found with full citations. Hopefully, the appendices will help you begin creating your own versions of the analyses contained here—expand them, extend them, argue with them, etc. Chapters of the book were organized thematically into a larger story that has proved effective in the classroom, but Appendix A is organized chronologically from 2006 forward. That way, you can find your own starting point, jump to your favorite song, mix and match in the margins, or create something entirely new. Choose your own adventure. Some songs and videos have cycled through many readings; others have been loyal to one. I don't include it on formal syllabi, but I've listed general themes underneath each pairing in Appendix A too, since some are less obvious than others, and we can't all hold class together in person to tease out a pairing's intent. Though I wish we could. Even the master syllabus is far from exhaustive; it certainly doesn't include every Beyoncé song. Add your own pairings and carry them forward. It's another beginning, certainly not an ending. Create a conversation; start a larger discussion—with friends, reading groups, anyone. Prepare yourself to enter an alliance of which Flo Kennedy would approve. Use Beyoncé's work as an example of a new center, and work to further shift the world.

Beyoncé was obviously being disingenuous when she sang, "Maybe we've reached the mountain peak / And there's no more left to climb" in "Start Over." Beyoncé doesn't believe in peaks—just look at her career. She believes in and works hard toward a continuous ascent. The mountain "peak" is consistently raised as one outdoes the past, becomes better. She also knows there are ways to subvert power, get around the system even as it quickly shifts to patch its holes and disguise itself anew. She stays one step ahead of the game. And so there's always somewhere left to climb or something left to work toward. She offers a hopeful example, constantly striving for more; better. So let's start over, imagine a better way to live. Imagine a better world. Go back to the beginning and imagine something different. Let's start over, like Beyoncé said, because the alternatives of giving up or giving in are unacceptable. There's too much at stake. In one of a few post-2013 interviews, Beyoncé told *Elle* magazine, "Power is making things happen without asking for permission." Follow Beyoncé's example—don't ask for permission. Read a book, play a song, watch a video. Think deeper. Listen to Black women. Go make something happen. Use Beyoncé's lyrics as a mantra: "Maybe you like it / Well, I don't / Maybe you'll settle / Well, I won't." Keep going. Then start over.

ACKNOWLEDGMENTS

I STILL CAN'T BELIEVE I WROTE A WHOLE GODDAMN book. Wow! I didn't do it alone though.

Mom, thanks for birthing me so I could ultimately put together sentences. But seriously: for modeling the kindness, open-mindedness, and resilience that shaped me. Hilary and Rachel, you always had my back growing up and stuck up for me when I refused to blend in. You're the best sisters I could ask for. Dad, you tried, and I guess that's something; but your politics and views directly harm the family you claim to support. I hope one day you understand that.

Mr. Curt Sousa, you're the most supportive, patient boyfriend, and I love you very much. I don't tell you enough, but thank you for putting up with me through all the ups and downs. I wouldn't want to be on this ride with anyone but you. And thanks to the whole Sousa family for always making me feel at home.

Some of my best friends are dogs: Honey and Rusty, you were my best thing and I'll miss you forever.

Marshall, you're a devil but you make me smile every day. (PSA: Reader, please consider senior dog adoption. Seniors are the most overlooked and neglected group at shelters and their hearts are bigger than anything you'll ever know!)

To all my friends—old, new, and no longer here—you've kept me going over the years. I can't possibly name everyone, but "I owe my life to the people that I love."

Reading Black women's words taught me to see the world critically, care-fully, correctly. A simple thanks for that shift in perspective is woefully inadequate. I hope to pay it forward, always.

Alyea Canada, you believed in me and took a chance on my manuscript when others wouldn't. You suggested outrageous cuts and revisions (getting rid of "Haunted" in a chapter on ghosts—WHAT?!), but you were never wrong. Your razor-sharp editing gave this book life and I can't thank you enough. To Lauren Rosemary Hook and Jamia Wilson, too, for masterfully bringing these chapters to the finish line. I'm so honored and grateful to be part of the Feminist Press's family and legacy, one I've long admired as a reader and teacher. Working with FP truly feels like being drafted onto an all-star dream team; I will forever play my heart out to make you all proud. To the entire FP collective—xoxoxoxo!!

Emerald Pellot, you created the most perfect, kick-ass illustration for the cover. Thank you! Readers: check out Emerald's GRL TRBL (www.grltrbl.com) and buy some amazing pins, shirts, or other swag for yourself and your friends!

Having my own book introduced with words from the legendary Cheryl Clarke means the world, the moon, the stars, everything. Cheryl, you've been an inspiration to me since I first read your essays and poetry as a teenager. The prospect of studying with you was the reason I applied to Rutgers for graduate work years ago. It was transformational to be in your classroom and soak in a tiny portion of your wit, humor, and brilliance. A mere thank-you doesn't suffice. My gratitude for your introduction can't be quantified.

I owe so much to two other formative educators that inspired me, believed in me when I didn't believe in myself: Andrea Tinnemeyer and Shirley Tang. Every time I want to give up, I think of you both and I keep going.

None of this would be possible without my badass students, in all my classes, even when Beyoncé wasn't on the syllabus. Thank you for signing up, for standing and speaking up for me, especially when others threw me under the bus (special shout-out to Knowledge and Power, Fall 2016). Thank you, above all, for allowing me the opportunity to learn, think, and grow with you all. To the additional folks who invited me to share my Beyoncé curriculum at your schools/venues, I'm throwing countless prayer-hand emojis in your direction too!

Amber E. Hopkins-Jenkins thrust "Politicizing Beyoncé" into the spotlight with an article back in 2012, and I'm forever thankful. Without her piece, the course would have faded away. Thanks to all the other writers and journalists who gave press and attention to the class and me since. Especially Hillary Crosley Coker, who went undercover as a student for *Jezebel*, wrote one of my favorite profiles of PB, and helped me think/talk through a lot during car-ride conversations back to NYC.

Others saw smaller pieces of this book, chatted with me about my work, or let me brainstorm while offering insight/editorial feedback in a variety of ways and settings: Sam Bobila, Zeba Blay, Janet Mock, Jake Sisco, Hillary Williams, DoctorJonPaul Higgins, Spectra Asala, Yari Gutierrez, Sara Perryman, Rachel Zaslow, Tom Bardwell, Ryan Harbage, LaShawn Adams, Ebony Johnson, Maximiliano Goiz, and more I'm likely forgetting. Thank you!

As much as my petty ass wants to dole out anti-thank-yous too, let me keep it cute and classy because my big mouth always gets me in trouble. I'll focus on the good: Carlos Decena approved the first version of "Politicizing Beyoncé" back in 2010, and Ethel Brooks and Yana Rodgers supported it for years to come. Louis Masur recognized its cross-departmental potential when some wanted to throw it away. Monique Gregory, Suzy Kiefer, and Feronda Orders never failed to support me and the class at an administrative level, while also always doing too much for way too little pay and recognition.

Related (and then I'll bite my tongue): Dismantle the ivory tower, don't get seduced into joining it! Demand higher wages and job security for adjunct instructors and staff! Bow down to the administrative workers that do the daily dirty work off which others profit!

Shout-out to the informal office spaces where I turned my course into a book. Over lots and lots of coffee, food, and sometimes whiskey. So many of these chapters were written and revised at Eagle Trading Co. in Greenpoint (Sam Bates—you're the best and now a good friend!). Honorary mention to the Habitat (RIP) and Moonlight Mile.

BeyHive, thank you for your staunch support of the course and me. I'm proud to consider myself among your ranks and will turn up any time you need me!

Beyoncé and Parkwood have been so generous. Jenan Matari, you connected me with Queen Bey's superwoman publicist Yvette Noel-Schure. I'll be forever in your debt. And thank you, Yvette, for supporting, believing in, and validating what I was doing in the classroom. For letting me know I wasn't imagining things. You, Parkwood, and Beyoncé gave my students and me the coolest field trip ever! None of us will ever forget it.

Finally, thank YOU for reading this book. I hope you find/found it useful. The world is beyond fucked up right now—take the things you love in pop culture and use them to start a conversation that might shift someone's perspective. You are powerful, and you were here. You *are* here. We are here.

MASTER SYLLABUS:
POLITICIZING BEYONCÉ

COURSE DESCRIPTION:

Beyoncé Giselle Knowles-Carter is known as many things: singer, songwriter, actress, performer, business woman, half of music's most powerful couple, wife, mother. But few take her seriously as a political figure even as politics continue to become more explicit in her work. This course will attempt to think about contemporary US society and its current class, racial, gender, and sexual politics through the music and career of Beyoncé. At times, she might deploy messages about race, gender, class, and sexuality that align with certain social norms, but during this interdisciplinary course we will ask: How does she also challenge our very understanding of these categories? How does Beyoncé push the boundaries of these categories to make space for and embrace other, perhaps more "deviant" bodies, desires, and/or politics? We will attempt to position Beyoncé as a progressive, feminist, and even queer figure through close examination of her music alongside Black feminist readings, both historical and contemporary. Ultimately, we will attempt to answer the question: Can Beyoncé's music be seen as a blueprint for progressive social change?

REQUIRED READING/LISTENING/VIEWING:

B'DAY (2006)
"Déjà Vu"
> Toni Morrison, *Beloved*
> Melissa Harris-Perry, "Introduction" and "Disaster"
> in *Sister Citizen: Shame, Stereotypes, and Black*
> *Women in America*
> Natasha Trethewey, *Beyond Katrina*
> Charmaine Neville, "How We Survived the Flood"
> — Hurricane Katrina; Slavery; Historical loop

"Ring the Alarm"
> Patricia Smith, *Blood Dazzler*
> Joy James, "Afterword: Political Literacy and Voice"
> Gayl Jones, selections from *Eva's Man*
> — Katrina (continued) and material possessions;
> Anger

"Upgrade U" and "Suga Mama"
> Barbara Ransby, selections from *Ella Baker and the*
> *Black Freedom Movement*
> Andreana Clay, "I Used to be Scared of the Dick:
> Queer Women of Color and Hip-Hop Masculinity"

—Black women's political leadership; Gender
dynamics in hip hop

"Get Me Bodied" and "Freakum Dress"
Sierra Mannie, "Dear White Gays, Stop Stealing Black
Female Culture"
— Appropriation; Origins of LGBTQ+ slang

"Kitty Kat" and "Green Light"
bell hooks, "Selling Hot Pussy: Representations
of Black Female Sexuality in the Cultural
Marketplace"
bell hooks, "Continued Devaluation of Black
Womanhood" in *Ain't I a Woman*
Melissa Harris-Perry, "Myth" in *Sister Citizen*
Janell Hobson, selections from *Venus in the Dark*
— Empowered sexuality; Sex-positive feminism;
Consent

"Resentment"
bell hooks, "Killing Rage: Militant Resistance"
Brittney Cooper, "Black Autumn: On Black Anger,
Tiredness, and the Limits of Self-Care"
Carol Anderson, "Kindling" in *White Rage*
— Anger; Self-care

"Listen"
bell hooks, "Black Women and Feminism" in *Ain't I
a Woman*
Sojourner Truth, "When Woman Gets Her Rights
Man Will Be Right"

Barbara Smith, "Some Home Truths on the
Contemporary Black Feminist Movement"
— History of feminism; Intersectionality

"Flaws and All"
Tamara Winfrey Harris, "Beauty: Pretty for a Black
Girl" in *The Sisters Are Alright*
— Body image; Beauty standards

I AM . . . SASHA FIERCE (2008)
"If I Were a Boy" and "Single Ladies"
Janet Mock, *Redefining Realness*
Kara Keeling, "Introduction: Another Litany for
Survival" in *The Witch's Flight*
Hortense Spillers, "Mama's Baby, Papa's Maybe: An
American Grammar Book"
— Internalized gender and race binaries;
Racialized gender; Gendered race

"Diva"
Sojourner Truth, "Ain't I a Woman?" and selections
from *Narrative of Sojourner Truth*
Nell Irvin Painter, selections from *Sojourner Truth*
Frances Beale, "Double Jeopardy: To Be Black and
Female"
Angela Davis, "Class and Race in the Early Women's
Rights Campaign" in *Women, Race & Class*
Staceyann Chin, "Poet for the People"
— Political divas; Performance; Connections and
continuity across time

"Ego"

> The Lady Chablis, *Hiding My Candy*
>> — Social construction of race and gender; Drag and camp

"Halo" and "Ave Maria"

> Maria Miller Stewart, "Religion and the Pure Principles of Morality, the Sure Foundation on Which We Must Build"
> Alice Walker, "The Only Reason You Want to Go To Heaven Is That You Have Been Driven Out of Your Mind (Off Your Land and Out of Your Lover's Arms)" in *Anything We Love Can Be Saved*
> Melissa Harris-Perry, "God" in *Sister Citizen*
>> — Religion and spirituality

"That's Why You're Beautiful"

> Gloria Naylor, selections from *The Women of Brewster Place*
> Alice Walker, selections from *The Color Purple*
>> — Autonomy; Empowerment; Structural inequality

"Scared of Lonely"

> Angela Davis, "When a Woman Loves a Man: Social Implications of Billie Holiday's Love Songs" in *Blues Legacies and Black Feminism*
> Billie Holiday, selections from *Lady Sings the Blues*
>> — Infusing lyrics with alternative meaning through vocal manipulation

"Poison"
    Lucille Clifton, "Won't You Celebrate with Me"
    Audre Lorde, "The Master's Tools Will Never
        Dismantle the Master's House"
    Angela Davis, "The Meaning of Emancipation
        According to Black Women" in *Women, Race &
        Class*
        — Toxic systems; Counterintuitive demands;
            Inside/outside dynamic

"Save the Hero"
    Melissa Harris-Perry, "Shame" and "Strength" in
        Sister Citizen
        — Negative/harmful aspects of the "strong Black
            woman" stereotype

"Why Don't You Love Me"
    Audre Lorde, "The Uses of Anger"
    Tamara Winfrey Harris, "Anger: Twist and Shout"
        from *The Sisters Are Alright*
    Pauli Murray, "The Liberation of Black Women"
    Alice Childress, selections from *Like One of the
        Family*
        — Anger; Resentment; Second wave feminism
            and history

4 (2011)
    "I Care"
        Audre Lorde, "Age, Race, Class and Sex: Women
            Redefining Difference"
        Frances Ellen Watkins Harper, "Women's Political
            Future"

— Connecting/caring across difference; Black
women's political engagement

"1+1," "I Miss You," and "Love on Top"
June Jordan, *Haruko/Love Poems*
Nikki Giovanni, "A Poem of Friendship"
— Love; Connection; Relationships

"Start Over"
Angela Davis, "Imagining the Future" in *Women,
Culture & Politics*
Mary Church Terrell, "The Progress of Colored
Women"
— Learning from the past

"End of Time"
Paule Marshall, *Praisesong for the Widow*
— Cultural history and legacy; Dance

"I Was Here"
Anna Julia Cooper, "The Status of Woman in
America"
Nikki Giovanni, "I Plant Geraniums"
Gwendolyn Brooks, "Old Mary"
Audre Lorde, "The Transformation of Silence into
Language and Action"
Audre Lorde, "A Litany for Survival"
Wendy S. Walters, "The Personal" in *Multiply/Divide*
— Time and temporality; Direct action; Making a
mark on history

"Run the World (Girls)"
    Angela Davis, "Radical Multiculturalism"
    Cathy Cohen, "Punks, Bulldaggers, and Welfare
        Queens: The Radical Potential of Queer Politics?"
    Nell Irvin Painter, selections from *The History of
        White People*
    Jewelle Gomez, "Land of Enchantment: 2050"
        — Feminism; Political coalition; Origins of
            whiteness; Visions of the future

"Schoolin' Life"
    Assata Shakur, selections from *Assata*
    Audre Lorde, "Poetry Is Not a Luxury"
    Barbara Christian, "The Race for Theory"
    Gloria T. Hull, Patricia Bell-Scott, and Barbara Smith,
        "Introduction: The Politics of Black Women's
        Studies" in *All the Women Are White, All the
        Blacks Are Men, But Some of Us Are Brave: Black
        Women's Studies*
    Gloria Joseph, "Black Feminist Pedagogy and
        Schooling in Capitalist White America"
        — Formal/informal education; Alternative forms
            of learning

Life Is But a Dream (2013)
    Zora Neale Hurston, *Dust Tracks on a Road*
    Nina Simone, *I Put a Spell on You: The
        Autobiography of Nina Simone*
    Audre Lorde, *Zami: A New Spelling of My Name*
        — Autobiography; Memoir; Celebrity; Privacy and
            publicity

***BEYONCÉ* (2013)**

"Pretty Hurts"
  Patricia Hill Collins, "Mammies, Matriarch, and
    Other Controlling Images" in *Black Feminist
    Thought*
  Zora Neale Hurston, "How It Feels to be Colored Me"
  Stephanie Covington Armstrong, *Not All Black Girls
    Know How to Eat*
  Morgan Jerkins, "The Stranger at the Carnival" in
    This Will Be My Undoing
  Cheryl Clarke, "hair: a narrative"
  Janet Mock, "Beauty Beyond Binaries: Being Pretty Is
    a Privilege, But We Refuse to Acknowledge It"
    — Beauty standards; "Pretty" as control

"Ghost" and "Haunted"
  Katherine McKittrick, "I Lost an Arm on my Last Trip
    Home: Black Geographies" in *Demonic Grounds*
  Wendy S. Walters, "Lonely in America" in *Multiply/
    Divide*
    — Music industry as metaphor for slavery; Power
    dynamics; Ghosts

"Blow," "Yoncé," and "Rocket"
  Audre Lorde, "The Uses of the Erotic: The Erotic as
    Power"
    — Sexuality; Sex-positive feminism; Agency;
    Eroticism

"No Angel"
  Jesmyn Ward, selections from *Men We Reaped*

"XO"

Zora Neale Hurston, *Their Eyes Were Watching God*
— Love as a force

"Superpower"

Octavia E. Butler, *Parable of the Sower*
Paula Giddings, "SNCC: Coming Full Circle" in *When and Where I Enter*
Audre Lorde, "Learning from the Sixties"
— Political organizing and protest; Visions of the future

"*Flawless"**

Chimamanda Ngozi Adichie, *We Should All Be Feminists*
Chimamanda Ngozi Adichie, "We Should All Be Feminists" (TEDx talk)
Roxane Gay, "Introduction: Feminism (n.): Plural," "Bad Feminist: Take One," and "Bad Feminist: Take Two" in *Bad Feminist*
bell hooks, "Feminism: A Movement to End Sexist Oppression"
Tricia Rose, "Hip Hop Demeans Women" and "'There are Bitches and Hoes'" in *The Hip Hop Wars*
— Feminism; Intersectionality

"Blue"

June Jordan, "Poem for South African Women"
Patricia Hill Collins, "Black Women and Motherhood" in *Black Feminist Thought*

Kay Lindsey, "Poem"
Joanna Clark, "Motherhood"
Dorothy Roberts, "Introduction" in *Killing the Black Body*
— Motherhood; Generational bonds

"Grown Woman"
Melissa Harris-Perry, "Crooked Room" in *Sister Citizen*
Alice Walker, definition of "Womanism" and "In Search of Our Mothers' Gardens" in *In Search of Our Mothers' Gardens*
Monique Morris, selections from *Pushout*
Barbara Smith, "Toward a Black Feminist Criticism"
— Womanism vs. feminism; Structural constraint; Rewriting history

"7/11"
Toni Cade Bambara, selections from *The Salt Eaters*
Alice Walker, *Hard Times Require Furious Dancing*
Flo Kennedy, selections from *Color Me Flo*
Audre Lorde, "A Burst of Light: Living with Cancer"
— Healing; Dancing; Self-care; Fun

"Ring Off"
Tamara Winfrey Harris, "Marriage: Witches, Thornbacks, and Sapphires" from *The Sisters are Alright*
— Marriage; Partnerships; Relationships

"Flawless (Remix)"
Alice Walker, "Be Nobody's Darling"

Joan Morgan, "The F Word" and "Hip-Hop Feminist" in *When Chickenheads Come Home to Roost*
Imani Perry, "The Venus Hip Hop and the Pink Ghetto: Negotiating Spaces for Women" in *Prophets of the Hood*
— Hip hop feminism; Coalition

LEMONADE (2016)

Part I:
"Pray You Catch Me," "Hold Up," "Don't Hurt Yourself," "Sorry," "6 Inch"

Saidiya Hartman, "Prologue: The Path of Strangers" in *Lose Your Mother*
Christina Sharpe, selections from *In the Wake*
Claudia Rankine, *Citizen: An American Lyric*
Brittney Cooper, "Refereeing Serena: Racism, Anger, and US (Women's) Tennis"
Pat Parker, "Where do you go to become a non-citizen?"
— Slavery; Ghosts; Citizenship; Capitalism

Part II:
"Daddy Lessons," "Love Drought," "Sandcastles," "Forward," "Freedom," "All Night"

Sherley Anne Williams, *Dessa Rose*
ntozake shange, *for colored girls who have considered suicide / when the rainbow is enuf*
Maya Angelou, "These Yet to Be United States"
Mari Evans, "I Am a Black Woman"
Warsan Shire, *Teaching My Mother How to Give Birth*

  — Intersectionality; Concept of freedom;
   Redefining America; Rewriting citizenship
   contract

"Formation"
 bell hooks, selections from *Teaching to Transgress*
 Kimberlé Crenshaw, "Demarginalizing the
  Intersection of Race and Sex"
 Kimberlé Crenshaw, "Mapping the Margins"
 Kimberlé Crenshaw, "Why Intersectionality Can't
  Wait"
 Jewell Parker Rhodes, selections from *Voodoo
  Dreams*
 Pat Parker, "Movement in Black" and "Where Will
  You Be?"
  — Intersectionality; Mapping the margins; Public
   education; Conjuring and resurrecting ghosts

BONUS TRACKS:

"Apeshit" from *Everything Is Love*—The Carters (2018)
 June Jordan, "Civil Wars" in *Civil Wars*
  — Limits of civility

"Crazy in Love" from *Dangerously In Love* (2003)
 Patricia Hill Collins, "Black Women's Love
  Relationships" in *Black Feminist Thought*
  — Love and relationships

"Yes" from *Dangerously In Love*
 June Jordan, "Notes Toward a Model of Resistance"

June Jordan, "Poem About My Rights"
— Consent; Rape culture

"Me, Myself and I" from *Dangerously In Love*
Michele Wallace, "Anger in Isolation: A Black
Feminist's Search for Sisterhood"
— Community; Coalition

"Bootylicious" from Destiny Child's *Survivor* (2001)
Elizabeth Alexander, "The Venus Hottentot"
— Body image; Stereotypes

"Survivor" from *Survivor*
Ann Petry, selections from *The Street*
— Survival in a toxic system

"Nasty Girl" from *Survivor*
Evelyn Brooks Higginbotham, selections from
Righteous Discontent
— Respectability politics; Sexuality

"Independent Women Part 1" from *Survivor*
Mary Ann Weathers, "An Argument for Black
Women's Liberation as a Revolutionary Force"
— Independence; Autonomy

"Bills, Bills, Bills" from Destiny Child's *The Writing's on
the Wall* (1999)
Sadie Tanner Mossell Alexander, "Negro Women in
Our Economic Life"
— Money; Wealth; Financial independence

APPENDIX B
MORE INFORMATION

Adichie, Chimamanda Ngozi. 2012. "We Should All Be
  Feminists." TEDxEuston. https://www.ted.com/talks/
  chimamanda_ngozi_adichie_we_should_all_be_
  feminists.
——. 2015. *We Should All Be Feminists*. New York: Anchor
  Books.
Alexander, Elizabeth. 2004. *The Venus Hottentot: Poems*.
  Minneapolis, MN: Graywolf Press.
Alexander, Michelle. 2010. *The New Jim Crow: Mass
  Incarceration in the Age of Colorblindness*. New
  York: New Press.
Anderson, Carol. 2016. *White Rage: The Unspoken Truth
  of Our Racial Divide*. New York: Bloomsbury.
Angelou, Maya. 1990. *I Shall Not Be Moved*. New York:
  Random House.
Baker, Josephine, and Jo Bouillon. 1977. *Josephine*,
  translated by Mariana Fitzpatrick. New York: Harper
  & Row.
Bambara, Toni Cade. 1980. *The Salt Eaters*. New York:
  Vintage Books.
Bambara, Toni Cade, ed. 1970. *The Black Woman: An
  Anthology*. New York: Washington Square Press.

Benbow, Candice Marie. 2016. "Lemonade Syllabus."
CandiceBenbow.com, May 6. http://www.
candicebenbow.com/lemonadesyllabus/.

Brooks, Daphne A. 2006. "Suga Mama, Politicized." *The
Nation*, November 30. https://www.thenation.com/
article/suga-mama-politicized/.

———. 2008. "'All That You Can't Leave Behind': Black
Female Soul Singing and the Politics of Surrogation
in the Age of Catastrophe." *Meridians* 8, no. 1:
180–204.

Brooks, Gwendolyn. 1960. *The Bean Eaters*. New York:
Harper & Brothers.

Butler, Octavia E. 1979. *Kindred*. Boston: Beacon Press.

———. 1993. *Parable of the Sower*. New York: Grand
Central Publishing.

———. 1998. *Parable of the Talents*. New York: Grand
Central Publishing.

Childress, Alice. 2017. *Like One of the Family:
Conversations from a Domestic's Life*. Boston:
Beacon Press.

Chin, Staceyann. 2007. "Poet for the People." In *Word
Warriors: 35 Women Leaders in the Spoken Word
Revolution*, edited by Alix Olson, 361–73. New York:
Seal Press.

Christian, Barbara. 1987. "The Race for Theory." *Cultural
Critique*, no. 6 (Spring): 51–63.

Clarke, Cheryl. 1983. "Lesbianism: An Act of Resistance."
In *This Bridge Called My Back: Writings by Radical
Women of Color*, edited by Cherríe L. Moraga and
Gloria E. Anzaldúa, 128–37. New York: Kitchen
Table: Women of Color Press.

———. 1983. *Narratives: poems in the tradition of black*

women. New York: Kitchen Table: Women of Color Press.

Clifton, Lucille. 1993. *The Book of Light*. Port Townsend, WA: Copper Canyon Press.

Cohen, Cathy J. 1997. "Punk, Bulldaggers, and Welfare Queens: The Radical Potential of Queer Politics?" *GLQ* 3, no. 4 (May): 437–65.

Collins, Patricia Hill. 2000. *Black Feminist Thought*. New York: Routledge.

Combahee River Collective. 1983. "A Black Feminist Statement." In *This Bridge Called My Back: Writings by Radical Women of Color,* edited by Cherríe L. Moraga and Gloria E. Anzaldúa, 210–18. Latham, NY: Kitchen Table: Women of Color Press.

Cooper, Anna Julia. 1892. *A Voice from the South: By a Black Woman of the South*. Xenia, OH: Aldine Printing House.

Cooper, Brittney C., Susana M. Morris, and Robin M. Boylorn, eds. 2017. *The Crunk Feminist Collection*. New York: Feminist Press.

Covington Armstrong, Stephanie. 2009. *Not All Black Girls Know How to Eat: A Story of Bulimia*. Chicago: Chicago Review Press.

Crenshaw, Kimberlé Williams. 1989. "Demarginalizing the Intersection of Race and Sex: A Black Feminist Critique of Antidiscrimination Doctrine, Feminist Theory and Antiracist Politics." *University of Chicago Legal Forum* 1989, no. 1: 139–67.

———. 1991. "Mapping the Margins: Intersectionality, Identity Politics, and Violence Against Women of Color." *Stanford Law Review* 43, no. 6 (July): 1241–99.

——. 2015. "Why Intersectionality Can't Wait." *Washington Post*, September 24.

——. 2017. "Kimberlé Crenshaw on Intersectionality, More than Two Decades Later." Columbia Law School Website. June 8. https://www.law.columbia.edu/pt-br/news/2017/06/kimberle-crenshaw-intersectionality.

Daughters of the Dust. 1991. Directed by Julie Dash. New York: Kino International.

Davies, Carole Boyce, ed. 2011. *Claudia Jones: Beyond Containment.* Oxfordshire, UK: Ayebia.

Davis, Angela Y. 1974. *Angela Davis: An Autobiography.* New York: Random House.

——. 1981. *Women, Race, & Class.* New York: Vintage Books.

——. 1990. *Women, Culture & Politics.* New York: Vintage Books.

——. 1998. *Blues Legacies and Black Feminism: Gertrude "Ma" Rainey, Bessie Smith, and Billie Holiday.* New York: Vintage Books.

——. 2012. *The Meaning of Freedom: and Other Difficult Dialogues.* San Francisco: City Light Books.

DePrince, Michaela, and Elaine DePrince. 2014. *Taking Flight: From War Orphan to Star Ballerina.* New York: Penguin Random House.

Evans, Mari. 2007. *Continuum: New and Selected Poems.* East Orange, NJ: Just Us Books.

Francis, Terri. 2007/2008. "What Does Beyoncé See in Josephine Baker?: A Brief Film History of Sampling La Diva, La Bakaire." *The Scholar and Feminist Online*, 6.1/6.2 (Fall/Spring).

Gay, Roxane. 2014. *Bad Feminist*. New York: Harper Perennial.

Giddings, Paula J. 1984. *When and Where I Enter: The Impact of Black Women on Race and Sex in America*. New York: William Morrow.

Giovanni, Nikki. 1978. *Cotton Candy on a Rainy Day*. New York: William Morrow.

———. 1994. *Racism 101*. New York: William Morrow.

Gomez, Jewelle. 1991. *The Gilda Stories*. Ithaca, NY: Firebrand Books.

Guy-Sheftall, Beverly, ed. 1995. *Words of Fire: An Anthology of African-American Feminist Thought*. New York: New Press.

Harris-Perry, Melissa V. 2011. *Sister Citizen: Shame, Stereotypes, and Black Women in America*. New Haven, CT: Yale University Press.

Hartman, Saidiya V. 2007. *Lose Your Mother: A Journey Along the Atlantic Slave Route*. New York: Farrar, Straus and Giroux.

Higginbotham, Evelyn Brooks. 1993. *Righteous Discontent: The Women's Movement in the Black Baptist Church, 1880–1920*. Cambridge, MA: Harvard University Press.

Hobson, Janell. 2005. *Venus in the Dark: Blackness and Beauty in Popular Culture*. New York: Routledge.

———. 2016. "Beyoncé as Conjure Woman: Reclaiming the Magic of Black Lives (That) Matter. *Ms.*, February 8. http://msmagazine.com/blog/2016/02/08/beyonce-as-conjure-woman-reclaiming-the-magic-of-black-lives-that-matter/.

Hobson, Janell, and Jessica Marie Johnson. 2016. "#Lemonade: A Black Feminist Resource

List." *African American Intellectual History Society*, May 12. https://www.aaihs.org/lemonade-a-black-feminist-resource-list/.

hooks, bell. 1981. *Ain't I a Woman: Black Women and Feminism*. Boston: South End Press.

———. 1984. *Feminist Theory: From Margin to Center*. Boston: South End Press.

———. 1992. *Black Looks: Race and Representation*. Boston: South End Press.

———. 1994. *Teaching to Transgress: Education as the Practice of Freedom*. New York: Routledge.

———. 1995. *Killing Rage: Ending Racism*. New York: Henry Hold and Company.

———. 1997. "Hardcore Honey: bell hooks Goes on the Down Low with Lil' Kim." *Paper Magazine*, May 1997.

Holiday, Billie, and William Dufty. 1956. *Lady Sings the Blues*. New York: Doubleday.

Hull, Gloria T., Patricia Bell Scott, and Barbara Smith, eds. 1982. *All the Women Are White, All the Blacks Are Men, But Some of Us Are Brave: Black Women's Studies*. New York: Feminist Press.

Hurston, Zora Neale. 1928. "How It Feels to Be Colored Me." *The World Tomorrow*, May 11.

———. 1937. *Their Eyes Were Watching God*. New York: Harper Perennial.

———. 1942. *Dust Tracks on a Road*. New York: Harper Perennial.

Jackson, Janet. *Janet Jackson's Rhythm Nation 1814*. A&M Records, compact disc.

Jerkins, Morgan. 2018. *This Will Be My Undoing: Living at*

the Intersection of Black, Female, and Feminist in (White) America. New York: Harper Perennial.

Jones, Gayl. 1987. *Eva's Man*. Boston: Beacon Press.

Jordan, June. 1980. *Passion: New Poems, 1977–1980*. Boston: Beacon.

——. 1981. *Civil Wars: Observations from the Front Lines of America*. New York: Simon & Schuster.

——. 1992. *Technical Difficulties: African-American Notes on the State of the Union*. New York: Pantheon Books.

——. 1994. *Haruko/Love Poems*. New York: High Risk Books.

——. 1998. *Affirmative Acts: Political Essays*. New York: Anchor Books.

Keeling, Kara. 2007. *The Witch's Flight: The Cinematic, the Black Femme, and the Image of Common Sense*. Durham, NC: Duke University Press.

Kennedy, Flo. 1976. *Color Me Flo: My Hard Life and Good Times*. Englewood Cliffs, NJ: Prentice Hall.

Kitt, Eartha. 1989. *I'm Still Here: Confessions of a Sex Kitten*. New York: Barricade Books.

Knowles-Carter, Beyoncé Giselle. 2013. "Miss Millenium: Beyoncé." Interview by Amy Wallace. *GQ*, January 10. https://www.gq.com/story/beyonce-cover-story-interview-gq-february-2013.

——. 2016. "Beyoncé Wants to Change the Conversation." Interview by Tamar Gottesman. *Elle*, April 4. https://www.elle.com/fashion/a35286/beyonce-elle-cover-photos/.

——. 2017. *How To Make Lemonade*. New York: Parkwood Entertainment.

Knowles, Solange Piaget. 2016. "An Honest
   Conversation with Solange Knowles."
   Interview by Anupa Mistry. *Fader*, September
   30. https://www.thefader.com/2016/09/30/
   solange-knowles-a-seat-at-the-table-interview.
Lady Chablis and Theodore Bouloukos. 1997. *Hiding My
   Candy: The Autobiography of the Grand Empress of
   Savannah*. New York: Pocket Books.
Life Is But a Dream. 2013. Directed by Beyoncé Knowles,
   Ed Burke, and Ilan Benatar. New York: HBO and
   Parkwood Entertainment.
Lorde, Audre. 1973. *From a Land Where Other People
   Live*. Detroit: Broadside Press.
———. 1978. *The Black Unicorn*. New York: W.W. Norton &
   Company.
———. 1982. *Zami: A New Spelling of My Name*. Berkeley,
   CA: Crossing Press.
———. 1984. *Sister Outsider: Essays & Speeches*. Berkeley,
   CA: Crossing Press.
———. 1988. *A Burst of Light*. Ithaca, NY: Firebrand Books.
Mannie, Sierra. 2014. "Dear White Gays, Stop Stealing
   Black Female Culture." *Daily Mississippian*, July 8.
   http://thedmonline.com/dear-white-gays/.
Marshall, Paule. 1983. *Praisesong for the Widow*. New
   York: Plume.
McKittrick, Katherine. 2006. *Demonic Grounds: Black
   Women and the Cartographies of Struggle*.
   Minneapolis: University of Minnesota Press.
Mock, Janet. 2014. *Redefining Realness: My Path to
   Womanhood, Identity, Love & So Much More*. New
   York: Atria Books.

——. 2016. "*Lemonade* Is Beyoncé's Testimony of Being Black, Beautiful, and Burdened." JanetMock.com, April 26. https://janetmock.com/2016/04/26/beyonce-lemonade-testimony-black-women-burden/.

——. 2017. "Beauty Beyond Binaries: Being Pretty Is a Privilege but We Refuse to Accept It." *Allure*, June 28. https://www.allure.com/story/pretty-privilege.

Moraga, Cherríe L., and Gloria E. Anzaldúa, eds. 1983. *This Bridge Called My Back: Writings by Radical Women of Color*. New York: Kitchen Table: Women of Color Press.

Morgan, Joan. 1999. *When Chickenheads Come Home to Roost: A Hip-Hop Feminist Breaks It Down*. New York: Simon & Schuster.

——. 2016. "Beyoncé, Black Feminist Art, and This Oshun Bidness." *Genius*, April 30. https://genius.com/a/beyonce-black-feminist-art-and-this-oshun-bidness.

Morrison, Toni. 1987. *Beloved*. New York: Vintage Books.

Murray, Pauli. 1999. *Proud Shoes: The Story of an American Family*. Boston: Beacon Press.

Naylor, Gloria. 1980. *The Women of Brewster Place*. New York: Penguin.

Oluo, Ijemoa. 2018. *So You Want to Talk About Race*. New York: Seal Press.

Painter, Nell Irvin. 1996. *Sojourner Truth: A Life, A Symbol*. New York: W.W. Norton & Co.

——. 2011. *The History of White People*. New York: W.W. Norton & Co.

Parker, Pat. 1999. *Movement in Black (Expanded Edition)*. Ithaca, NY: Firebrand Books.

Parker Rhodes, Jewell. 1993. *Voodoo Dreams: A Novel of Marie Laveau*. New York: Picador.

Parks, Suzan-Lori. 1990. *Venus: A Play*. New York: Theatre Communications Group.

Perry, Imani. 2004. *Prophets of the Hood: Politics and Poetics in Hip Hop*. Durham, NC: Duke University Press.

Petry, Ann. 1946. *The Street*. Boston: Mariner Books.

Pough, Gwendolyn D., Elaine Richardson, Aisha Durham, and Rachel Raimist, eds. 2007. *Home Girls Make Some Noise!: Hip Hop Feminism Anthology*. Mira Loma, CA: Parker Publishing, LLC.

Randolph, Sherie M. 2015. *Florynce "Flo" Kennedy: The Life of a Black Feminist Radical*. Chapel Hill: University of North Carolina Press.

Rankine, Claudia. 2014. *Citizen: An American Lyric*. Minneapolis, MN: Graywolf Press.

Ransby, Barbara. 2003. *Ella Baker and the Black Freedom Movement: A Radical Democratic Vision*. Chapel Hill: University of North Carolina Press.

Roberts, Doria. 2011. *Blackeyed Susan*. Hurricane Doria Records, compact disc.

Roberts, Dorothy. 1997. *Killing the Black Body: Race, Reproduction, and the Meaning of Liberty*. New York: Vintage Books.

Rose, Tricia. 2008. *The Hip Hop Wars: What We Talk About When We Talk About Hip Hop—and Why It Matters*. New York: Basic Books.

Shakur, Assata. 1987. *Assata: An Autobiography*. Chicago: Lawrence Hill Books.

Shange, Ntzoke. 1975. *for colored girls who have considered suicide / when the rainbow is enuf*. New York: Scribner.

Sharpe, Christina. 2016. *In the Wake: On Blackness and Being*. Durham, NC: Duke University Press.

Shire, Warsan. 2011. *Teaching My Mother How to Give Birth*. United Kingdom: Mouthmark.

Simone, Nina. 1965. *I Put a Spell on You*. Phillips, vinyl.

———. 1966. *Wild Is the Wind*. Phillips, vinyl.

Simone, Nina, and Stephen Cleary. 1999. *I Put a Spell on You: The Autobiography of Nina Simone*. Boston: De Capo Press.

Smith, Barbara. 2000. *The Truth That Never Hurts: Writings on Race, Gender, and Freedom*. New Brunswick, NJ: Rutgers University Press.

Smith, Barbara, ed. 1983. *Home Girls: A Black Feminist Anthology*. New Brunswick, NJ: Rutgers University Press.

Smith, Barbara, and Lorraine Bethel, eds. 1979. *Conditions 5, The Black Women's Issue (November)*. Brooklyn, NY: Independent Publishing Collective.

Smith, Patricia. 2008. *Blood Dazzler*. Minneapolis, MN: Coffee House Press.

The South End Press Collective, eds. 2007. *What Lies Beneath: Katrina, Race, and the State of the Nation*. Boston: South End Press.

Spanos, Brittany. 2016. "How Beyoncé's 'Lemonade' Reclaims Rock's Black Female Legacy." *Rolling Stone*, April 26. https://www.rollingstone.com/music/music-news/how-beyonces-lemonade-reclaims-rocks-black-female-legacy-67463/.

Spillers, Hortense J. 2003. *Black, White, and in Color: Essays on American Literature and Culture*. Chicago: University of Chicago Press.

St. Félix, Doreen. 2016. "A Love Profane: On *Lemonade*, Beyoncé Visual Album." *MTV News*, April 28. http://www.mtv.com/news/2874454/ beyonce-lemonade-a-love-profane/.

Stenberg, Amandla, and Quinn Masterson. 2015. "Don't Cash Crop My Cornrows." YouTube. https://www.youtube.com/watch?v=O1KJRRSB_XA.

Taylor, Keeanga-Yamahtta, ed. 2017. *How We Get Free: Black Feminism and the Combahee River Collective*. Chicago: Haymarket Books.

Trethewey, Natasha. 2010. *Beyond Katrina: A Meditation on the Mississippi Gulf Coast*. Athens: University of Georgia Press.

Truth, Sojourner. 1998. *Narrative of Sojourner Truth*, edited by Nell Irvin Painter. New York: Penguin.

Turner, Tina. 1985. "We Don't Need Another Hero (Thunderdome)." On *Mad Max Beyond Thunderdome: Original Motion Picture Soundtrack*. Capitol Records, compact disc.

Walker, Alice. 1973. *Revolutionary Petunias*. New York: Harcourt Books.

——. 1982. *The Color Purple*. New York: Harcourt Books.

——. 1983. *In Search of Our Mothers' Gardens: Womanist Prose*. New York: Harcourt Books.

——. 1997. *Anything We Love Can Be Saved: A Writers' Activism*. New York: Ballantine Books.

——. 2010. *Hard Times Require Furious Dancing*. Novato, CA: New World Library.

Walker, Kara. 2014. "At the behest of Creative Time Kara E. Walker has confected: A Subtlety, or the *Marvelous Sugar Baby* — an Homage to the unpaid and overworked Artisans who have refined our

Sweet tastes from the cane fields to the Kitchens of the New World on the Occasion of the demolition of the Domino Sugar Refining Plant." Installation. Williamsburg, NY: Domino Sugar Factory.

——. 2014. *An Audience*. New York: Sikkema Jenkins & Co.

Walker, Margaret. 1966. *Jubilee*. Boston: Houghton Mifflin.

Walters, Wendy S. 2015. *Multiply/Divide: On the American Real and Surreal*. Louisville, KY: Sarabande Books.

Ward, Jesmyn. 2013. *Men We Reaped: A Memoir*. New York: Bloomsbury.

Washington, Harriet A. 2006. *Medical Apartheid: The Dark History of Medical Experimentation on Black Americans from Colonial Times to the Present*. New York: Anchor Books.

Wells, Ida B. 2014. *The Light of Truth: Writings of an Anti-Lynching Crusader*, edited by Mia Bay and Henry Louis Gates Jr. New York: Penguin.

Williams, Sherley Ann. 1986. *Dessa Rose*. New York: HarperCollins.

Winfrey Harris, Tamara. 2015. *The Sisters Are Alright: Changing the Broken Narrative of Black Women in America*. Oakland, CA: Berret-Koehler Publishers.